To Zosia, Magda and Piotrek

Contents

List of Plates

Acknowledgements

This book would not have been possible without several visits to Poland and I am grateful to the British Academy, the Polish Academy of Sciences and the University of Exeter who have at various times helped finance these visits. To the international fraternity of Chopin scholars I am greatly indebted, both directly and indirectly. Their willingness to share knowledge and expertise is in the best traditions of unselfish scholarship and I have been greatly heartened by it. Jeffrey Kallberg in particular has been an invaluable help, responding promptly to my numerous queries, reading the manuscript and offering several helpful suggestions. My debt to Dr Kallberg's own research will very soon be apparent to the reader. I have also benefited from the advice and encouragement of Derek Carew. He too read the manuscript, and his wide knowledge of early nineteenth-century piano music and concert life was placed freely at my disposal.

To my many friends in Poland I owe a special debt. Hanna Wróblewska and Dalila Turło of the Chopin Society could not have been more helpful. Several of my thoughts on Chopin took shape through discussions with Dr Turło, though in a few cases I have stuck to my guns. I am also grateful to the staff of the Institute of Musicology at the Polish Academy of Sciences, to Katarzyna Morawska, Władysław Malinowski, Elżbieta Malinowska and Elżbieta Witkowska in particular. It is impossible to express adequately my gratitude to Zofia Chechlińska, not only for her advice and help on early nineteenth-century Polish music, but for her generous hospitality and the warmth of her friendship.

I am grateful to Professor Carl Schachter for permission to quote Ex.41; to Professor Wallace Berry for Ex.39; to Betty Jean Thomas Berk for Ex.36; to University of Chicago Press for Ex.38 and to Longman Inc. for Ex.40 and Ex.50. Finally I must thank Tabitha Collingbourne who typed the music examples, and Sue Daley, who helped with proof-reading and prepared the index.

Jim Samson   Exeter 1985

Prologue

Books on Chopin proliferate. There is even a book about the books. Yet surprisingly few of them examine his music in any but a loosely descriptive, impressionistic fashion. Biography has proved more alluring. From the Liszt book of 1852[1] onwards the flood of biographies has continued to swell and it shows little sign of abating. In English alone there have been five books since 1976.[2] Quality is another matter. I seriously doubt whether an adequate biography can be rendered by anyone whose understanding of the music is casual. If there is a single overwhelming defect of recent English biographies it is their exiguous and shallow treatment of creative process, which is after all central to the 'life' of any composer. In this and in other respects they fall short of the high standards set by Gastone Belotti in his three-volume study in Italian and by Józef Chomiński in his concise but penetrating book in German.[3] Perhaps translations are the answer.

Critical studies of Chopin's music, then, are few and far between, at least in English. Gerald Abraham's book[4] was of immense importance as an early and perceptive introduction, the first serious attempt since Niecks[5] to provide English-speaking readers with an anatomy of the composer's style. Abraham's book was published in 1939 and since then there has only been one book in English which deals primarily with the music, a symposium edited by Alan Walker.[6] There may be some value then in a fresh study, one which aims to provide a detailed analysis of the style and structure of the music in the light of recent Chopin scholarship on the one hand and recent analytical methods on the other.

Quite apart from the many books on Chopin in Polish, French and German, there is a wealth of scholarship which has been channelled into formats other than the full-length book and which is therefore little known outside specialist circles. Much of this has been work at the rock face, involving text-critical methods and other forms of source study. Since the First International Chopin Congress of 1960[7] there has been an explosion of such scholarship in Poland itself, resulting in several major studies in dissertation form [8] and in *Rocznik Chopinowski*, and culminating in Krystyna Kobylańska's monumental catalogue of Chopin's manuscripts.[9] The *Katalog* is a triumph of patience and method, an indispensable work of reference which must now supersede Maurice Brown's earlier Thematic Index,[10] though this too was of immense value in its day. Other source study has been undertaken by the Swiss scholars Bertrand Jaeger and J. J. Eigeldinger and by the Americans Thomas Higgins, Ferdinand Gajewski and Jeffrey Kallberg. Kallberg's work has been especially valuable. He has looked in particular at the sketches and rejected public manuscripts of Chopin's later music for the information they yield about his musical style and working methods, and his continuing work on the sources will certainly prove of the utmost importance for later Chopin research.[11]

Even where the primary focus of study is analytical, as in my own book, manuscript research is an essential tool, conveying a wealth of information about compositional process. Its most concrete achievement, however, has been to facilitate the preparation of reliable texts. Many of the notorious uncertainties about Chopin sources have now been eliminated, thanks to recent scholarship. Yet problems will always remain, for they are an inevitable by-product of the flexible composer-performer relationship which obtained in early nineteenth-century piano music. Any attempt to prepare a source-chain for a Chopin piece will involve difficulties at almost every stage, due to the multiplicity of sources, including autographs, and the substantial variation among them. Where editions are concerned the sketches need present relatively few problems, but often there are several 'public' autographs for a single work (including rejected manuscripts, engraver's exemplars and presentation manuscripts) and stemmatic analysis is often complex as to chronology. In relation to copies much has now been clarified. Kobylańska has distinguished no fewer than seventy-four separate hands other than Chopin's, so there can be little excuse for the mistaken identifications which dogged earlier editions, especially with Fontana copies. Further difficulties arise, however, over the extent of Chopin's contribution at the proof stages of a work, over divergent 'simultaneous' first editions and over the significance of his glosses in editions belonging to students and friends.[12] Faced with a plethora of material, the most an editor can do is to seek a uniform basis of sources for each work, and even here there will be ample room for disagreement. Of the various complete editions, the best all-round contenders are the Henle *Urtext*, edited (mostly) by Ewald Zimmermann, and the Polish National Edition (not to be confused with the older Paderewski Complete Edition), under the general editorship of Jan Ekier.

However we evaluate the *Urtext* editions of Chopin, we may be grateful that the blatant errors and fanciful inventions of nineteenth-century editors need no longer trouble us. Yet these early editions are well worth examining for other reasons. They are a fascinating cypher to changing fashions in nineteenth-century performance practice and more generally to changing patterns of reception. Chopin reception has been a fruitful area of research in Polish musicology, much of which, like its German mentor, is devoted to the aesthetics and social history of music. Under the guidance of Zofia

Lissa and Józef Chomiński, several younger scholars have turned their attention to early editions and to early critical writing on Chopin in order to assess the changing tastes and preconceptions of particular periods and particular nationalities.[14] Even the many biographies are useful in this kind of study. The myths about Chopin the man are worth examining not only in a negative and destructive way,[15] but also in recognition of their value as stages in the interaction of unchanging historical materials and changing receptive attitudes, a process which continues today.

It is a process which has been extended to the music itself. This has been performed and described in many different ways and there is little reason for our own age to assume undue privilege. The historicist performance practice of today is of course a useful corrective to an earlier generation's creative collaboration with the text, but it presents its own difficulties, of a conceptual as well as a pragmatic character. It is enough to record that the aims have changed, just as they have changed in the world of criticism and analysis. The proselytising tone of a critic such as James Huneker[16] may be unacceptable today, but it was at least consistent with the author's objective. For Huneker the task was to enhance (vicariously) the reader's experience of the music by conveying his *own* experience as vividly as possible, relying above all upon an imaginative, if at times over-exuberant, use of metaphor. Heinrich Schenker, model for so much contemporary analysis in England and America, aimed higher, seeking nothing less than the elusive sources of unity, coherence and value in a work.[17] Schenker's analyses have yielded penetrating insights into the structural heart of Chopin's music, but their capacity to demonstrate the 'unity' of a work in some exclusive, all-embracing sense remains questionable.

The distinction between description of style and analysis of structure, polarised in Huneker and Schenker, continues to haunt contemporary writing about music.[18] The matter will be discussed in a later chapter, but it should be pointed out now that this book proceeds from the premise that there is interest and value in both approaches. The narrative addresses issues relating to both style and structure throughout, but there is a discernible change of emphasis from the former towards the latter as the book unfolds. Early chapters deal mainly with the sources and the characteristic profile of Chopin's musical style. Later chapters look rather at the structure of his music and try at least to arrive at some useful generalisations about how it functions.

The music will of course survive without the help of an apologist or an analyst. Its lasting popularity, reaching, as Arthur Hutchings puts it, 'from salon to slum', owes little to the descriptions of Huneker or to the analytical graphs of Schenker, though our understanding and enjoyment of it can be enhanced by both. That popularity is the more remarkable when we consider that Chopin rarely ventured beyond the environment of his own instrument. Here indeed lies the source of one of the most enduring myths about his music, a false equation between limitation of medium and limitation of expressive range which has often tagged him a mere 'salon composer'. The label proved the more appealing in the nineteenth century, given the aesthetic pre-eminence assigned, in some quarters at least, to vocal music. In reality Chopin's total involvement with the piano was right at the heart of his creativity. A composition would begin life at the piano, its overall conception already formed and its melodic and harmonic details often already realised before he set pen to paper. He drew much of his inspiration directly from his exploration of novel keyboard textures and sonorities and he allowed the limitations of the instrument to define the boundaries of an enclosed musical world which could 'contain' the expressive extremes of a widely ranging language. As George Sand remarked, 'he made a single instrument speak a language of infinity.' Where Beethoven's genius reached always outward, expanding the corpus of forms until it could embrace a tiny bagatelle and a massive choral symphony, Chopin rather absorbed into his deliberately restricted world elements drawn from the vocal styles of *Lieder* and opera as well as from the orchestral literature. In penetrating to the heart of the piano he managed to suggest through it, and often to draw together and synthesise, salient characteristics of other media, both intimate and epic. 'Chopin is the greatest of them all', said Debussy, 'for through the piano alone he discovered everything.' This filtration of different media into the language of the piano is paralleled in a way by the permeation of elements from different genres and forms into a single work. A Chopin piece will often travel from one manner to another in a discreet counterpoint of styles, where a polonaise will enclose a mazurka, a sonata will incorporate a nocturne and a study, a waltz will be subsumed by a ballade. His major extended works go even further in this direction, often blending elements of different formal archetypes – sonata-form, rondo and variations – with remarkable resource and ingenuity.

At its best it is a music rich in ambiguities, implicative on several levels, shy of congruence and of the predictable course. And this multi-levelled character, enabling a listener to move around within a work, to expand his or her awareness laterally, so to speak, is extended by the dialogue which Chopin permits between 'cultivated' and 'vernacular' elements. His light music is more sophisticated than that of Mozart, Beethoven and Schubert, while even his most epic works derive much of their energy from the idioms of folk or bourgeois music-making. In this fusion of the accessible and the sophisticated he was in the long run cutting against the grain of his age, an age which was increasingly to separate the popular and the significant. Yet there is a sense in which this aspect of his achievement does reflect contemporary concerns. Chopin would hardly have rationalised it, but there was a prevalent tendency among the early Romantics to idealise popular materials, to view them as expressive of a generalised notion of the natural, unpolluted culture of the 'people', and, as Raymond Williams reminds us,[19] the notion grew in attractiveness in proportion to the Romantic artist's growing dependence on a more tangible middle-class 'public'. As one of the few composers of the early nineteenth century whose income from sales of his published music was substantial, though it could never have supported him, Chopin certainly relied upon that public and on occasion he deliberately pandered to its whims. But he had little inclination to communicate directly to it. Unlike most composer-pianists of the age he shunned the public concert, directing his music-making to a small circle of initiates, to many of whom 'popular' materials, including those of folkloristic origins, would have assumed something of the character of an exoticism, a lively local colour.

Chopin was not averse to exploiting this aspect of folk materials, particularly in his early years. Increasingly, however, they came to assume for him a much deeper significance, as a symbolic representation of the nation's spiritual identity. Throughout his lifetime it had of course no political identity. Again he was responding in part to a theme of his age, an age in which growing national awareness, often answering concrete political needs, gained a philosophical dimension in the writings of, among others, Fichte in Germany and Mickiewicz in Poland. Chopin responded, but after his fashion. He probably never read Fichte and he rejected the mystical, messianic nationalism which was propounded by Mickiewicz and which characterised much Polish nationalism in exile. More crucially he rejected the kind of overtly political gesture which might have been made through opera or programme music, a gesture which was urged upon him often enough from his earliest days. This he left to Polish composers at home and the results speak for themselves.

He was a reticent nationalist then, but a nationalist all the same. Certainly much of his inspiration was drawn from his private, doubtless idealised, image of Poland, and this reached some way beyond historical evocations and rustic vignettes. The unhappy destiny of the country was an enduring preoccupation and it must surely have been a contributory factor in the prevailing tragic or melancholy *Affekt* of much of his greatest music. Nor was this any less real to him when it acted as a focus for more personal discontents. For Polish audiences Chopin's music retains to this day powerful nationalist associations, and commentators from that country are inclined to view it as expressive of essentially Polish, and more generally Slavonic, characteristics. In reality Chopin can be no more labelled a 'Slavonic composer' than a 'salon composer', but it is perhaps not too fanciful to pinpoint certain qualities which his music shares with that of other Slavonic composers. The affinities with later nineteenth-century Russian music are particularly striking. One thinks of the greater structural status assigned to texture and sonority, of the episodic designs, of the preference for melodic variation and decoration rather than motivic dissection and of the tendency to raise the emotional temperature of the individual moment in an impulsive, apparently spontaneous way.

But these are esoteric matters, an easy prey to wishful thinking. The certainty is that Chopin laid the foundations upon which a 'Polish' style might have been built, which is not at all to claim that his music embodies indigenous qualities of Polishness. He was aware that if his music were to be nationalist rather than merely provincial it must not be isolated from the great achievements of European music. Many years later his great compatriot Karol Szymanowski was to write of him: 'Chopin was an eternal example of what Polish music was capable of achieving – a symbol of Europeanised Poland, losing nothing of his national features but standing on the highest pinnacle of European culture.'[20] Today, when we tend to view his music as a variety of European Romanticism, it is perhaps worth remembering that to many of his contemporaries the novel and individual features of his art were associated with his Polish origins. Even Niecks, writing in the 1880s, attributed much of the personal character of Chopin's music to his 'Polishness', though he warned against a prevailing tendency to overstate that particular case. Chopin may not have been a 'Slavonic composer' first and foremost, but his music contributed in its way to that swelling tide of nationalism which characterised the art of the nineteenth century.

In other respects he seemed a child of an earlier age, his tastes and sympathies untouched by many aspects of the spirit of early Romanticism. Certainly he was anything but the archetypal Romantic composer of popular imagination. His mind was characterised by a love of order and precision, by a rejection of over-exuberant types of thought, and these qualities are reflected in his music. He found no room there for extravagant rhetoric and theatricality or for mawkish sentimentality. Nor had he much sympathy with the big, abstract ideas which fired the imagination of the age, including its composers. Chopin had no 'new word' for mankind and this in turn had a bearing on the relative stability, the lack of any radical change, in his musical style, once established. In an age in which growth and development were the watchwords of artistic expression, as the music of Beethoven, Berlioz, Liszt and Wagner amply demonstrates, Chopin constantly refined but did not change fundamentally the main components of his style.

In any case he showed only moderate interest in the music of his contemporaries, reciprocating little of the enthusiasm expressed by Berlioz, Schumann and Mendelssohn for *his* music and reserving his unqualified admiration for those masters of an earlier age, Bach and Mozart. Even more uncharacteristically for a composer writing in the second quarter of the century, he was fairly indifferent to the major political and ideological issues of the day (the Polish question apart) and to the various extra-musical stimuli, from nature imagery to the supernatural and the world of the exotic, which seemed an obligatory source of inspiration to the Romantics. Nor was he greatly interested in the other arts. This was a period characterised in the aesthetic sphere by a strengthening impulse towards a fusion of the arts. For Berlioz, Schumann and Liszt, literature was more than just an outside interest: it was a direct generator of musical ideas. Chopin, by contrast, had only a passing interest in literature and painting, though he counted among his friends great exponents of both arts and may indeed have been influenced by one of them, Delacroix. He shunned the fashionable interest in programme music and his few contributions to that most typical of all Romantic forms – the art song – are hardly among his major, or his most characteristic, achievements.

Chopin avoided then many of the surface manifestations of Romanticism in music, the 'Achilles' heels', as Szymanowski was later to describe music's links with poetry, nature and the exotic (Bourniquel called them the 'mirages of Romanticism'). Yet in a deeper sense he did capture and express the spirit of the age, its ardour and idealism, its 'longing and restlessness',[21] its love of spontaneity, with an authority which his contemporaries immediately recognised. His music has an intensity born of introspection and it became a natural focus for the growing preoccupation of the Romantics with the evocative and affective powers of music, a preoccupation evidenced alike in contemporary criticism and in more serious philosophical writing. In a manner which reached right to the heart of the Romantic impulse, Chopin *lived* in his music, engaging there in an interior play of powerful emotions, marshalled and controlled by a compulsive need for order. The best of his music reflects that tension, taming or freezing the impetuosity which often seems about to erupt, harnessing a tumult of feeling in the lucidity of its forms. In a way it presents a model, classically perfect, of the impulsive spirit of early Romanticism.

1

A biographical sketch

Here is a young man who, abandoning himself to his natural impressions and without taking a model, has found, if not a complete renewal of pianoforte music, at least a part of what has been sought in vain for a long time – namely an abundance of original ideas of which the type is to be found nowhere. We do not mean by this that M. Chopin is endowed with a powerful organisation like that of Beethoven, nor that there arise in his music such powerful conceptions as one remarks in that of this great man. Beethoven has composed pianoforte music, but I speak here of pianists' music, and it is by comparison with the latter that I find in M. Chopin's inspirations an indication of a renewal of forms which may exercise in time much influence over this department of the art.

These were the reactions of François-Joseph Fétis (*Revue Musicale*, 3 March 1832) to Chopin's first public concert in Paris. It was held at Pleyel's rooms on 26 February and the programme included the E minor Concerto and the *La ci darem* Variations, both played as solos.[1] Fétis's comments were prophetic. Others had remarked on the originality of Chopin's music, but Fétis recognised that this went some way beyond mere novelty, that the music bore the stamp of genius and might in due course lead to a fresh start, a new direction, for piano music. His review is instructive in other ways. It draws our attention to the clear division in early nineteenth-century concert life between the 'high art' of the Viennese Classical masters, especially Beethoven, and the more popular arena of the virtuoso composer. Beethoven's shadow loomed large over the most earnest endeavours of instrumental composition and Fétis's observations are symptomatic of a general tendency at the time to measure new creative talents against his achievements. It was a primary aim of some of the smaller, more prestigious concert organisations to bring to their subscribers some understanding of Beethoven's powerful and disturbing musical voice. These were predominantly orchestral and chamber music concerts and their audiences were small, dedicated and élitist, little interested in the more superficial aspects of instrumental technique. Other forums were even more exclusive, notably the private *réunions* in which musicians, amateur and professional, would gather with the aim of playing music of the highest quality.

Such activities remained a world apart from the remarkable growth of a commercial concert life in the early nineteenth century, a phenomenon justly described by William Weber as a 'cultural explosion'.² Public concerts soon began to rival even opera in popularity, and they had the merit of being cheaper and easier to promote. Many were so-called 'benefit' concerts organised by professional virtuosi who earned their living by performance and composition and had to be able to turn their hand to concert promotion and management as well. Their income could then be supplemented through the sales of published music and teaching, a response in both cases to an expanding and eagerly receptive amateur market centred on the piano. The piano was at the heart of the benefit concert. Display pieces for piano and orchestra – concertos, rondos, variations and pot-pourris – were its staple diet, with the composer-performer expected to demonstrate his acrobatic technique and, equally important, his powers of improvisation. This was the world of 'pianists' music' carefully distinguished by Fétis from 'pianoforte music' and it was towards a successful career in the former world that Chopin's earlier activities and energies had been directed.

The works for piano and orchestra composed during the five years or so before his first Paris concert were tailored to a career as a virtuoso-composer on the concert platforms of major European cities, and the success of that concert would have seemed a natural springboard to such a career. As Fétis went on to remark: 'If the subsequent works of M. Chopin correspond to his début, there can be no doubt but that he will acquire a brilliant and merited reputation.' It was success of a kind, though we should certainly take *cum grano salis* the loyal report of Chopin's friend Antoni Orlowski that 'all Paris is stupefied'. There was a strong Polish representation at the concert and then – as now – the Pole abroad would support his own, often allowing national pride to inhibit objective evaluation. The fact is that Chopin had great difficulty in following up the success of that first Paris concert, and once more Fétis put his finger on the problem. 'He brings little tone out of the instrument,' he remarked later in the same review, unwittingly reiterating a criticism which had dogged Chopin's earlier public appearances. The limitation was part and parcel of a temperamental discomfort with the role of 'public' pianist.

The acclaim in Paris was timely, for earlier attempts to establish himself outside his native Poland had met with only moderate success. A short trip to Vienna in the summer of 1829 had augured well. Chopin had just completed his three-year course at the Warsaw conservatory and he was understandably dazzled by his first contact with a city which had once been the musical jewel of Europe, even if its glitter was fading rapidly. There had also been a brief and rather less eventful trip to Berlin the previous year, and on both occasions he soaked himself in opera – Cimarosa, Weber and Spontini in Berlin, Boieldieu, Meyerbeer and Méhul in Vienna. More to the point, he scored a personal success in Vienna. Before the visit Chopin's teacher Józef Elsner sent copies of the Op.2 Variations and the Op.4 Sonata to the eminent publisher Haslinger. Haslinger listened to

Chopin play the variations and was so impressed that he arranged for a concert on 11 August at the Kärntnerthor Theatre, then managed by Graf Gallenberg. The Kärntnerthor had been the venue for many a distinguished concert in the past, including the première of Beethoven's Choral Symphony a mere five years earlier, and it was a prestigious setting for the young Chopin's début outside Poland. He played the Variations and improvised on the popular Polish wedding-song *chmiel* and the concert was such a success that it had to be repeated a week later with the inclusion of the *Krakowiak-Rondo*, Op.14.[3]

Vienna approved of Chopin. Once more there was a recognition in some quarters that both his music and his performance style represented something new. 'On account of the originality of his playing and compositions one might almost attribute to him already some genius, at least insofar as unconventional forms and pronounced originality are concerned,' wrote one critic.[4] Another observed, this time of the second concert, that 'his style of playing and writing differs greatly from that of other virtuosi'[5]. And this in Vienna which was used to the finest performers of the day. In keeping with the fashions of the public concert, Chopin included elements of national colour both in the orchestral pieces and in his improvisation, and this was no doubt part of the attraction of the concerts for Viennese audiences. It was a good selling point, and he was careful to include national dance rhythms in the finales of the two piano concertos which he composed on his return to Warsaw and which were intended to launch his career as an international virtuoso-composer.

Vienna gave Chopin a foretaste of success and he made the city his first stopping-point when he left Warsaw again the following year to establish his reputation in the wider world of music. He arrived there in November, accompanied by his close friend from school days, Tytus Woyciechowski. The plan was for a triumphant two-month stay which would consolidate his earlier success and which would form the prelude to a grand tour, with Italy as the next stop. But the timing was unfortunate. One week after their arrival in the Austrian capital Poland erupted. The effect of the Congress of Vienna in 1815 had been to confirm the partition of Poland between Russia, Prussia and Austria, while at the same time creating a small, so-called 'Kingdom of Poland' with the Russian Czar Alexander I as 'King'. Initially Alexander seemed well intentioned towards Poland and policies were broadly liberal, but after various political intrigues reform quickly conceded to repression. The Grand Duke Constantine, who trained the army, became the most hated and feared man in Poland, and his brutal methods were intensified when Alexander's death made way for the reign of Nicholas I. During Chopin's last few years in Warsaw there was seething discontent among the Polish people, and he must have been familiar with an atmosphere in which secret societies of artists and intellectuals plotted revolution in the cafés of the city. A few months after Nicholas visited Warsaw to open the Polish Diet of 1830, a rather clumsy attempt to assassinate the Grand Duke Constantine touched off a general uprising which was to continue for the better part of a year before it was finally suppressed.

When news of the uprising reached Vienna, Tytus returned to Warsaw to take part in the fighting, leaving Chopin in a city where Poles were no longer welcome. He was never to see Tytus again. His anticipated contacts with the grander elements in Viennese society simply did not materialise in the new political climate, and this no doubt accounted partly for his failure to arrange a concert. But there were other reasons, unrelated to the Polish question. Count Gallenberg had been obliged to leave the Kärntnerthor Theatre and the new manager Louis Dupont showed little interest in Chopin. Nor was Haslinger so helpful now that money was involved. Another factor was Vienna's current infatuation with the young Sigismond Thalberg, whose meteoric rise to fame just preceded Chopin's visit and left little room for competition. Czerny apart, there had been a steady exodus of Vienna's pianists in the early nineteenth century (Hummel left in 1816, Moscheles in 1825) and in 1830 Thalberg was *the* pianist in the city, though he was himself soon to depart for Paris and London. Several of Chopin's remarks about Thalberg in letters to Poland may smack a little of sour grapes, but doubtless the shallow virtuosity of Thalberg's actual music, much of it exploiting his famous 'three-hand effect,' just about gave the measure of Vienna's musical tastes.

Personal misfortunes aside, Chopin had good reason to feel disenchanted with post-Congress Viennese cultural life, now that he had time to view it at leisure. Metternich was successfully choking any truly vital artistic and intellectual life in the city through the ruthless application of rigorous censorship. Where music was concerned the Viennese lived off their glorious memories or retreated into the innocuous and charming worlds of light Italian opera, salon orchestras and bandstands, the music in short of balls and banquets. 'Here they call waltzes *works*, and Strauss and Lanner who play dance music are called *Kapellmeisters!*' Chopin wrote to Poland, 'which all goes to show how the taste of the Viennese public has declined.'[6]

The success of 1829 completely eluded Chopin during his second visit to Vienna, and as a result he idled away some ten months in the city, achieving little. His lifestyle was by no means as unpleasant as has sometimes been suggested, but it was indolent and unproductive, and his confused and at times rather affected letters to Poland make little attempt to conceal his insecurity and uncertainty. 'Shall I go to Paris? Shall I stay here? Shall I put an end to myself? Shall I stop writing to you? Tell me what to do.'[7] He was after all living off his father with no clear prospects for future employment and his understandable homesickness was compounded by the troubles in Poland and by his youthful hankering after a young Polish singer whom he had admired from a safe distance. He was not, however, friendless in Vienna. Loneliness was mitigated by the kindness of the distinguished physician Dr Malfatti, he of Beethoven's acquaintance, and by his friendships with younger musicians in the city, the Polish composer Tomasz Nidecki, the cellist Josef Merk and the brilliant young violinist Josef Slavik. He continued to compose, of course, working halfheartedly on such big public pieces as a concerto for two pianos (never completed) and the *Grande Polonaise Brillante*, as well as lighter 'salon' pieces such as the *Valse Brillante*, Op.18. At the same time he was working on pieces which transcended the demands of the salon or the public concert. Above all he worked on several of the studies which were later to be included in Op.10, pieces which belong to his full stylistic maturity.

The proposed two-month visit was prolonged indefinitely and Chopin was characteristically incapable of reaching a firm decision about future plans. His eventual departure on 20 July 1831 was no doubt precipitated by the lack of response to, or even interest in, his only two public appearances in the city in April and June. Munich was the first stop, and while there he played the E Minor Concerto and the *Fantasy on Polish Themes*, Op.13 with some success. A month later in September he was in Stuttgart, and a week after that he arrived in Paris, where he was to make his home. It was while in Stuttgart that he heard of the final suppression of the Polish uprising. It was a key moment in Chopin's life, bringing into sharp focus the conflicting claims on his emotions, the call of the world which he knew, but whose limitations were all too apparent to him, and the call of the international world of music, in which he had yet to prove himself. The frequent depressions to which he had been susceptible in Vienna now gave way to a single cry of despair, articulated in the so-called 'Stuttgart Diary'. For all the extravagance of its language, the diary has a ring of sincerity which distinguishes it from some of the earlier letters to Poland.

> Oh God! You are there! You are there and yet you do not take vengeance! Haven't you witnessed enough crimes from Russia? . . . Oh father, so this is how you are rewarded in old age! Mother, sweet suffering mother, you saw your daughter die, and now you watch the Russian marching in over her grave to oppress you! . . . Oh Tytus, Tytus! . . . What has become of *her*, where is she now, poor girl? . . . Perhaps she is already in Russian hands? The Russians may be touching her, stifling her, murdering her! . . . I am helpless, sitting here powerless, suffering through the piano, in despair. . . . And what now? God, god, move this earth – let it swallow the people of this century.[8]

Such was Chopin's despair over family and friends, over adolescent love, over a Poland to which he could not now return. Ten months earlier, when news of the uprising had reached him in Vienna, he had been in an agony of indecision. To return with Tytus or to remain in Vienna and serve the Polish cause through his music, as Tytus urged? 'Why can't I beat the drum?' he had written to Jan Matuszyński. There is clearly no simple cause and effect in this, but it seems possible that the added depth and richness of the works whose inception dates from his year in Vienna, together with their tragic, passionate tone, reflect at least in part a new commitment to express Poland's tragedy in his music. 'Guns smothered in flowers', was Schumann's famous phrase.

Yet for all the nostalgia and despair, and the sincerity of his patriotism, it is probable that Chopin would not have returned to Poland after Stuttgart, even if that had been feasible. His final year in Warsaw, between the two visits to Vienna, had confirmed the need to broaden his horizons. 'You can't imagine how I lack something in Warsaw now,' he wrote to Tytus. The fact is that Warsaw could never have sustained Chopin's genius either as a composer or as a pianist. By comparison with leading European cities, including of course Vienna which he had just visited, it was a cultural backwater, and that despite something of an intellectual renaissance in the early years of the century. This was some time before the rigorous suppression of the Polish language and its literature which followed the defeat of the 1830 rising. On the contrary, since Poniatowski, Polish had been encouraged as the official language of the courts and administration. In addition there were Polish-language journals, a monumental dictionary compiled by Samuel Linde (a colleague of Chopin's father), and an upsurge of creative writing which registered the impact of the new wave of German Romantic poetry; Adam Mickiewicz's *Ballads and Romances*, heralding the Romantic age in Polish poetry, appeared in 1822.

Musical life, too, was picking up in the early decades of the century. At the National Theatre there was a fashionable Italian opera repertory, frowned upon by some of the more serious musicians in the city but adored by Chopin and of no little significance for the evolution of his musical language. Orchestral concerts were more of a rarity, but there were performances of Beethoven symphonies promoted by E. T. A. Hoffman and Elsner at the Resursa Muzyka. There were also public concerts organised by the Society of National and Religious Music and by the Society for Amateur Music at rooms in the National Theatre. Most important of all, the Warsaw Conservatory, soon to play host to Chopin, was established in 1821. By then Alexander's reforming zeal had cooled considerably and for the next decade – Chopin's teenage years – artistic and intellectual life was distinctly less lively. There were few outstanding concerts, and the one or two occasions when Chopin caught sight and sound of truly distinguished visiting performers such as Hummel and Paganini must have served only to underline the need to leave Poland.

The one mitigating factor was a thriving musical life far from the public gaze in the salons of that small group of very wealthy families who made up Poland's upper class in the early nineteenth century. Several of these aristocrats were themselves composers, and they often had their own small orchestras and mounted their own opera productions. Musical evenings were organised by society hostesses at the palaces of the Czartoryskis, Sapiehas, Potockis and Radziwills, modelled of course on the mores of contemporary French salons. The 'Blue Palace' salons were famous, and so too were the concerts organised by the so-called Warsaw Benevolent Society. The piano was at the heart of the salon. In Poland, as elsewhere in Europe, it had become a symbol of gentility, a necessary accomplishment for well-bred young ladies, and the focal point of any social evening. Polonaises were the most fashionable salon pieces in early nineteenth-century Warsaw, though minuets and contredanses were also popular and the waltz was in the ascendant. The repertory was well known to the young Chopin. He frequently improvised dance pieces as a boy, and his earliest written compositions were influenced by the many distinguished, if minor, Polish composers of such keyboard pieces in the early years of the century.

Chopin was much in demand at the salons from an early age. He was well known in Warsaw as a child prodigy, the 'heir of Mozart', having given a public concert at the age of eight (a concerto by Gyrowetz) and played to the internationally famous singer Catalani two years later. At fifteen he even played to Czar Alexander at the opening of the 1825 Diet and received a diamond ring for his efforts. From the start, moreover, he was treated as a social equal, and not merely as a 'musician'. We need only read Spohr's vivid accounts of aristocratic *soirées*[9] to remind ourselves that this kind of acceptance was far from typical. As a child, for instance, Chopin frequently visited the Grand Duke Constantine at Belvedere and played there with the Duke's son. A little later he became friendly with the governor of the Principality of Poznan, Prince Radziwill of Antonin, himself a composer, and he spent several weeks at Antonin between the two Vienna trips, playing music with the Prince's daughters and composing works for the family. Chopin moved easily in this society, and to a large extent he continued to move in it when he left Poland and eventually settled in Paris. It seems he had a natural air of distinction, the manner and reserve of a 'gentleman'. 'Aristocratic bearing', 'princelike charm' – we encounter such descriptions again and again in the literature, and no doubt that bearing and charm made their own discreet demands on Chopin's hosts. He was of course aware of the limitations of the salon, recognising only too clearly that much of its music was modish and trivial – 'music for the ladies' was his own phrase and he meant it disparagingly. Yet he never rejected the salon and he was in due course to invest its music with new dimensions of quality and beauty.

If Chopin felt at ease in aristocratic circles, with all the social graces carefully cultivated, there was nevertheless a quite different side to his make-up. He was not of course of aristocratic stock. Indeed his family background was staunchly middle class. His father Nicholas Chopin, a Frenchman who had settled in Poland in 1787, was a teacher at the Lyceum, many of whose staff were of foreign origins and some of them distinguished scholars too. He had been a tutor at the Skarbek estate in Żelazowa Wola, a small village some sixteen miles from Warsaw, and it was here that he met and married Justyna Krzyzanowska, an impoverished relative of the Skarbeks who acted as their housekeeper. Frederick, their third child, was born in Żelazowa Wola on 22 February 1810, and the family moved to Warsaw when he was just seven months old. The Chopins finally settled in a large house near the university, and Nicholas supplemented his income by taking in boarders from the Lyceum. Several of these, notably Tytus Woyciechowski, Dominik Dziewanowski, Jan Białoblocki and Jan Matuszyński, became Chopin's close friends, and his letters to them and to Julian Fontana, whom he got to know a little later, reveal him at his least reserved. Often there is a streak of bluntness, of healthy vulgarity and even cutting sarcasm in these letters which would perhaps have surprised his aristocratic acquaintances.

As several biographers have suggested, Chopin's personality was undoubtedly much influenced at formative stages by this interaction of the very different worlds of home and school on the one hand and the grandest Warsaw society on the other. There was yet another world which he encountered briefly but tellingly during several summer holidays at the Szafarnia country estate of Dominik Dziewanowski. Szafarnia introduced him to Polish folk music and dance not in the polite form encountered in fashionable drawing-rooms, but in its authentic rural setting. He was captivated by this music, by its harmonic astringencies and rhythmic energy, and there are signs in some of his letters that already as a fourteen-year-old he sensed its potential to renovate musical language.[10]

For the most part, however, his early dance pieces belong in style to the salon manner of his Polish contemporaries and immediate predecessors. That manner was tempered to an extent by a thorough grounding in Bach and the Viennese classics initially through his piano teacher Adalbert Żywny and later at the conservatory. Żywny was primarily a violinist, so that in some respects at least Chopin's piano technique was self-acquired, a factor which may well have had some bearing on its pronounced individuality. Yet whatever his qualities as a piano teacher, Żywny was clearly no ordinary musician. He laid the foundations for Chopin's lifelong love of Bach, and this was to be of the utmost importance for his developing musical thought. Later Chopin turned to the more eminent Józef Elsner for private lessons in music theory and he continued to work with Elsner when he entered the conservatory in 1826. The conservatory offered an intensive training in theory and counterpoint in the first two years with free composition in the third year, and Chopin emerged, predictably enough, as an exceptional student. In his final report Elsner referred to his 'outstanding abilities' and described him as a 'musical genius'. Certainly his reputation in Warsaw musical circles was of the highest and the concerts which he gave before departing for Vienna, when he played for the first time his two piano concertos, were accorded extravagant praise. The one adverse criticism was the smallness of tone, echoing the Viennese press a year earlier and presaging Fétis's comments a year or so later.

Such criticisms must have served to underline Chopin's own doubts about his future as a virtuoso-composer. 'I am not fit to give concerts,' he was later to write to Liszt. 'The crowd intimidates me and I feel asphyxiated by its eager breath, paralyzed by its inquisitive stare, silenced by its alien faces.'[11] Following an unsuccessful appearance at a charity concert two months after the Paris début, Chopin more or less abandoned the concert platform. Indeed it is remarkable that he could have established such a widespread reputation as a pianist on the basis of a mere handful of public concerts (barely one a year during his first decade in Paris and then none until the English concerts of 1848). In all probability his rejection of the career of virtuoso-composer was no snap decision, but the result of a gradual and growing awareness that he was temperamentally unsuited to the role. Indeed his letters suggest that already in his Warsaw days he thought of himself first and foremost as a composer. Nonetheless the change of direction was of momentous importance for his life and music, and the path he chose to follow subsequently was an unorthodox one. In the early nineteenth century it was usual to establish a reputation either as a *virtuoso* composer, whose creative work centred primarily on display pieces for the piano or violin, or as a *composer*, with a corpus of symphonic works, operas, choral music and so on. Chopin followed neither course. He rejected the mantle of the virtuoso, but continued to write almost exclusively for the piano and to work within the stylistic framework of public virtuosity and salon music. His achievement was to transform both worlds utterly, to elevate them to a plane where they need yield nothing in stature and importance to the more prestigious worlds of the symphony and the opera-house.

That he was in a position to follow this course was due at least partly to the contacts he established in Paris with wealthy Polish families, many of whom had settled there after the uprising, and through them with the cream of Parisian society. After an initial sluggishness such contacts ensured that his services as a teacher to the children of the wealthy were much in demand. He enjoyed the teaching at first, and it had some bearing on the nature of his creative output in the 1830s, encouraging the production of short, manageable pieces, but for the most part his pupils were only modestly talented[12] and were unable to benefit fully from his novel and often ingenious teaching methods. The pleasure he took in teaching soon began to wane, but the income was no small compensation. At twenty francs a lesson, Chopin could afford to live very comfortably, even luxuriously, and he found it more congenial to restrict his appearances as a performer to small groups of initiates in society drawing-rooms, where his reputation as a pianist and improviser soon became legendary.

In the salon Chopin's best qualities as a performer could be appreciated. Although the point has occasionally been exaggerated, it does seem that he found heaviness in playing distasteful, preferring a discriminating sensitivity of touch to a show of power. All those nuances which were lost in the concert-hall, the carefully shaded dynamics, intricate pedal effects, delicate washes of passagework and discreet rubato, came into their own in the *soirée charmante*. His contemporaries were not slow to express their admiration. 'The marvellous charm, the poetry and originality, the perfect freedom and absolute lucidity of Chopin's playing cannot be described – It was perfection in every sense. . . '[13] 'The whole man appeared to tremble, while under his fingers the piano sprang to life with its own intensity.'[14]

Chopin's income from teaching was supplemented by his earnings from the sales of published music. Apart from the private publication of some very early music, he first went into print at the age of fifteen when his C minor Rondo was published by Brzezini & Co. Other early pieces were published by Haslinger (Op.2) and Mecchetti of Vienna (Op.3), but shortly after arriving in Paris he sold publishing rights to Schlesinger (after tentative negotiations with Farrenc) and from 1834 onwards his music was published 'simultaneously' in France, England (Wessel) and Germany (Kistner, and later Breitkopf & Härtel). This necessitated a large number of engraver's exemplars, and indirectly created no end of trouble for future editors.

Simultaneous publication was already a fairly well-established practice among composers by Chopin's time. Its purpose was to avoid piracy due to the complex copyright laws in different countries, though it must be said that in practice Chopin rarely achieved true simultaneity. Many different options existed for the mechanics of music publishing. With Schlesinger Chopin gave autograph manuscripts directly to the publisher, proof-reading himself in early and later periods and often allowing others to do so in the intervening period (1835–1841). With his German publishers he sent proof sheets from the French edition until late 1835, after which he sent manuscripts, though until 1841 these were often by copyists. Once the work had left his hands he had no editorial control. His dealings with Wessel in England were more complicated. Until 1843 proofs, copyists' manuscripts and autographs were variously sent, after which autograph manuscripts seem to have been the norm. There were difficulties over Wessel's editorial emendations, his practice of imposing picturesque titles, and his methods of payment. In general, as Jeffrey Kallberg has pointed out,[15] Chopin's trouble with his publishers arose from attempts to co-ordinate a variety of options to obtain maximum advantage both financially and in terms of widespread dissemination.[16]

As Chopin's publications grew in number, his bargaining power increased, and so too did his reputation and income. Very soon he was achieving the success in Paris which had eluded him in Vienna. In the 1830s Paris could well claim to be the cultural capital of Europe, now that the Viennese star had faded, and Chopin's arrival coincided with the glorious flowering of French Romanticism in all the arts. Musically Paris was second to nowhere in Europe. In the orchestra of the Societé des Concerts du Conservatoire (founded in 1828) it could boast one of the finest ensembles in Europe, and it attracted to the Opéra, the Opéra-Comique and the Théâtre Italien the leading singers and composers of the day. Rossini himself lived in the city, of course, and Cherubini was still active at the conservatoire when Chopin arrived. Spontini had left in 1820, but the grand opera tradition was ably continued by Meyerbeer and Halévy. Chopin's love of opera could not have been better served. Paris was a magnet, moreover, for the best pianists of the day. Chopin particularly admired Kalkbrenner and even considered having lessons with him, while of the younger generation he made friends quickly with Ferdinand Hiller and Franz Liszt. His relations with Liszt were never much more than cordial, but Hiller partly replaced Tytus Woyciechowski as Chopin's intimate *confidant*, sharing that role to an extent with the cellist Auguste Franchomme.

Socially the early Paris years were nothing if not lively. Very soon he was part of a circle of artists and musicians which seems dazzling in retrospect. The poets Heine and de Vigny were among his acquaintances, as was the artist Delacroix, later to become a close friend. Berlioz too was part of the circle, and Chopin had much affection for the man, even if he could not share Liszt's and Hiller's enthusiasm for the music. Much the same was true of his relations with Schumann and Mendelssohn, both of whom he got to know in the early 1830s.[17] He had nothing but admiration for the playing of Clara Wieck, but could find little to interest him in the music of her husband-to-be, though Schumann's enthusiastic advocacy of *Chopin's* music was a considerable factor in its growing popularity.

Such company was congenial, but Chopin always claimed that he could only relax fully with his compatriots and he was greatly cheered by the arrival in Paris of his old friends from Warsaw, Jan Matuszyński and Julian Fontana, and by his growing friendship with an older and rather more colourful Pole Albert Grzymala. All three soon became indispensable to his well-being. For Matuszyński Chopin had the deepest feelings, but he tended to use Fontana rather shamelessly, before the latter's departure for America in the early 1840s. Even Grzymala, who saw himself as a sort of father figure, was pressed into Chopin's service on trivial matters on more than one occasion. Later he was to become marginally involved with another group of Poles in Paris. The Polish Literary Society acted as a focus for many Polish artists and intellectuals who gravitated to the city after the collapse of the uprising. With Mickiewicz at their head they were committed to the task of furthering the cause of Polish nationalism abroad, and their artistic talents were viewed as a means to that end. Chopin's attitude to this group was always ambivalent, and he was certainly a disappointment to them, though he did befriend Cyprian Norwid in the 1840s. As Mickiewicz saw it, he frittered away his prodigious talents entertaining the French aristocracy rather than serving the Polish cause.

The fact is that Chopin, for all his patriotism, was enjoying his success in Paris. His standard of living improved steadily during the first few years there, and he moved in due course to elegant rooms in the Rue de la Chausée d'Antin, spending freely on the best clothes, a hired coachman and furnishings of quality. The city agreed with him and he put to the back of his mind any thought of returning to Poland; he could easily have done so when the Czar offered the first of many amnesties in 1833. At the same time Poland, his family and his friends at home were constantly in his thoughts, and when he heard that his parents had left for Karlsbad in August 1835 he immediately set off to join them. They spent a happy month together before Chopin had to return to Paris. This was to be his last meeting with his parents, though after the trauma of his father's death in 1844, and again in his own last year, he saw something of his older sister Ludwika, herself a talented pianist who had once entertained artistic ambitions. It was in Dresden, on his return to Paris from Karlsbad, that he met again the Wodziński family, whose sons had been among Nicholas Chopin's boarders in Warsaw. Chopin was immediately taken with their sister Maria, a sixteen-year-old beauty whom he had last seen five years earlier, and he stayed two weeks in Dresden in the company of the Wodzińskis before moving on to Leipzig and Paris.

Chopin's relationship with Maria Wodzińska ended unhappily. The following July he visited Maria and her mother at Marienbad and formally asked for her hand in marriage. He was given some initial grounds for optimism, but was told that much would depend on his state of health, already precarious. In the winter he became very ill and in Warsaw there were even reports of his death. The Wodziński family was alarmed, and by the spring of 1837 the letters from Maria's mother (with brief postscripts from Maria) became less frequent and less encouraging. In July, while still waiting for a definite answer from the family, he travelled to England with Camille Pleyel, head of the firm of piano manufacturers whose product Chopin admired above all other instruments. He visited London and the surrounding countryside but, apart from a single performance at John Broadwood's house in Bryanston Square and a meeting with his English publisher Wessel, he kept his distance from English musical life, and his opinion of the country was less than wholly favourable. It was while there that he must have received a letter from Maria's mother making it clear that his suit was not accepted.

Maria Wodzińska was not the first object of Chopin's amorous intentions. He had hankered after a young singer Konstancja Gladkowska during his final year in Warsaw, composing the slow movement of the F minor Concerto and the Waltz Op.70 No.3 under the influence of that youthful love. It seems that there was little in the way of concrete declaration.[18] It was an adolescent love, though none the less sincere for that, and Konstancja continued to act as a largely unwitting focus for Chopin's emotional deprivations during his sojourn in Vienna. Like most people, he needed a close relationship, but he seemed to find it easier to communicate emotionally with men than with women. While he craved Konstancja from afar, he poured his heart out to Tytus. At the same time there is no firm basis for the assumption, occasionally made, that his emotional dependence on men such as Woyciechowski and Hiller ever had a physical dimension. This was almost certainly reserved for the opposite sex. That he had some sort of casual sexual encounter just before his arrival in Paris is certain, and it is also possible (though unlikely) that he had a brief affair with the beautiful Countess Delfina Potocka soon after his arrival there.[19] But the relationship with Maria Wodzińska was a different matter. From the start Chopin viewed her as a suitable match, and the break-up of the relationship disturbed him as much as anything because it dashed his hopes of a settled, stable family life.

A year after that disappointment Chopin found himself becoming increasingly involved with the novelist George Sand, whom he met through Liszt's mistress Marie d'Agoult. The next ten years of his life were to be dominated by that relationship. In almost every respect it was an attraction of opposites. Even their backgrounds point up the contrast, Chopin's conservative, middle-class and devoutly Catholic, Mme Sand's radical and liberal-minded. In their lifestyles too the couple could hardly have been more different, Chopin anxious to preserve proprieties, refined in manners, aloof, Sand flaunting her unorthodox lifestyle and advanced views, he living only and narrowly for music, she embracing the whole world of ideas, however insecurely. While it has sometimes been over-stressed, there was undoubtedly a strong maternal element in Sand's feelings for Chopin, a need to give what she had never received. She herself recognised this, though she argued that it 'could not for a moment struggle against the love born of the entrails', by which she meant her love for her own children.[20] Her earlier search for a fulfilling relationship had taken her through a long succession of affairs following her separation from Casimir Duvenant. There were Jules Sandeau, Prosper Merimée, de Musset, Pietro Pagello, Louis-Chrystom Michel and Charles Didier. Indeed the early stages of her relationship with Chopin acquired a touch of melodrama through the almost comical jealous intrigues of her current lover Félicien Mallefille, himself a Chopin devotee. It was a factor in the couple's plan to leave Paris in search of an idyllic retreat in Majorca. Typically Chopin was in an agony of indecision about the move and, again typically, he insisted for appearance's sake on leaving Paris for Perpignan independently of Mme Sand and her two children, finally arriving by mail coach on the evening of 31 October 1838. The group then took a steamer to Barcelona, where they spent a few days, and on 7 November they set off in a small packet boat for Palma.

The story of Chopin and Sand in Majorca has been told many times.[21] They were greeted by inhospitable and disapproving islanders and by a multitude of inconveniences, not the least of which was the difficulty in finding acceptable accommodation anywhere in Palma. When they eventually found a villa in the country, it proved quite incapable of withstanding the rains of an unusually severe winter, and the conditions took a dreadful toll of Chopin's deteriorating health. As news of his consumption spread rapidly, the couple were further ostracised, and they were even obliged to pay to have the villa disinfected and redecorated. In despair Mme Sand managed to move her entourage to a monastery at Valldemosa where she had already rented rooms. Life here was hardly less difficult, particularly as the pious villagers, who clearly regarded the group as heathens, banded together to make the purchase of even basic foodstuffs all but impossible. The resourcefulness of George Sand during this traumatic period was remarkable. She was a provider (purchasing a goat and a sheep to ensure some reliable nourishment), a teacher (spending most of the day instructing her children), a nurse (looking after the ailing Chopin), and a writer, (continuing to work on her manuscripts at night, including a revision of *Lélia* and the completion of *Spiridion*). Her industry on these books was a product of dire financial necessity, for the family was incurring substantially greater expenses in Majorca than had been anticipated.

The same imperative drove Chopin to work, despite his illness, acute depression and the lack of a decent piano. At last the Pleyel piano sent from Paris arrived in Palma, and at considerable expense Mme Sand had it delivered to Valldemosa. On 22 January 1839 Chopin was able to write to Pleyel: 'I am forwarding the *Préludes*. I finished them on your little piano which arrived in perfect condition, despite the sea, the storms and the Palma customs.'[22] Exhausted after completing the preludes, Chopin sank into ever-declining health and spirits, until Mme Sand decided that it was essential to leave the island. Once more the problems multiplied – the sale of the piano, the uncertainty about the departure date of the boat, and so forth. Chopin was now coughing blood and haemorrhaging badly, and he deteriorated during the voyage to Barcelona. While he convalesced there, George Sand was his constant attendant. 'She nursed me by herself', he wrote to Grzymala. 'I have seen her . . . deprive herself of everything for my benefit. . . . Besides everything else she manages to write.'[23] Increasingly she was looking upon Chopin as a second son. 'I care for him like a child and he loves me like his mother.' For a time at least this was a fulfilling enough role for Mme Sand. In late February the group sailed to Marseilles, where Chopin continued to regain his strength and addressed himself once more to his affairs, writing petulant letters of complaint about his publishers to Fontana and Grzymala, and requesting all sorts of chores to be done in preparation for his arrival in Paris. His capacity to use his devoted Polish friends was one of his least attractive attributes.

In June Chopin and Sand finally arrived at Sand's chateau at Nohant, and in the peaceful atmosphere there he was able to devote himself to composition, completing the B flat Sonata, three new mazurkas (Op.41), the Second Impromptu and the G major Nocturne, Op.37 No.2. Life at Nohant was a pleasant routine enlivened by visits from friends such as Grzymala and by evening entertainments. The couple returned to Paris in the autumn, and for the next few years Nohant and Paris were both to be essential for his well-being and work, the security and peace of the one preparing him for the livelier social and musical life of the other. Fontana and Grzymala had found apartments for Sand and Chopin in Paris, a small bachelor flat for the composer and two twin-storey apartments for Sand

and her children. They led semi-separate lives, meeting around five o'clock for the family dinner, usually with only a few close friends present. Chopin continued to teach and to grace the salons, but there were some more formal appearances too, a concert at Pleyel's rooms in April 1841, a performance for Louis-Philippe at the Tuileries in December and a recital with his close friends Pauline Viardot and Auguste Franchomme in February 1842.

Two months after that recital Chopin received a blow which left him emotionally paralysed. His childhood friend Jan Matuszyński died in George Sand's apartment of pulmonary tuberculosis. When they returned from Nohant in September Chopin and Sand were unable to face living in the Rue Pigalle, where Jan had died, and moved instead to two apartments in the Square d'Orléans, close to their friend Charlotte Marliani. From this period onwards, as Jeffrey Kallberg has pointed out,[24] there was a major change in Chopin's attitude to his work, in particular a dramatic drop in his rate of production and a comprehensive review of all the elements of his craft. It was at this time that he studied counterpoint treatises by Cherubini and Kastner, a study which contributed to significant new directions in his later piano music. His flow of ideas was undiminished, as accounts of his improvisations indicate, but he became increasingly self-critical about arriving at a finished version of a piece and committing it to paper in a final form. 'He spends days of nervous tension and almost terrifying desperation. He alters and retouches the same passages endlessly and paces up and down like a madman.'[25] It may be too that he was influenced by his close friendship and many discussions with Delacroix, who in the early 1840s began to move away from the Romantic spontaneity of his earlier painting towards a more controlled style, formally balanced and restrained.

In any event Chopin's rethinking of his art was doubtless encouraged by and certainly facilitated by a fairly uneventful lifestyle during these years. Yet beneath the placid exterior of their routines in Paris and Nohant there were serious tensions developing in the Sand-Chopin relationship, tensions which were to become exacerbated in the mid-1840s. It would seem that they were lovers in the accepted sense for only a very brief period, possibly no more than a year. Whatever the reason for this, Chopin, according to Sand, was susceptible to morbid and obsessive jealousies about both her past and her present. All this, together with discord involving the children Maurice and Solange, was fictionalised in the novel which occupied Sand in the summer of 1846, *Lucrezia Floriani*, a novel whose theme is the death of a romance. It is a cruel depiction of Chopin and, while it is clearly anything but impartial, it cannot be completely disregarded. 'Karol did not have minor faults. He had one major one, great, involuntary, fatal intolerance of mind.'[26]

Adam Zamoyski has drawn our attention to another portrait of Chopin during these years. It emerges from the diary of his pupil Zofia Rozengardt, examined by Count Zamoyski in Cracow. 'There is a strange mixture in his character, vain and proud, loving luxury and yet disinterested and incapable

1. *Chopin's father (1771–1844), from a portrait by Miroszewski*

2. *Chopin's mother (1782–1861), from a portrait by Miroszewski*

3. *Chopin's birthplace in Żelazowa Wola*

4. *A view of Warsaw, from the Sapieha Palace*

5. *Chopin in 1847. Pencil drawing by F. X. Winterhalter*

6. *Chopin. A watercolour by Maria Wodzińska, painted in Marienbad, 1836*

7. *Chopin in 1849. From a photograph by L. A. Bisson*

8. *One of two surviving Pleyel pianos, on which Chopin played. It is on display in the Chopin Society in Warsaw*

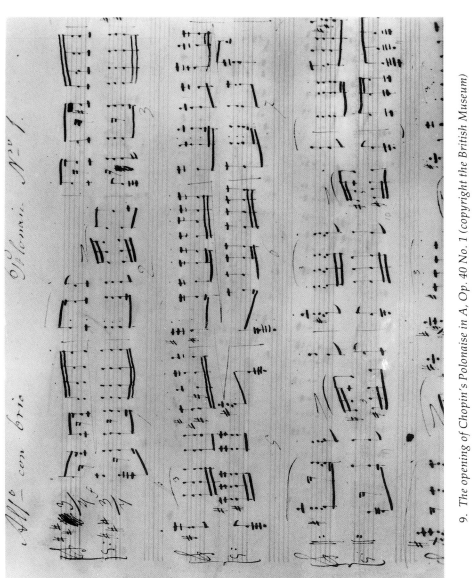

9. *The opening of Chopin's Polonaise in A, Op. 40 No. 1 (copyright the British Museum)*

of sacrificing the smallest part of his own will or caprice for all the luxury in the world. He is polite to excess and yet there is so much irony, so much spite inside it.'[27] This is a telling description and it tallies well with some of the conclusions of that most committed of Chopin biographers Arthur Hedley. Hedley refers to Chopin's ironic attitude to mere sentimentality, 'whatever form it appeared in, whether in the shape of adoring woman admirers or the Germanic soulfulness of a Schumann' – perhaps a little unfair to Schumann! – to his 'strong waves of anger or contempt . . . sarcasm . . . contemptuous silence' and beneath it all that 'imperious craving for perfection' which 'dominated and tormented Chopin's whole life.'[28]

During the summer of 1846 the estrangement between Chopin and Sand became more serious. The differences in their social attitudes became increasingly a source of friction, as Sand became more and more involved with progressive social and political ideologies. But this was merely the surface of more fundamental tensions, many of them arising from Chopin's ambiguous position in the household, especially where the children were concerned. Their eventual separation was brought about largely by family disputes involving Maurice and Solange. Sand and Chopin disagreed fundamentally over the character of the sculptor Auguste Clésinger who proposed to Solange in Nohant in April 1847. Chopin had become increasingly fond of Solange, and he recognised that Clésinger was simply a bounty hunter. Because of his disapproval of the relationship he was not informed of the proposal until May, when the first banns were published, a delay which he strongly resented. There were further complications stemming from Sand's earlier adoption of a cousin's daughter Augustine Brault, to whom Maurice became attached, but who was also courted by the young painter Rousseau. The family intrigues were labyrinthine, but the outcome was that Chopin sided with Solange against her mother, Rousseau backed out of his proposed marriage with Augustine (largely due to rumours spread by Solange and Clésinger) and an irreparable breach was driven between Chopin and Sand. For the latter it became 'clear' that all along the focus of Chopin's affection had shifted from her to her daughter, and it is true that Chopin was close to Solange for the brief remainder of his life.

The rest of the story is quickly told. Following the break with Sand, Chopin's health and spirits declined rapidly, with the winter of 1847–8 reducing him to a shadow of his former self. On 16 February, just a week before revolution broke out in Paris, he gave his last concert in the city, joining Franchomme and Alard in a performance of a Mozart trio and three movements of the Cello Sonata at Pleyel's rooms. Two months later he left for England, having promised to visit his pupil Jane Stirling and her sister Mrs Erskine at their home in Scotland. By then he was dangerously ill, though he was obliged to play for his supper, performing to the English aristocracy and even the Queen, and giving public concerts at Eaton Place and St James's Square, all to great acclaim. In August the season was over

and Chopin, now short of funds as well as health, made his way to Edinburgh where he was pampered to distraction by the devoted, well-meaning,
but tiresome Miss Stirling. He gave a concert in Manchester on 28 August,
where his playing was on the whole well-received but was deemed too
delicate for such a large hall. Back in Edinburgh his mood was black and
dejected, as he grew increasingly intolerant of the Scottish climate and of
the attentions of Jane Stirling. His last public concert, given for the benefit
of Polish refugees, was on 31 October in London, and a month later he
returned to Paris. His creative output had now reduced to a trickle, and
with his failing health he was no longer able to teach. The last days were
a struggle with consumption, cheered only by the presence of his sister
Ludwika, who had made the journey to Paris to be by his side. She had
always been close to him, and she was with him when he died on 17
October 1849. His last work was almost certainly a mazurka, though not, as
Fontana reported, Op.68 No.4, which he left in the form of a rather chaotic
sketch. The aptness of the frame enclosing Chopin's surviving music has
often attracted comment. His creative life ended with a mazurka. It had
opened thirty-three years earlier with a polonaise.

2

Apprenticeship

'Polonaise in G minor, dedicated to Her Excellency Countess Victoria Skarbek, composed by Frederick Chopin, a musician aged eight.' This is how Chopin described his first surviving piece, published privately by Canon Cybulski in 1817. Most of the music he composed during these years of early childhood remained in manuscript and a great deal of it has disappeared.[1] There is one other surviving piece from 1817, a Polonaise in B flat major, and after that we have nothing until the A flat major Polonaise of 1821, which he dedicated 'to M. Żywny, from his pupil Frederick Chopin'. In general style and character the two early polonaises probably differed in no essential respects from the many short pieces which he was in the habit of improvising on the piano from an early age. Most of them he would not have bothered to write down.

It is not surprising that Chopin's earliest surviving written compositions should have been polonaises, for the polonaise reigned supreme in the drawing-rooms of early nineteenth-century Poland. The dance itself was of course Polish in origin, but its musical characteristics, while not quite so distinctive as those of the more familiar nineteenth-century polonaise, had attracted the interest of French and Austro-German composers throughout the eighteenth century and even before.[2] J. S. Bach, Couperin and above all Telemann[3] included polonaise movements in their suites, while rondos 'à la polacca' and independent polonaises appear in W. F. Bach, Schubert, Mozart and Beethoven. The finale of Beethoven's Triple Concerto is one of the more celebrated of many such movements. Not unnaturally, Polish composers turned to the polonaise with more commitment, and there is a plentiful repertory of eighteenth-century concertos, rondos and variation sets, to say nothing of operatic songs and theatre entr'actes, which draw upon its familiar characteristics. Little of this music has travelled beyond the Polish frontier and little deserves to. It is for home consumption only, as are the rather later polonaises of Prince Michał Kleofas Ogiński (1765–1833).[4]

Ogiński's pieces do have some historical importance, however, for it was above all in his hands that the polonaise was moulded into an independent miniature of distinctive character for harpsichord or piano, designed for the salon rather than the ballroom or the opera house. Ogiński was one of a family of musicians who bore eloquent witness to the lengthy tradition of amateur composers drawn from the Polish aristocracy. His polonaises have a simple, homespun character, melancholy in tone and largely untainted by contemporary Western European influences, and they defined the basic framework of the form as a clearcut 'da capo' type, often with a short introduction. They set the tone for the countless polonaise songs and piano pieces composed in the early nineteenth century (many with a patriotic programme), though later composers considerably widened the scope of Ogiński's model. Karol Kurpiński, whose polonaises were usually composed for orchestra in the first instance[5] and later transcribed for keyboard, maintained the simplicity of the Ogiński 'polonaise triste' but enriched it through devices, and often literal themes, drawn from the opera-house. In the hands of Chopin's teacher Józef Elsner, on the other hand, the polonaise acquired something of the finesse of the early classical keyboard sonata and sonatina. Yet another line of development, evidenced particularly in Franciszek Lessel and Maria Szymanowska, invested the dance piece with something of the virtuoso manner of composers such as Hummel, Field and Weber.

Such stylistic shadings on a simple dance form were just the surface of a much deeper pluralism which attended Polish music as it journeyed from the Enlightenment into the era of Romanticism. There is a general tendency in music historiography to view pre- and early nineteenth-century Slavonic music as a kind of poor relation to a Western European 'mainstream'. This approach has done scant justice to pioneering developments in Bohemian music, and it is in any case a dubious *modus operandi*, but it does correspond closely enough to the realities of Poland's music in the early nineteenth century. Polish composers at this time did seem to be in constant pursuit of yesterday's Western European styles, particularly in the fields of symphonic and chamber composition. Admittedly the music of Haydn, Mozart and (to a lesser extent) Beethoven was familiar in the Warsaw of Chopin's formative years and there are ample signs that Polish composers were sensible of the uniqueness of their achievements. Józef Elsner, Feliks Janiewicz[6] and Józef Brzowski in particular responded to the Viennese masters as models of excellence and were not slow to borrow from them gestures which might add weight and distinction to their own instrumental music. But the idiom of that music was often closer in essence to the 'galant' manner of the early classical period, then largely outmoded in Western Europe. The time-lag is no less apparent in the self-consciously 'learned' manner so often adopted in Polish devotional music of the period, reflecting a stylistic separation of sacred and secular which was much less marked in Western Europe, though it had by no means disappeared.

Neither the 'high-brow' art of the symphony nor the severity of the mass and the church cantata had much impact on the young Chopin. Nor did they hold much attraction for the wider musical public in early nineteenth-century Warsaw. Warsaw audiences were much more responsive to the rapidly spreading 'bravura' concert music composed by virtuosi such as

Hummel, Field and Weber, and to the growing body of lightweight miniatures designed for the drawing-room and centred on the piano. It was an international trend which again found Polish composers, Chopin included, in eager pursuit. It is only really in Chopin's early rondos, variations and concertos that we find a fully realised *stile brillante* in Poland, but the bravura pieces of violinists such as Karol Józef Lipiński[7] and of the pianist-composer Franciszek Lessel[8] moved some way in that direction and doubtless influenced Chopin himself. Maria Szymanowska too made her mark on the world of fashionable concert music. Aside from Chopin she was the only Polish composer of the first half of the century to reach a substantial non-Polish audience. Shortly after her introduction to the Warsaw salons in the second decade she gained international recognition as a gifted and sensitive pianist and as a composer of distinction, though she eschewed display pieces in favour of delicately drawn, evocative miniatures, echoing John Field (whom she knew in Russia) and at times pre-echoing Chopin's own lyrical pianism.

For all their growing popularity neither the concert-hall nor the salon could rival the opera-house as the nerve centre of fashionable music in Warsaw, and it was here that Chopin's enduring love of opera was born. From the 1820s onwards the opera was dominated by contemporary Italian styles, and above all by Rossini. Several Italian composers made their home in the Polish capital, at least until the uprising of 1831, and one of them, Carlo Evasio Soliva, played a major role in musical circles as principal of the School of Singing and Declamation. It was in Soliva's opera *Aniela* that Chopin's much-admired Konstancja Gladkowska made her début in 1830. From Maciej Kamienski's *Nędza uszczęśliwione* (1778) onwards, native Polish composers had made a growing contribution to the operatic repertory of the National Theatre, excelling in comic operas on rustic themes, particularly in the form of *Singspiele* or 'vaudevilles'. Jan Stefani's *Cud mniemany* (1794) is considered by Polish historians as a landmark of the period immediately preceding the more substantial achievements of Elsner and, above all, Karol Kurpiński, the leading Polish opera composer before Moniuszko. Kurpiński was a prominent figure in Warsaw's musical life and the young Chopin crossed his path on numerous occasions. We read of him improvising on one Kurpiński theme and he included another in his Op.13 *Fantasy on Polish Themes*. Kurpiński was the conductor, moreover, at Chopin's farewell concerts in Warsaw when he performed the two piano concertos for the first time.

A representative cross-section of Polish music composed during Chopin's years in Warsaw would reveal then a heterogeneous range of styles: high Baroque church cantatas by Jacob Goląbek, Classical symphonies and chamber music by Elsner, bravura concertos and solos by Lessel and Józef Desczyński, mood miniatures by Szymanowska, Italianate operas by Kurpiński and vaudevilles by Stefani. Ironically, in view of this range of styles, the concept of a national Polish idiom was much in the air in the early nineteenth century, discussed not only in treatises by Wacław Sierakowski and Elsner, but in popular newspapers of the day. For obvious political reasons Polish composers were encouraged and expected to write music which affirmed a sense of Polish identity. In practice, however, 'Polishness' in music had not progressed much further than an appropriate choice of subject matter and the introduction of modal and rhythmic characteristics derived from the polonaise, mazurka and (slightly later) krakowiak.

For the most part such characteristics were simply grafted on to familiar styles, so that Polish elements in Lessel and Elsner, for example, do not differ in many respects from Polish elements in Hummel and Weber; the difference lies above all in the frequency of their occurrence. It is doubtful if a progressive Polish 'school' of composers could have grown from this scanty soil, even if political change had not scotched any such possibility in the wake of 1831. The sad truth is that music in early nineteenth-century Poland, for all its variety, was dominated by amateurs and dilettantes, and even the professional composers submitted to their insular and conservative tastes. 'National' music amounted to little more than colourful songs and dances.

Considerations of national style played little part in Chopin's response to the music surrounding him as a boy. One is struck by the certainty with which his lifelong tastes and sympathies were formed in these early years. From the start he showed little interest in symphonic and chamber compositions or in church music. Even in his third-year composition course at the conservatory he was allowed to pursue his own inclinations while his fellow students worked industriously on the statutory cantatas. Chopin turned instead to more accessible quarters, to fashionable Italian opera and to the music of the salon and the concert virtuoso. These were the worlds of display and sentiment which shaped his emerging musical personality and it was to be his achievement immeasureably to enrich their materials and gestures in his own musical language, revealing in them a capacity to shape music of lasting quality.

Needless to say there are few signs of that quality in the little G minor Polonaise presented to Countess Skarbek in 1817. Like the B flat major piece from the same year, it is a straightforward response to the music which the young Chopin must have played himself, including polonaises by Ogiński, Elsner and his own teacher Żywny. Wacław Poźniak has shown the near identity of the trio of the B flat piece and an Ogiński polonaise, and Józef Chomiński has demonstrated similar links between the openings of the G minor work and an F minor Polonaise by Elsner.[9] Such parallels could be multiplied, for in design and character the Chopin pieces are similar to countless other polonaises turned out by Polish composers at the time. Formally they adopt the Ogiński model, with both the main sections and the trios governed by simple statement and response patterns in conventionally articulated periods. Technically the pieces are undemanding, with the clean textures and simple harmonies which we might expect of an eight-year-old. Yet at the same time it is clear that the young composer was in his simple way deliberately exploring the potential of his medium, trying out contrasting textures and registers and sampling a variety of accompaniment patterns and simple hand-crossing devices. Right at the outset his creativity was inseparable from the physical limitations and potentialities of the piano.

Four years separate the two pieces of 1817 from the next surviving piece, a polonaise in A flat major, which provides us with the composer's earliest known autograph, bereft of dynamics, phrasing or tempo indication. It is appropriate that he should have dedicated this piece to Żywny, for he had just come to the end of his period of study with the old man, and the much greater assurance of this polonaise and of its successor in G sharp minor no doubt reflects the benefits of this tuition.[10] These are no longer pieces for the dance, but dance pieces designed for the salon and directed above all towards display. The sophistication of the G sharp minor in particular is remarkable for a composer in his early teens. Right from its confident opening flourish the piece marks a distinct advance on the three earlier polonaises. Even a glance at the left-hand part is enough to demonstrate the new technical command. Here for the first time classical accompaniment patterns give way to characteristically widened and differentiated configurations, with hints too of the kind of concealed left-hand melody which Chopin was later to make his own.

Already the A flat major and G sharp minor polonaises are more viable than most of the polonaises composed by Chopin's older compatriots. Polish writers make much of native influences, but it is possible to overstate the case. Ogiński, Elsner and Żywny have certainly been left behind, though there are affinities with the bravura polonaises of Lessel and Szymanowska (especially the trio of her F minor). The cut of the themes and the nature of the passage-work in the Chopin pieces indicate clearly, however, that he was now responding to a much wider range of influences. In particular some of the textures suggest striking parallels with the music of Hummel and Weber, neither of whom was a stranger to the polonaise. One of Hummel's most popular pieces, running to no less than thirty-eight editions in the early nineteenth century, was a rondo 'à la polacca' *La Bella Capricciosa* Op.55 and Ex.1(i) indicates some of the affinities between this piece and Chopin's A flat major Polonaise. There are similar parallels between Weber's *Grande Polonaise* Op.21 and the Chopin G sharp minor, as Ex.1(ii) shows.[11]

Such affinities need not, of course, imply that Chopin was using the Hummel and Weber works as direct models, but they do serve to demonstrate his assimilation of the characteristic gestures of a virtuoso style which was gaining more and more international currency in the solo piano literature of the early nineteenth century. Such fingerprints were beginning to assume something of the character of the stock-in-trade materials of the virtuoso composer, and the list can easily be extended. Another conventional pattern used in the G sharp minor Polonaise comprises various types

Hummel, *La Bella Capricciosa* Op.55

Chopin, Polonaise in A flat major

Ex.1(i)

Weber, *Grande Polonaise* Op.21

Chopin, Polonaise in G sharp minor

Ex.1(ii)

of *Rollfiguren* to break up a simple chromatic descent (bars 9–10). Yet another, found in the trio, is the rising arpeggio or skip followed by descending scalar thirds as a gesture of temporary closure (Ex.1(iii)).

These devices are part and parcel of the remarkable right-hand virtuosity of the G sharp minor Polonaise, where little is presented without adornment. This is especially so in the trio. Here the right hand sweeps over most of the keyboard in an astonishing parade of double trills, parallel thirds and cascades of demisemiquavers over a steady left-hand pulse. Of course it is easy to criticise the piece on the grounds that this exuberant ornamentation disguises a poverty of genuine melodic interest and a pain-

Kalkbrenner, Fantasy in F major Op.68

Chopin, Polonaise in G sharp minor

Ex.1(iii)

fully turgid harmonic rhythm, particularly at the beginning of the trio. But for Chopin the piece was first and foremost an essay in virtuosity and ornamentation, two notions which were closely allied in early nineteenth-century concert pianism and nowhere more so than in the music of his mentor Hummel. Moreover, like Hummel, Chopin was already a master of improvisation, a factor which had a significant bearing on his emerging compositional style. The art of embellishment took much of its impetus from the contemporary practice of improvising on familiar themes, presenting them in many different guises, often of progressively increasing virtuosity. We know that many of Chopin's dance pieces began life as improvisations and the ornate melodic tracery of the G sharp minor Polonaise has something of the rhapsodic, apparently spontaneous flow of a written-out improvisation.

There is little enough of that spontaneous flow in the Rondo in C minor which was published as Chopin's Op.1 by Brzezini & Co. in 1825. The vogue for independent rondos was strong in the early nineteenth century and the term carried clear connotations for the general mood of a piece as well as for its formal organisation.[12] The character of the instrumental rondo was much influenced by *opera buffa* and inclined towards an appropriately tuneful, buoyant mood, texturally clean and with a pace which would be lively, yet modest enough to leave room for rapid passage-work. The latter point is important, for in the hands of the virtuoso composer the rondo acquired something of a bravura character, and this, combined with a tendency to use colourful national elements, ensured its popularity with concert audiences and of course publishers. Chopin's Op.1 belongs to this tradition, and the large stretches and wide left-hand leaps of a passage such as bars 101–108 argue for his own highly developed technique as a performer as well as his precocious compositional command of all the resources of the piano.

For all that, virtuoso elements have been somewhat subordinated to an earnest preoccupation with classical methods of construction. It was after all Chopin's first attempt at an extended musical structure, and we should not be surprised that its materials lack distinction and that its structure is insecure. The weaknesses are apparent in the construction of the rondo theme itself. This begins on a dominant harmony and is therefore introduced by a four-bar tonic affirmation whose banality is scarcely mitigated by an attempt at retrospective justification (bars 28–30 ff.). We may be thankful that it is omitted from the two later statements of the rondo theme. The theme itself describes a melodic arc, a design which was to be used to impressive ends in later Chopin, particularly when allied to a subtle harmonic organisation, but which here comprises little more than a chain of scales and arpeggios supported exclusively by tonic and dominant harmonies. Both melodic contour and harmonic support stress the self-contained nature of the eight-bar sentence, so that subsequent statements, 'lifted' to the relative major, dissipate any sense of momentum which has been generated and leave us with an impression of three blocks of material laid rather artlessly end to end.

The second part of the theme is even closer to classical procedure, with rhythmic and textural contrast highlighted by two-bar periodic phrasing. Ex.2 indicates the Mozartian statement and response pattern. Subsequent

Ex.2 Op.1

sequential working is again clearly in the manner of classical practice, though it is worth noting that the pattern is based on an underlying chromatic symmetry at the major third which foreshadows later Chopin passage-work. In context this sequential working fails to maintain the tension generated by the initial contrast of Ex.2 and the ensuing link to E major through an exposed German sixth (another later fingerprint) is rendered unconvincing.

It is clear from the opening paragraph of Op.1 that at this stage Chopin was far from comfortable with classical formal types. His problems were twofold. He had difficulty in mediating convincingly between the contrasts which were dictated by classical thought and in sustaining the tension and momentum present in the initial statement of an idea. Viewed as a fifteen-year-old's exercise in pastiche the paragraph would have exceptional merit, of course, but it lacks the freshness and fluency which characterised the G sharp minor Polonaise. Something of that freshness is recaptured in the E major second theme (bars 65–99), whose sprightly manner suggests reference points in the rondo themes of the early Classical sonata and through them with the opera-house. Once more it is the continuation which disappoints. The vitality of the theme is sapped through excessive repetition and the subsidiary idea (bars 81–92) is weak.

The ensuing material is dominated by bravura passage-work, now involving both hands. Increasingly it takes on the character of a cadenza in preparation for the third theme, whose tonal setting of A flat major is symmetrically distanced from the C minor and E major of the first and second themes. Here we find the first appearance in Chopin of those nocturne-style accompaniments – rippling semi-quavers in wide arpeggiation – which were popularised by John Field but which found their way into a good deal of early nineteenth-century piano music, including that of Maria Szymanowska (parts of her B flat major Nocturne, for example). Chopin's melody grows out of a rhythmic motive which is all but ubiquitous in the virtuoso style. It was to reappear in the main theme of the 'Adieu' Polonaise in B flat minor, composed the following year (1826), and again in the themes of both piano concertos. The motive is used to form a bridge to the second statement of the rondo theme, the central pivot of the work's loose arch structure. Moreover the same motive is at the heart of the D flat major episode which follows that pivot. An immediate repetition of the third theme, required by exact formal symmetry, would have been unacceptable so soon after its first appearance and its replacement by a new episode which nevertheless preserves elements of the third theme in its rhythm and accompaniment pattern is a felicitous detail. The return of the other themes closes the symmetry thus:

Principal Themes	A	B	[X]	C	A	D[Y]	B	A
Principal Tonal Regions	c	E	g sharp	A flat	c	D flat	D flat	c

Capital letters indicate major keys; small letters indicate minor keys.

Close examination of the rondo theme of Op.1 suggests that Chopin had difficulty in pacing the bar-by-bar progression of a classically constructed paragraph. An overall view of the work indicates further weaknesses, particularly in the crude juxtaposition of materials which are too widely differentiated to form a cohesive whole. Such formal imperfections are underlined in a sense by the much greater assurance of the two polonaises dating from around the same time as Op.1. They are sharply contrasting in character, reflecting two distinct varieties of the earlier polonaise in Poland. The D minor Op.71 No.1 (1824–5)[13] is a bravura piece, close in manner to the earlier G sharp minor and with no less elaborate and mannered ornamentation. The B flat minor, on the other hand, evokes a gentler world. It was composed in 1826 as a farewell gift to his schoolfriend Wilhelm Kolberg and its use in the trio of an air 'au revoir' from Rossini's

La Gazza Ladra,[14] together with its rather melancholy, even sentimental, tone, relate it to the opera-inspired 'polonaise triste' which was common in early nineteenth-century Poland. There are occasional turns of phrase here which hint unmistakably at the later Chopin.

Neither polonaise is a masterpiece, but they have much more fluency and spontaneity than the rondo, emphasizing that at this stage Chopin felt more at home with simple dance miniatures than with extended forms. It was to be some time before he found his own way of coming to terms with more ambitious structures, but the *Rondo à la mazur* Op.5, composed in 1826–7, is at least a marked improvement on Op.1. It was in 1826 that Chopin began his formal musical education at the Warsaw conservatory, and it is tempting to draw comparisons between Op.5 and the two rondos 'à la mazur' composed by his teacher Józef Elsner. Chopin may well have been familiar with the Elsner pieces, but it is difficult to see much evidence of it in Op.5.[15] Rather, one is impressed by the strong personal stamp of the music. Undoubtedly it was in large measure Chopin's stylisation of mazurka features, of which the Lydian fourth is only one, which gave Op.5 its individual character and its sense of greater overall unity and homogeneity. Like many genuine folk mazurkas the melodies are built from elaborations of one or two tiny motives, with momentum and variety achieved through changes in rhythmic detail and ornamentation. The rondo theme itself is typical. Its lengthy melodic paragraph – thirty-six bars in all – is constructed entirely from elaborations of the opening two-bar cell, with rhythmic variations and melodic embellishments. The melodic shapes here and in the second theme in the sub-dominant are close to folkloristic sources and their harmonisation too owes something to these. Gerald Abraham has drawn attention to Chopin's harmonisation of the Lydian fourth by means of a diminished seventh chord,[16] but this if anything represents a gesture of accommodation, drawing the folk inflection into a familiar enough enhancement of diatonic relationships. It is more striking that in the context of the relative minor the sharpened fourth is presented against an unchanging tonic harmony, suggesting an independence of linear and vertical elements which may well have its origin in peasant drone harmonies. This independence is responsible for much of the spiciness of individual harmonies in Op.5. In the second and fourth bars of the theme in its harmonised version, for example, the harmonic rhythm and part-movement dictate a semitonal friction with the melody, and there are similar sharp points of dissonance when the second theme is harmonised by a pedal *bourdon*, clearly a folkloristic stylisation, together with an ostinato figure in mazur rhythm.

The suppression, or at least containment, of bravura elements in the piano writing of Op.5 has been taken by some commentators as an indication that Chopin had not yet fully mastered the virtuoso style, especially when the rondo is compared with a work such as the *Variations on 'La ci darem'* Op.2, composed the following year. But we have already noted his command of keyboard gymnastics in earlier works and it seems more likely that in turning to the mazurka for his inspiration he deliberately restrained such gymnastics in favour of the expressive qualities of folk materials. Throughout his life he was to reserve for the mazurka his most private thoughts, perhaps partly because, unlike the polonaise, it had never been appropriated by non-Polish composers as a conventional means of creating Polish colour. It is obviously difficult to draw firm lines about such matters, but it seems that the mazurka only became recognised as a national dance in the late eighteenth century, absorbing and synthesising elements of older regional dances such as the mazur, oberek and kujawiak. The composed mazurkas of the early nineteenth century (salon pieces and songs, often for the vaudevilles) stylised some features of these dances, even down to foot stamping and exclamations, and preserved the character and tempo differences of the three principal regional types, but they tended to rationalise folk materials, smoothing out many of their more dynamic features. Chopin was familiar with these urban mazurkas from childhood and he became acquainted with their rural prototypes during summer visits to Szafarnia. He was in the habit of improvising mazurkas from an early age, and this no doubt accounts for the fact that some of his earliest written-out mazurkas – the G major 'Kulawy' and the B flat major, both of 1825–6, and the D major of 1829 – exist in two different versions. Indeed there is an account by Oskar Kolberg of Chopin improvising the prototypes for all three during dancing at the home of Dr Samuel Linde.[17] There are hints of future things in all three mazurkas, but nothing so 'advanced' as an early version of Op.7 No.4, bearing the date 1824 in Wilhelm Kolberg's hand.[18]

The mazurka was clearly an essential part of Chopin's early musical sustenance and its influence doubtless encouraged the simpler textures and greater consistency of idiom in the *Rondo à la mazur*. The work is not without its flaws, however. There is still at times an uncomfortable stylistic distance between the pleasing spontaneity of folk-inspired material and passages of self-conscious development on the one hand or fairly shallow passage-work on the other. But the nature of the rondo scheme, where the ritornello can remain at least partially closed, renders this distance acceptable if not desirable, and Chopin now shows greater resource in effecting smooth transitions between contrasting components of the structure.

In its containment of virtuosity, the *Rondo à la mazur* stands apart not only from Op.1, but from its successors, the Op.73 and Op.16 rondos. Op.73 was written initially for solo piano in 1828, but later in the year presented in a version for two pianos.[19] It is a bravura piece, technically more assured than Op.1, but with little enough of Chopin's individual features visible beneath the finery. He was writing *à la mode*, drawing freely upon clichés which some earlier pieces had already discarded. As with most composers in their formative years, his evolution towards a personal voice was far from tidy and consistent, and we need not be surprised that Op.73 has little of the individuality of the *Rondo à la mazur*, composed two years earlier. It does have features of considerable stylistic interest, however, and in particular the suggestion of a peripheral influence from Beethoven, resting easily enough on the prevailing virtuoso manner. Chopin's view of Beethoven was ambivalent. In general he felt that his music exceeded the boundaries of good taste and that Hummel offered a more rounded and balanced musical experience, but he recognised the disturbing power and originality of Beethoven's work from an early age. 'I have not heard anything so great for a long time – in this work Beethoven makes fools of us all', he wrote to Woyciechowski after playing a Beethoven trio.[20] Some of Chopin's mature music offers concrete indications that Beethoven's achievement was not lost on him,[21] but already in Op.73 there are hints of an influence. The rondo theme itself, with its Weber-like glitter, remains immune, but the introduction suggests Beethoven in its intensification of classical rhythmic and textural contrasts into an opposition of commanding semiquaver octaves and chorale-like harmonies (the *sf* markings here are Chopin's own, stressing his affinities with other virtuoso composers[22]), while the A minor theme (bars 73–81) also recalls Beethoven. These are no more than tentative affinities, the more so in that the obvious and immediate influences on Op.73, Hummel and Weber, were themselves much indebted to the same source. But whether direct or indirect the connection serves to underline the extent to which composers even temperamentally distant from Beethoven could not escape his influence. His music was a sounding-board for the efforts of an entire generation of later composers, Chopin included.

The bravura manner of Op.73 is again the dominant feature of the Op.16 rondo, begun in Warsaw in 1829 and completed in Paris a few years later. Only in the slow introduction are there clear signs of the later Chopin and in particular the remarkable *agitato* section whose impassioned recitative grates mercilessly on an obstinately unchanging harmonic pedal. Yet even here Chopin was meeting the expectations of a *brillante* rondo, where an introduction, in the manner of improvised preluding, would tend towards exploratory harmonies and impulsive changes of mood and tempo. Hummel is the obvious model for Op.16, as for much of Chopin's music in the later Warsaw years. Indeed his fondness for the rondo at this time is itself an indication of his commitment to a *stile brillante*.[23] Rondos were after all among the most popular concert pieces in the early nineteenth century.

They were rivalled only by the many *airs variées* which were consumed voraciously by the music-listening and music-buying public. Composers such as Hummel, Moscheles, Kalkbrenner, Field and Weber wrote dozens of these. They were only moderately interested in the special formal challenges posed by variation-form, challenges which had been faced squarely by Bach, Haydn and Beethoven and which in the post-Beethoven era were addressed principally in the slow movements of cyclic forms, especially piano sonatas and string quartets. Rather they saw variations as an impetus towards virtuosity and ingenious ornamentation, with formal cohesion of subsidiary importance.[24] Their variation sets were *pièces d'occasion*, not so different from the ubiquitous improvisations on well-known operatic melodies or folksongs, and they tended to be strung together fairly loosely. There would often be a slow introduction, followed by variations of progressively increasing virtuosity, a minor key variation emphasizing harmonic quality and a popular dance, or alternatively fugal, finale. Leaving aside questions of quality, Mozart was the most important single influence on the development of early nineteenth-century ornamental variations, but the most characteristic exponents and the strongest influences on Chopin's early sets were again Hummel and Weber.

The connection is immediately apparent in his *Introduction and Variations in E major on a German National Air (Der Schweizerbub)*, which was tossed off 'in a few quarter-hours'.[25] The introduction, prefiguring the theme melodically, is improvisatory in character, with rapid changes of texture and mood and 'gestural' cascades of scalar figures in free rhythm. Davis's description of some of Hummel's introductions as a 'recorded example of his art of improvisation'[26] might well apply equally to Chopin. The theme itself, characteristically a familiar national air,[27] is marked *senza ornamenti* which speaks volumes about contemporary performance practice. The five variations are classical in technique, preserving phrase lengths and harmony, with a statutory journey to the tonic minor in the fourth. There are hints of Weber in the left-hand semiquavers of the third variation and more obviously in the closing waltz, though such time changes in the finale were common practice. The demands on the performer and listener are modest, as they are also in the *Souvenir de Paganini*, composed in 1829 after the violinist gave a series of concerts in Warsaw; indeed Paganini may well have played his Op.10, incorporating 'Le Carnival de Venise' on which Chopin based his *Souvenir*, at the Warsaw concerts. Chopin was later to give a deeply considered response to Paganini in his own Op.10 studies. The *Souvenir* by contrast is a trivial piece, a continuous chain of right-hand variations over an unbroken and unchanging barcarolle bass, and its chief claim on our attention is its conceptual similarity to the much later and greater *Berceuse*.[28]

In later years Chopin was to draw upon elements of both rondo and variations to help him model the form of extended single-movement works, blending these elements subtly with other formal archetypes. His interest in them as independent forms belonged only to these early formative years, however, finding its most public expression in two works for piano and orchestra, the *Variations on 'La ci darem'* Op.2 of 1827–28 and the *Krakowiak–Rondo* Op.14 of 1828. Their last significant appearance in his music comes in the Op.16 Rondo and the *Variations brillantes* Op.12, the latter composed in Paris in 1833 at a time when the *stile brillante* was rapidly losing its attraction for Chopin.

Already during his Warsaw years there were influences which counteracted the virtuoso style. His training at the conservatory clearly affected all aspects of his developing creative talent, not least his attempts at variation-form. But under the guidance of Józef Elsner he was required to address himself to other, more rigorous, disciplines. Elsner was a leading figure in Warsaw's musical life, helping to run the opera as well as the conservatory, founding the Society for Religious and National Music and co-founding the Resursa Muzyka (Music Club). He was a respected pedagogue as well as a composer, and his course at the conservatory involved Chopin in several lessons a week in counterpoint, theory and figured bass and in the compo-sition of Viennese-modelled sonata movements, none of them areas which we readily associate with his music. The indirect, long-term effects of these studies were undoubtedly important, for Chopin was to become a master of 'concealed' counterpoint in his mature music and he was to draw upon sonata principles in a highly individual way in his later extended structures, and not only the sonatas. In the short term, however, his study gave rise to some less happy results.

Two works composed during his years at the conservatory, the Sonata in C minor Op.4 and the Piano Trio Op.8, attempt to come to terms with the traditional four-movement cycle. The sonata was composed in 1828 and was one of the works sent by Chopin to Haslinger in 1829, along with *Der Schweizerbub* and the *'La ci darem' Variations*. Critical opinion has been universally unkind to Op.4, and with good reason. It is appropriate that the sonata should have been dedicated to Elsner, for it bears all the marks of a highly gifted student's laboured attempt to impress his teacher with an ambitious, 'learned' work. The natural lyricism abundantly displayed in earlier miniatures has been rigorously trimmed in the interests of motivic unity and economy. The imitative element embodied in the opening theme, whose resemblance to Bach's Two Part Invention in C minor has caught the eye of more than one commentator,[29] is entirely characteristic (Ex.3). It is present again in the minuet and in the trio. This attempt to tighten the texture motivically is pursued at the expense of the melody and accompani-ment textures which came much more naturally to Chopin at this stage of his development, and it is taken very far in the first movement of the sonata. A variant of the motive in bar 2 is worked exhaustively in the normal sequential fashion to the exclusion of any significant thematic contrast, rather as though the driest developmental passages from Op.1 and Op.73 had been inflated into a full-length movement. In the process there are some fairly tortuous harmonic excursions, though in the exposition these invariably return to the C minor tonic.

The monothematic and monotonal character of this exposition calls for some comment. Parallels with late Haydn or late Beethoven, initially tempting, are not really to the point here. If anything Chopin is rather harking back to pre-Classical procedures, and in particular to Bach, whose music he had studied from an early age. The development section, with its constant quaver movement, earnest imitative working and sequential

Ex.3 Op.4

journey through the fifths cycle, is also close at times to Baroque procedures, without any real attempt to bring these procedures into an accommodation with Classical periodisation and Classical contrast. The chromatic elements in the harmony are of interest not so much because of their extent, which is considerable, but because they arise out of a rigorous motivic working and intricate part-movement which are far from characteristic of Chopin at this stage and which result, incidentally, in cramped, lifeless keyboard textures far removed from the sparkle of the rondos. Something of that sparkle is recaptured in the *moto perpetuo* of the finale, certainly the closest of the four movements to more congenial and accessible contemporary styles. But it is in the $\frac{5}{4}$ slow movement that we catch brief glimpses of the more familiar Chopin. To be sure, the rhythmically pliable tracery of bars 21–31 and the lightly decorated repetition of the main theme (bar 32 ff.) have clear origins in the ornamental melody of Field and Hummel, but they also capture a little of that elusive quality which we identify retrospectively as Chopinesque.

There are no less happy thoughts in the Piano Trio, Op.8, composed for private performance at 'Antonin' where Chopin spent a few convivial weeks in 1829. The musical ideas here 'breathe' a great deal more easily than in the sonata, but in relation to the medium the work is hopelessly inept. Chopin was clearly incapable of writing interestingly for the strings (the poor violinist rarely escapes first position in the whole of the first movement[30]) and there is little understanding of that *concertante* interplay of forces which makes for good chamber music. Even where the thematic substance is fresh and lively, Chopin seems to have been at a loss to know how to occupy the accompanists, whether strings or piano. When the piano has the tune, the strings as often as not provide an amorphous sustained background, merely doubling the bass and an inner voice, or worse still fall back on the most hackneyed string-crossing devices.

As in the sonata the key scheme of the trio's first movement is intriguing, to say the least. In Op.4 the exposition is monotonal and the recapitulation begins a tone lower in B flat minor, before making the necessary tonal adjustments. In the first movement of the trio the exposition is again monotonal, and this time the recapitulation begins with a thematic *and* tonal reprise, but it moves to the dominant minor for the second subject, a curious reversal of classical procedure which was to be echoed in the first movement of the E minor Concerto. The concertos indeed were to confirm Chopin's unorthodox view of the relationship between tonality and formal design in sonata movements during his Warsaw years. It is easy to attribute this to a lack of experience with the larger forms and to an insecure grasp of the significance and power of tonal architecture (as Charles Rosen drily puts it: 'They evidently did not have very clear ideas about sonatas out there in Warsaw'[31]). But the fact remains that even in the later sonatas Chopin's conception of tonal relationships is a far cry from classical procedure. In relation to formal design (though not, as we shall see, underlying structure), there is a relaxation of that dominant-tonic polarity which is so critical to classical thought. The development was to be as much a source of new possibilities as a destruction of old principles, but as yet Chopin had little to add on the positive side.

The sonata and trio are among the least beguiling of Chopin's efforts during the later Warsaw years, demonstrating a failure of means and ends which is far from typical. The other extended works of these years – the rondos and variations – are remarkable rather for the skill and finish of their workmanship, if not for their stylistic individuality. In particular they demonstrate a confident control over every aspect of bravura keyboard 'facture'. There is an engaging exuberance in Chopin's demonstration of his powers in these works. The entire gamut of pianistic resources is explored, and the textures are formulated with a meticulous care and an attention to detail which are astonishing for a composer not yet twenty and which certainly transcend the provincial context of Warsaw's music. Much the same panache is exhibited in the three polonaises of the later Warsaw period. They belong fairly and squarely to the world of the *stile brillante,* remaining as close to Weber as to the mature Chopin, though there are of course hints of things to come. Of the three the B flat major Op.71 No.2 is the most prophetic, foreshadowing the majestic manner and the formal expansion of the mature polonaises and permitting the ornamentation to build a cumulative momentum which is directed towards power rather than mere virtuosity. Even the details are prophetic, the chains of dominant-quality sevenths at bar 71, for example, the contrary motion 'bridge' in the trio[32] and the use of bass trills and melodic closure formulae which were later to be distinguishing features of the Chopin polonaise. The F minor Op.71 No.3, probably composed in 1828, and the G flat major of 1829 are more traditionally conceived and less ambitious in scope. The F minor was especially popular at 'Antonin' when Chopin visited there in 1829 and this may have stimulated him to write another polonaise during his visit. Prince Radziwill was himself a composer and cellist, and Chopin scored his new piece for cello and piano, so that the prince could perform it with his daughter. Later he added an introduction and the piece was published as Op.3 and dedicated to Josef Merk. The composer's own assessment of the music does it no great injustice. 'It is nothing but glitter, for the drawing-room, for the ladies.'[33]

It would be fruitless to look for a consistent development during Chopin's formative years in Warsaw. He was gradually acquiring a command of *métier*, and in this respect the Op.2 Variations of 1827–8 mark a significant step forward, especially in the control of bravura keyboard textures. But the technical assurance of Op.2 and of subsequent concert pieces was achieved somewhat at the expense of stylistic individuality. In mastering the tools of the virtuoso-composer, Chopin remained necessarily close to his models, though in due course he would learn to use those tools in fresh and individual ways, investing virtuosity with a new substance and power. In the meantime a more personal, distinctive voice was gathering strength in some of the less pretentious miniatures of the later Warsaw period, pieces which eschew completely the virtuoso manner. There is the A flat major Waltz, for instance, whose phraseology is already close to that of the mature waltzes. This extends beyond the flowing *moto perpetuo* theme to the rhythmic motive and melodic contour of the trio, strikingly similar to the main theme of Op.34 No.1. Then there is the A minor Mazurka, issued by Fontana as Op.68 No.2, where the Lydian fourth influences harmonic structure as well as melodic shape, in that Chopin refuses to accommodate it diatonically. Other details are prophetic in this mazurka, the association of tonal 'relatives' in the response to the main theme (bars 17–28), the *bourdon* fifth of the trio and the brief hints of harmonic adventure at bars 34–5 and again at bar 39. Above all there is the E minor Nocturne, important not just as the first of the nocturnes but because there are indications here of a new approach to melody and ornamentation. The successive ornamental variations of the opening idea are less concerned to dress it with fancy frills than to enhance and intensify its expressive qualities and to reveal it in constantly changing lights. The ornamentation becomes in short integral to the melody. Harmonically too there is a new subtlety and sophistication, not so much in the range of materials employed but in the control and pacing of the large-scale movement. In particular we might note the importance of bars 14–22 as a means of offsetting the harmonic stability of both the main theme and the secondary idea.

Chopin's apprenticeship equipped him, then, not only with a formidable command of *métier* in big concert pieces but with the tentative beginnings of a personal, highly idiomatic voice in some of the miniatures. Yet even the most forward-looking of these lack the authority of the mature composer. The recent performance history of Chopin's music tells its own story in this regard. The works of the Warsaw years are given statutory airings, but they have kindled the enthusiasm of performers and audiences only intermittently and have failed to secure a place in the standard concert repertoire. The only significant exceptions to this general rule are the two piano concertos.

3

Stile brillante

The concertos were not Chopin's first attempts at writing for the orchestra. He had already made his mark outside Poland with his performance in Vienna of the *'La ci darem' Variations*, the work which elicited Schumann's famous 'Hats off, gentlemen! A genius.' He began the work in 1827 and by the following year he had completed not only the variations but two other works for piano and orchestra, the *Krakowiak-Rondo* Op.14 and the *Fantasy on Polish Themes* Op.13. The rondo was performed at the second of his 1829 Vienna concerts and both works were given at several concerts in Poland before his final departure.

It would be fruitless to expect formal cohesion and a closely reasoned thematic argument in pieces which were conceived first and foremost as showcases for virtuosic display. In a letter from Vienna Chopin described the rapturous applause which followed each variation of Op.2. This was quite usual at the time and, if nothing else, it would have made short work of a composer's pretensions to unity. Since the Bach-Abel concerts in London it had become customary for pianist-composers to establish their reputations with display pieces for piano and orchestra.[1] London began the trend and for some time it remained the principal centre for such concerts. Clementi did a long stint at Hanover Square beginning in the 1780s and the London pianists were joined by Dussek in the 1790s. Dussek was not to be held fast by any single centre, however. He travelled widely and it is not unrealistic to view him as a prototype of today's touring concert pianist. From Dussek onwards it was standard practice for the virtuoso to hawk his wares from city to city. As the century turned, the geography of concert life began to change, with Vienna emerging to rival London as a centre for international pianism. Beethoven was there, of course, along with Czerny and Ries, while Moscheles and Thalberg spent their early years in the Austrian capital. By the time Chopin passed through it, however, Vienna's star was already fading. Weimar, Dresden and Leipzig were taking precedence in the German-speaking states, but it was Paris above all which offered the real challenge to London, even if native French and English pianists were conspicuous by their absence. 'The virtuosos come to Paris every winter like swarms of locusts . . .', wrote Heine.[2] In the 1830s Paris could boast Liszt and Chopin, Kalkbrenner, Hiller and Pixis, to name only the more spectacular talents. These men plied their skills in the salons, in the publishers' rooms and in public benefit concerts, sharing the programme with a seemingly indiscriminate array of genres and forces. The solo recital, as we understand it today, was of rather later vintage,[3] and a benefit concert programme would resemble rather a vast musical feast, with perhaps an overture or sinfonia, an obligatory selection of songs and arias, some move-ments from a chamber work, an improvisation and a concerto or rondo for solo instrument and orchestra.[4] It was quite usual for the movements of a concerto to be separated by other items in the programme – Chopin's concertos were presented in this way in Warsaw – and even for a 'concerto' to be assembled from a movement each of three separate works. Concertos were of course part of the staple fare of the benefit concert, but bravura solos and improvisations were no less in demand and lighter pieces for piano and orchestra – rondos, variations or pot-pourris – were especially popular. Usually these would have a brilliant virtuosic coda, an unmistake-able cue to the 'claquers'.

It is to this category of light orchestral piece that the three Chopin works belong, and in keeping with the type they are based either on familiar operatic melodies (Op.2) or on national airs (Op.13) or dances (Op.14). In the early nineteenth century the enthusiasm for folk music, especially that of the Celtic regions and Eastern Europe, became increasingly widespread, and composers and publishers were not slow to exploit it. In all three works Chopin's use of folk materials is of this order, little more than a sop to current fashions. The forms of the works – variations, rondo and fantasy ('pot-pourri' would be an equally appropriate title for Op.13 and it was so described by Chopin himself) – were also a direct response to popular taste. Already in Dussek we find many rondos and variations for piano based on popular tunes and a later generation took the practice very much further. There is a plethora of such works by Hummel, Kalkbrenner, Moscheles, Thalberg and others. If the titles 'Grande' or 'Brillante' were omitted by the composer they would very often be supplied by the publisher. Such works were composed as pièces d'occasion, very much in the spirit of giving the public what it had come to hear, which meant catchy (and preferably familiar) tunes smothered by virtuosity. The orchestral accompaniment is of minimal importance. It is often marked 'ad libitum' and could be performed if necessary by a string quintet or omitted altogether.[5] Chopin himself was in the habit of playing all his works for piano and orchestra, including the concertos, as solos, emphasising that the spotlight should be clearly focused on the pianist as virtuoso.

By Chopin's time the piano had emerged as the virtuoso instrument par excellence, but it was a late starter in the field. The virtuosi of the seventeenth and eighteenth centuries were to be found above all in the opera-house, where leading sopranos and castrati were lauded by the public in a manner reserved in the nineteenth century for the great pianists and in our own time for conductors. The dangers are obvious enough in all three cases and in the early nineteenth century there seemed to be general critical agreement that singers were the arch perpetrators of bad taste, particularly in their excesses of ornamentation. Yet it was precisely that vocal ornamentation which had such a widespread influence on keyboard writing of the late eighteenth and early nineteenth centuries, an influence to which Chopin was certainly not immune.

The virtuosity of the violin, supported by a long and vigorous tradition, was second only to that of the voice, and again there was a marked deterioration of taste in the early nineteenth century, with concert performances often amounting to little more than parades of circus tricks. The more distinguished virtuoso-composers rose above such things, naturally enough, and could turn the bravura manner to artistic account, while retaining it as a basic impulse of style. Spohr was a case in point. His early concertos take much of their inspiration from virtuosi such as Rode and Eck, but he went on to absorb more solid influences from Cherubini and Beethoven, turning them to good account in his orchestral and chamber music. His early career included extensive concert tours as a soloist and it is in this respect above all that his lifestyle differed from that of an earlier generation of violinist-composers. The touring virtuoso was becoming a familiar figure in early nineteenth-century musical life. He would still be expected to address aristocratic gatherings, but his music-making responded more and more to the tastes and fashions of an emerging middle-class audience, an audience which demanded above all novelty and display.

Novelty and display were precisely the attributes which most accurately characterised the compositions and performances of Nicolò Paganini, the man who came to epitomise the nineteenth-century cult of virtuosity. That cult was in its way an authentic reflection of the spirit of Romantic individualism, with the additional connotation of the performer heroically transcending the limitations of his instrument. Even the supernatural resonances which surrounded Paganini found a context in the age of the Gothic revival. Paganini's technical prowess was certainly remarkable, judging by contemporary accounts, and his compositions represented a considerable extension of the possibilities of the instrument, even if much of this was directed towards a rather superficial gimmickry. 'Connoisseurs say . . . that the very thing by which he fascinates the crowd debases him to a mere charlatan', remarks Spohr in his autobiography, and later, following a concert by Paganini, 'In his compositions and his execution I found a strange mixture of the highly genial and childishly tasteless. . . .'[6] Such complaints, a standard enough theme in music criticism long before the nineteenth century, grew in number and acerbity as the cult of the virtuoso gained impetus. And Paganini's role could scarcely be overemphasised. It was at least partly in response to his technical mastery that new developments in keyboard technique were instigated, with a mimetic element for which there were of course distinguished Baroque precedents. Liszt and Schumann were just two of many young pianist-composers who transcribed the caprices, stretching pianistic resources to their limits in doing so. Chopin avoided such transcription, but he responded nonetheless. He preferred to translate Paganini's achievement into more characteristically idiomatic keyboard terms, and the major outcome of that mediation was his early set of studies, published as Op.10.

While the new pianism leaned heavily on the virtuosity of the voice and the violin, its most immediate stimulus came from the development of the piano itself. Like music publishing, piano manufacture was a growth industry, or at least an expanding craft, in the first half of the nineteenth century, responding to a widening domestic market among the newly affluent middle class. The history of the early piano has been told many times,[7] and it will be sufficient to emphasise here the close relationship which existed at every stage of its evolution between the piano manufacturer, the performer, the composer and the publisher. In many cases indeed all four were the same man. Clementi, Cramer and Dussek were involved, with varying degrees of success, in all four professions. By Chopin's time greater specialisation of function was the order of the day, but it was still common for performers to maintain a close connection with a particular manufacturer, and demonstration concerts, once highly popular, continued to feature at the 'salles' of piano manufacturers. Chopin enjoyed the special qualities of several makes of piano, but he particularly admired the light sound of the Pleyel instrument and many of his Paris concerts took place at Pleyel's rooms.

By then the differences between pianos were less critical than formerly and their influence on compositional and performance styles less marked.[8] The pianist-composers of Chopin's generation drew freely upon the achievements of several earlier 'schools' of performance which had been more directly dependent on the different characteristics of the two main types of early piano, the Viennese and the English. Categories were anything but watertight,[9] but in general the light-toned, light-actioned and well-damped Viennese instrument encouraged a 'brillante' style of rapid, non-legato passage-work and a cantilena which would be subject to elegant embellishment. This was the manner favoured by Mozart and taken over in part by Hummel and Kalkbrenner. The heavier, deeper-toned English instrument, on the other hand, fostered a legato 'cantabile' style associated above all with Clementi and continued by Cramer and Dussek.[10]

Chopin's piano style owes something to both lines of development, but with a leaning towards the former in his earlier years. Of contemporary performance styles he was closer during these early years to the 'brilliant' manner of Kalkbrenner and Moscheles than to the soft melodious execution of Field.[11] He was aware of course of the limitations of the bravura style, of the ease with which today's sparkle becomes tomorrow's empty cliché, but he shared with Kalkbrenner and Moscheles an exhilaration in the exploration of every aspect of the developing instrument's potential. It was above all a process of discovery.

Something of this quality can be gleaned from an examination of the engraver's exemplar of the solo part of the Op.2 Variations (K.8)[12] Chopin has suffered much at the hands of editors, but it is sometimes wrongly assumed that a fecundity of dynamics, expression marks and phrasing indications automatically infers editorial enthusiasm. One is struck in the Op.2 autograph by the meticulous care exercised by Chopin himself over such details, though in the miniatures (as opposed to the concert pieces) of the Warsaw period such information is often omitted from those autographs which have survived. At the first entry of the soloist in Op.2 Chopin moulds every nuance of the unfolding line, articulating its contrasts, its ebb and flow, its impulsive changes of mood with the most explicit instructions as to phrasing, dynamics, expression marks and pedalling. The contrasts in texture here and throughout the introduction are striking, with imitative working of the main motive giving way to delicate *fioriture*, capricious skipping passage-work and a lyrical cantilena. The process owes a good deal to improvisation and it is time now to consider the importance of this as a seminal influence on composed music within the orbit of the *stile brillante*.

The art of keyboard improvisation had a lengthy history, of course, but its blossoming in the early nineteenth century blended well with an age which put a premium on spontaneity in all the arts. Its importance in the concert life of the time can be inferred from the fact that 'extemporaneous performance' often took pride of place on posters and advertisements and that piano methods tended to deal with the subject in some detail.[13] Such methods, together with a wealth of contemporary criticism, enable us to build up some sort of picture of the practice of improvisation, despite an obvious dearth of primary sources.[14] An element of improvisation entered into the widespread practice of decorating the cantilena of slow movements and this in turn had an influence on composed ornamental melody, and in particular on variation sets. Improvisation and ornamentation were closely allied, and both were further allied to the notion of virtuosity, as the methods make abundantly clear. Virtuosity was of course a primary aim of the cadenza, one of the most enduring forums for improvisation, and not only in concertos. Cadenzas appear in a variety of contexts in Chopin's music, from nocturnes to ballades, and the end of the introduction to Op.2 is entirely characteristic. Improvisation was also prominent in the practice of 'preluding' composed music, often using recitative-like material or arpeggiated passage-work, and this too left its mark on the composed slow introductions to rondos, variation sets and pot-pourris. But most important of all was the extempore performance on a given theme (often an operatic or folk melody), where elaborate ornamentation, explosions of virtuosity, motivic development and contrapuntal working of the theme, often in association with other well-known melodies, were all part of the expected armoury.[15] Accounts of such extempore performances make it clear that there were much greater and more frequent changes of mood, tempo and tonal region than would have been considered acceptable in composed music. In this way the improvisation would 'stretch the conventions',[16] permitting processes which only later became part of 'composition' and thus acting in a limited way as a determinant of style. We can sense something of this from those composed-out works in 'free' form in the late eighteenth and early nineteenth centuries, and especially works described as 'fantasia' or 'fantasy'. The abrupt contrasts and unexpected outbursts in C.P.E. Bach's fantasies, or for that matter in Beethoven's Fantasy Op.77, are cases in point, probably taking us close to the flavour of the improvisation.

For the early nineteenth-century composer-pianist the borderline between improvisation and composition was in any case a good deal less clear than it is today.[17] A composition would as often as not begin life as an improvisation, and there are accounts of Chopin's agonised attempts to formulate on paper an idea already perfectly realised at the piano. Certainly the flow of ideas and the infectious, sparkling passage-work in the introduction of Op.2 has something of the character of a composed-out improvisation, an extempore prelude to the main business of the piece, the theme and its variations.[18] The basic idea is an unfolding cantilena derived from the theme, but this alternates with exuberant figurations whose variety and inventiveness are remarkable, at times foreshadowing closely later Chopin textures. These figurations are of several classes. The most traditional are chord-outlining patterns which extend and widen similar textures in Mozart. More characteristic are the long *fioriture* over a steady left-hand pulse, decorative outgrowths of melody, but tending towards a chiaroscuro effect which would lose touch with melody. By 1827 such *fioriture* were common enough in piano music, with a major impetus coming from Hummel and Field, as Ex.4 suggests. Chopin was later to refine the device considerably, integrating it thoroughly with the melodic substance of a piece. Quite different in effect are those passages where the melody simply splinters into a 'coruscating shower of chromatic particles', as Gerald Abraham so aptly described bars 19–20.[19] Such passages are harmonically rooted by the left hand, but tend to lose touch with harmony, aspiring towards the status of a self-sufficient texture. Indeed both the *fioriture* and the 'coruscating particles' epitomise the delicate balance in Chopin's music at this stage between the subordination of figuration to melody and/or harmony and its growing emancipation from these controlling forces, its aspiration to model the form.

The virtuosity of this slow introduction sets the tone for what is to follow. There are many individual touches in the variations themselves, but in the main their characterisation is in conformity with current practice. In his *Dictionnaire de Musique Moderne* of 1825 Castil-Blaze rather drily described the typical ornamental variation set thus: 'First there are simple quavers and triplets, then arpeggios, syncopations and octaves,without forgetting the adagio in the relative mode and the *tempo di polacca*'.[20] The implication of a conformity taken to the point of stereotype is clear, and it is true that

Hummel, Sonata in F sharp minor

Field, Nocturne in A major

Chopin, *La ci darem*

Ex.4

Castil-Blaze's scheme fits Chopin's Op.2 rather neatly. The adagio in the minor and the *tempo di polacca* are both there (variations 5 and 6) and so too is the triplet variation (variation 1). The other three variations are rather different, but their characterisation echoes many another set at the time, a *moto perpetuo* in mainly conjunct motion, a flowing left hand with repeated notes and arpeggiation, close to Weber in manner, and a sequence of leaping figures for both hands which may well owe something to John Field.[21] Also characteristic of the genre is the progressive rhythmic animation and cumulative virtuosity of the set, with a dual goal in the last two variations, the drama and rhetoric of the fifth (typical of slow variations in its freer treatment of the theme) and the brilliance and *élan* of the polonaise, foreshadowing the *Grande Polonaise Brillante* of a few years later.

The virtuosity of Op.2 is extended in the *Fantasy on Polish Themes* Op.13. The work is really a pot-pourri of three themes and their variants, and it is even less tightly structured than the earlier variations, with which it has a good deal in common. Again there is a slow, improvisatory introduction, characterised by *fioriture* and sparkling passage-work, and again there is a dance finale, a kujawiak which culminates in the predictable blaze of virtuosity. The treatment of the other themes, a pastoral folksong and a melody from one of Kurpiński's operas, is akin to a linked pair of unrelated variation sets. The presentation of the sets follows a similar pattern with each of the themes elaborated melodically by the soloist and then 'worked' by the orchestra while the piano engages in non-thematic configuration. There is in short a unity of treatment which mitigates to some extent the disunity of substance. This sharpened differentiation of song and pattern within the piano part was a feature of the *stile brillante* and it is evidenced again in the two piano concertos.

There are other links with the concertos. The main theme of the kujawiak is presented by the soloist in octaves in a manner which directly foreshadows the folk-influenced episodes in the finales of both concertos. It also corresponds closely to the opening of the *Krakowiak-Rondo* Op.14, subtitled a 'Grande Rondeau de Concert'. The tonal charm of octaves at once gives a haunting quality to this opening (Chopin himself was very pleased with it) and it nicely prefigures the more personal idiom of the rondo. Despite the 'grande' of its title, it is an unpretentious piece, standing in relation to Op.2 and Op.13 rather as the *Rondo à la mazur* does to Op.1 and Op.73. Virtuosity is focused and moods and themes more closely unified, partly in response to the national dance idiom. Even the writing for orchestra holds more interest than in the two display pieces, as Gerald Abraham has suggested.[22]

It is easy to pinpoint in all three works details of piano texture and of thematic and harmonic procedure which foreshadow some of the greatest of the mature works.[23] It would be surprising indeed if such prophetic fingerprints did not exist. But the formal and stylistic framework within which they appear is still a conventional one, borrowed from the international concert platform. The framework is, as it were, infiltrated by details which we retrospectively identify as Chopinesque, but it is not itself seriously challenged. This process of infiltration is taken further in the two piano concertos, the first extended works in which Chopin's personal voice is strong and clear. Yet even in the concertos the originality lies more in the detail than in the overall conception and formal mould. These belong firmly to the world of the 'brillante' concerto, their closest points of contact with Hummel, Moscheles, Kalkbrenner and Field.

The virtuoso concerto of the early nineteenth century was a response above all to Mozart's concertos. It is seldom, however, that we find Mozart's delicate equilibrium (and at times creative tension) between the ritornello principle and symphonic thought, and between an almost operatic drama of moods and personae and a concern for structural strength. Virtuosity was a major consideration in Mozart, of course, but again there is an inspired balance between bravura passage-work and thematic elements, and between ornament and substance. It is difficult to generalise about the virtuoso-composers' response to the Mozart model, but two broad tendencies can be identified, both of them resulting in structural crudity when compared with Mozart. The changing role of the orchestral prelude is at the heart of the matter. Even in the most symphonically conceived of Mozart's concertos the prelude preserves a traditional ritornello function, achieved through open-ended thematic presentation and a monotonal framework which nonetheless sustains remarkable harmonic variety and generates a real sense of anacrusis to the entry of the soloist.[24] One direction followed by early nineteenth-century pianist-composers was towards a drastic compression of the prelude to a point where its structural function was little more than the opening of a simple frame which would enclose an 'accompanied solo'. Often indeed the preludes to the Chopin concertos were truncated in accordance with such contemporary mores.[25] A quite different tendency was to invest the prelude with the tonal and thematic dialectic of a symphonic exposition, as Beethoven does in his third concerto, so that the entry of the soloist becomes in effect a second exposition, never the case in Mozart. Weber's concertos were transitional in this respect, preserving a monotonal prelude, but replacing Mozart's taut procession of ideas with clear-cut, self-contained themes to be repeated more-or-less unchanged by the soloist. By moving a stage further and abandoning the monotonal prelude, Hummel and Field moved closer to the full symphonic exposition. Field's grasp of large-scale structure was at best insecure, and it is possible to attach too much significance to the tonal progression in his preludes, but Hummel, like Beethoven, poses the problem in a more direct way. The danger of formal redundancy is all the greater in Hummel, moreover, in that he lacks Beethoven's capacity for generative motivic processes, rhythmically propelled, which might take in the first solo as part of a single sweep of ideas. The thematic, and above all *tonal*, closures at the end of his preludes are problematical in that they tend to negate any sense of anacrusis to the first solo and thus to impede the 'flow' of the structure.

Undoubtedly Hummel's concertos were the most important formal and stylistic models for Chopin when he composed the two piano concertos, extending, as Gerald Abraham convincingly demonstrates,[26] to a near-identity of the motivic materials of the E minor Concerto and those of Hummel's A minor. Arnold Schering, argues Abraham, was 'led astray' by the dedication of the E minor Concerto to make a much less potent connection with Kalkbrenner's D minor. Yet such arguments only serve to emphasise that affinities need to be viewed in the wider context of a striking uniformity of gesture within the 'brillante' concerto, amounting really to an extensive common repertory of short, rhythmically propelled motivic shapes, syncopated accompaniment patterns and bravura configurations, many of them arising out of a need to generate momentum in the absence of genuine harmonic or motivic growth. It was an art of conformity in an age of growing individualism. The very opening motive of the F minor Concerto has a rhythmic characterisation found in Hummel's A minor, Field's A flat major and Kalkbrenner's D minor, to name only three of the more enduring of the many 'brilliant' concertos of the time,[27] and the syncopated pattern in the succeeding phrase is hardly less characteristic.

Such comparisons provide a revealing and necessary context for the F minor Concerto, but they tell us nothing about the skill with which Chopin welds his materials together, turning the conventional gesture to much greater artistic account than do any of his immediate predecessors and contemporaries. The prelude, for instance, similar on the surface to those of Hummel's A minor and B minor Concertos, is given a processional, anacrusic character through the use of discrete intercutting elements within its apparently seamless flow, with the introduction of new rhythmic motives carefully paced to prevent the structure from sagging and losing momentum. The technique is Mozartian. Mozartian too is the judicious balance between contrast and continuity, as Ex.5 suggests. The example

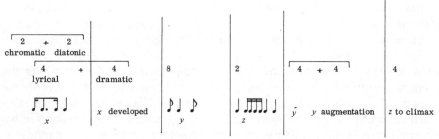

Ex.5 Op.21

outlines the three rhythmic motives which act as unifying and propulsive agents in the opening paragraph and illustrates the extent to which there is a 'Classical' balance of contrasting rhythmic and harmonic elements underlying the unbroken flow of the music. Such a presentation cannot fully convey the subtlety of the paragraph, the unobtrusive transference of y from accompaniment to melody, the later augmentation of y in the bass line and the barely noticed interpolation of a two-bar passage whose rhythmic profile z later assumes importance in different thematic contexts. The whole is a beautifully balanced play of contrasted yet related elements. Like Hummel, Chopin moves to the relative major for the second theme, following a short 'buffer' passage which becomes the unexpected source of later ideas. The second subject itself is conceived as an area of stability, though it barely sustains the exact repetition and sequential working which Chopin demands of it. The most felicitous touch is the reintroduction in this new thematic and tonal context of the rhythmic motive z, leading us back to the tonic for the entry of the soloist.

The solo entry, with its *fortissimo* octaves, itself conforms to familiar practice within the virtuoso concerto (Pixis, Ries, Klengel), but Chopin transforms the gesture into a powerful, superbly dramatic intrusion of a commanding soloist upon a hushed, expectant orchestra. From this point attention is centred on the soloist as the concerto takes on its true *genus* as an accompanied solo. The pianist carries us with him through a succession of impulsively changing roles – showman, combatant, poet – with an engaging spontaneity denied to the sonata or symphony. This is no mere decorated restatement of the prelude, moreover, despite the tonal duplication of its principal thematic elements. No sooner has the soloist presented the opening material than he moves into an unexpected 'new' theme which amplifies and softens the innocent 'buffer' passage linking the main tonal regions of the prelude, a gesture again more redolent of Mozart than of Hummel and his circle, and one which gives a quite new focus of interest to the first solo. Interestingly enough, Chopin decorates this new theme lavishly, but exercises much greater restraint with the soloist's version of the second subject, even to the point of simplifying rather than elaborating it on immediate repetition. This lends added significance and beauty to the florid ornamentation of the beginning of the theme in the reprise. The gesture is the more effective in that the reprise sacrifices the powerful resource of tonal synthesis, allowing only a passing mention to the first subject and presenting the second subject once again in the relative major.

In keeping with the conventions of the 'brilliant' concerto, bravura elements in the first solo are reserved for the two blocks of passage-work which follow each theme, effecting a bridge to the main points of tonal clarification, F minor, A flat major, and finally the C minor of the second ritornello. This clear duality of song and pattern in each tonal region confirms the general tendency of the *stile brillante* to sharpen the contrast between the lyrical and configurative elements of the Mozart concerto. As bravura material became more virtuosic, compensatory song passages became more extended and more obviously lyrical, though they tended to remain constrained by a Classical phrase structure. The song-pattern sequence is also followed in the second solo or middle section of the Chopin concerto. The pattern acts initially as an accompaniment to some development of the opening motive in the orchestral woodwind, but it is gradually emancipated from this status into a *spieltheme* which directs the music powerfully towards the third ritornello. It is a convincing enough sequence, but not quite the fusion of form and idea which we associate with the later Chopin, and its weakness is in part a weakness of the species. The heart of the virtuoso concerto is melody (susceptible to decoration and variation) and bravura pattern – poetry and display. Aspects of sonata thought rest uncomfortably on this base and the middle sections or 'developments' are often the least congenial stages of the process, falling back rather too easily on routine sequential patterns or unmotivated thematic working.

The second solo of the E minor Concerto follows exactly the same sequence as its predecessor and the parallel is strengthened by the similarity of the motives (Ex.6). But in the E minor the nocturne-like melody has a

Ex.6

beauty and spontaneity which mitigates the formal weakness. Again the *gesture* is familiar. It was common practice for the second ritornello to give way to just such a ruminative solo (Weber C major, Hummel A minor, Field A flat major and Kalkbrenner D minor), but Chopin's melody breathes a fresher air, uniquely his own. If anything, it is the formal setting which disappoints. We are offered individual moments of ravishing beauty (the second subject, for example), but the structure is less convincing than that of the earlier work. The broad, self-contained themes of the prelude lack that subtle balance of open-ended components which give the F minor prelude its fascination, so that the first solo entry is much less an inevitable outcome of the preceding argument. In general the responsibilities of tackling a much grander, more ambitious conception seem to have led Chopin to a more self-conscious reliance on his models in this work. It is tempting to rehearse again the Abraham-Schering argument. Abraham demonstrates a close affinity between the motivic material of Chopin's E minor and Hummel's A minor Concertos. Yet if we extend Schering's parallel with Kalkbrenner we find a remarkable correspondence of *gesture* throughout the first and second solos. The first solo entries are strikingly similar and they settle down to the same kind of dotted rhythm melody over a throbbing chordal left hand, followed by bravura patterns. The second solos are both nocturne-like, depending in each case for their effectiveness upon a sense of tonal distance, and both are succeeded by a driving semiquaver propulsion to the third ritornello.

In one major respect, however, Chopin departs from both Hummel and Kalkbrenner. The tonal structure of this first movement is eccentric, to say the least, and it has provoked censure from many quarters. Tovey called it 'suicidal'. The second theme appears in the tonic major both in the prelude and in the first solo, so that relief from the tonic region is delayed until the beginning of the second solo, investing that moment with very special beauty but hardly justifying the earlier lack of tonal contrast and tension. In the reprise, on the other hand, the second theme appears in the relative major, a strange reversal of classical procedure, and the problem is compounded by a slow movement also in the tonic major. Chopin's earlier cyclic forms had indeed prepared us for an unorthodox view of tonal relations within sonata-related structures. The monotonality of the exposition sections of Op.4 and Op.8 has been noted, while the reprises of the Trio and the F minor Concerto both place the second subject outside the tonic. The uneasiness one feels about all these tonal schemes is a result not of their flexibility – the Classical masters had already demonstrated this in large measure – nor even their violation of a fundamental principle of sonata thought, the tonal synthesis which results when material originally outside the tonic is brought within its fold. It comes rather from a failure to relate detail to whole. Ironically, Chopin's distance from the Austro-German tradition is never clearer than when he turns his hand to the formal archetypes most closely associated with that tradition, and this is apparent even in these early essays in extended forms. As yet, however, he had not learnt to *use* that distance to creative ends. It is clear from the concertos that he viewed tonal contrast less in terms of its structural potential than as a means of local colour change, where the contrast of major and minor was often in itself a sufficient resource. Now large-scale structural coherence can of course be achieved by other means than tonal architecture, as Chopin himself would later demonstrate. In the concertos, however, the harmonic language is primarily diatonic and tonal functions dictate the short-term chordal and linear movement. It is the failure to inflate these to a higher level which amounts to a structural weakness, an almost wilful negation of a formal resource which the material itself demands. Needless to say, voices have been raised in justification of Chopin's tonal practice in the concertos, at times on esoteric lines.[28] The most that can be said fairly is that the tendency to curtail or omit a first subject reprise (common enough in the virtuoso concerto) and to transfer the weight of tonal activity to the reprise rather than the exposition are early intimations of Chopin's later inclination to view the final stages of a work less as synthesis than as apotheosis. But this is tentative explanation, not justification. In the end the concertos linger in the memory for the poetry of their detail rather than the strength of their structures.

That poetry is given full rein in the slow movements of both works, where Chopin's delight in delicately embroidered threads of melody, at once suave and nostalgic, is given consummate expression. The F minor slow movement, apparently inspired by an awakening adolescent love, is an accompanied nocturne of rarest beauty, owing as much to the line of lyrical pianism which stretches from Clementi and Dussek to John Field as to the Viennese tradition of Mozart and Hummel. In the end, of course, it is pure Chopin. In the refinement and delicacy of its ornamental melody and in the impulsive ardour of its central recitative, Chopin's melody comes of age. If that melody was to reach its greatest heights in the later nocturnes, it nonetheless captures in these two early movements a freshness and innocence which is the more instantly beguiling for the comparative simplicity of its harmonic setting. We value the movements all the more because the orchestral backcloths render their particular charm unique in Chopin's output, or anyone else's.

In building his finales around national dance rhythms, a mazurka in the F minor and a krakowiak in the E minor, Chopin was following a practice long established in the keyboard concerto. The precedent can be traced even to J. C. Bach, but a more immediate stimulus would have come from concertos by Field and in particular the two concertos by Weber, whose finales have 'popular' episodes not unlike those in the Chopin works. Even the *cor de signal* in the virtuosic coda of the F minor reminds us of the solo horn in the bravura coda of Weber's Second Concerto. In any event it is a colourful moment. And in general the orchestral style of the *brillante* concerto was very colourful when it was not very dull. Eccentricities of scoring abound in these works, and the more striking details of Chopin's orchestration often call to mind very specific associations. The *col legno* strings in the finale of the F minor Concerto remind us of Hummel's A minor, for example, while the tremolando accompaniment to the slow movement's impassioned recitative is strikingly similar to the equivalent point in Moscheles's G minor Concerto. The time has long passed when we needed to make an aggressive case in defence of Chopin's much-maligned scoring in the concertos. It is adequate to its purpose.

It has been widely assumed that in the *Allegro de Concert* Op.46, published in 1841, Chopin salvaged what remained of his incomplete concerto for two pianos, or even a third piano concerto, though no precise evidence appears ever to have been adduced. It does seem at least a plausible hypothesis, though stylisations of ritornello-concertino contrasts were far from unprecedented in the solo keyboard literature. Attention has been drawn to the 'transparent inconsistencies of style'[29] between 'tutti' and 'solo' writing in this work, but really this would have been no more marked than in Chopin's frequent performances of the two concertos as solos. Whether or not the *Allegro de Concert* takes its origins in the third concerto, its structure is that of a compressed concerto movement played as a solo, and as such it has special interest as the only one of Chopin's concerto movements to adhere to a more-or-less conventional tonal scheme. There is a monotonal prelude, a first solo presenting song (new material) and bravura pattern in the tonic, followed by a second subject and bravura pattern in the dominant. After the second ritornello the second solo presents an elaborated, nocturne-like version of the second subject in the tonic minor, there is a further bravura writing and a closing ritornello linked thematically to the prelude.

Chopin worked on the concerto for two pianos during the year in Vienna just before his arrival in Paris, and we know from his correspondence that he had the greatest difficulty with it, a reflection no doubt of his growing disenchantment with the *stile brillante*. During that same year he wrote another work for piano and orchestra, the *Grande Polonaise Brillante* in E flat major Op.22, and a few years later in Paris he prefaced it with an *andante spianato*. The andante was composed in 1834 as an independent piece and its plangent lyricism fits uncomfortably with the polonaise. It is a fairly arbitrary coupling. The polonaise itself is in the bravura manner of the lighter orchestral pieces of the Warsaw period, taking over in a sense from the 'polacca' finale in Op.2.[30] In its unashamed showmanship it makes a fitting coda to Chopin's early involvement with the polonaise. When he returned to the dance form again in Paris it took on a very different significance.

4

Baroque reflections

The *Grande Polonaise* was a coda in another sense. For Chopin the orchestra held little attraction other than as a conventional enhancement of solo virtuosity, and his creative involvement with it ended with this work. It was his last big 'public' display piece, but not quite his farewell to the *stile brillante*. Some of the music which he produced during his early years in Paris still belongs firmly to that world. He completed the Rondo Op.16 (begun in Warsaw) and composed a set of *Variations Brillantes* Op.12 on a theme of Hérold, his last essays in the genres so beloved of the benefit concert. His *Grand Duo Concertant* for cello and piano on themes from Meyerbeer's *Robert le Diable*, a collaboration with Auguste Franchomme, is of much the same fashionable order, once again turning to popular opera as the melodic basis for an elegant, nicely turned pot-pourri. This was also the concept underlying a later collaborative *Hexameron*, where six pianist-composers contributed a movement each on the march from Bellini's *I Puritani*. But here Chopin departed from expectation. His contribution has a nocturne-like simplicity which almost seems to cock a snook at the surrounding virtuosity, and this more accurately reflects his aesthetic commitments during the early Paris years. We have already noted that some of the most revealing early glimpses of the mature composer are offered not by the bravura music of the Warsaw period, but by less pretentious miniatures – mazurkas, waltzes and above all the E minor Nocturne.

Not that Chopin ever entirely disowned the virtuoso style. His achievement was immeasurably to refine and enhance its materials, investing them with unsuspected power and beauty. Texture and configuration were divested of the conventional rhetoric and bravura of the concert-hall, gaining in the process a new subtlety and variety in their realisation and a new role as structural elements. Ornamentation lost its association with display and became rather an expressive device, ultimately inseparably fused with substance. The bravura codas of the concert pieces were translated from applause-winning gestures into formal components, agents of apotheosis. The *stile brillante* then provided the foundation for later development, but its gestures were transformed utterly. And the change was qualitative, evidenced even in apparently minor dimensions of the musical argument such as dynamics. Where autographs for the extended works of the

Warsaw period have survived, the contrasts and extremes of their dynamic markings stress that Chopin's musical thought took as its starting-point either inherited notions of Classical dualism or (and more often) the rhetoric of the virtuoso style.[1] A very different picture emerges from the autographs of the Op.10 Studies. Here dynamic markings tend to support the unitary, arch-like structures which operate both in small and large dimensions in these as in many other works of Chopin's maturity.[2]

The Op.10 Studies have a special importance in Chopin's output. More than any other works at the time they act as a bridge between the *stile brillante* of the apprentice years and the unmistakable voice of maturity. They were probably composed between 1829 and 1832 though only a few of them have been dated precisely.[3] It is likely that Chopin began work on some of the Studies which were to be published as Op.25 in 1833, completing this second cycle in 1836. The composition of both sets stretched therefore over some seven years. In the autumn of 1839 he wrote another three studies, the so-called *Trois Nouvelles Études*, for inclusion in the *Méthode des Méthodes* of Moscheles and Fétis. In all of them Chopin addressed himself systematically to the world of pianistic technique which had spawned the virtuoso style. But the result rises far above the dry exercises of a Czerny or the flashy acrobatics of a Thalberg. To a degree barely approached in earlier piano studies he gave substance and poetry to the genre, conquering virtuosity on its home ground, and in doing so lifting himself clear of the surrounding lowland of mediocrity. Later flirtations with the *stile brillante* were no more than the calculated concessions to public taste of a composer secure in his own aims and skills.

Short didactic keyboard pieces were of course common enough in the eighteenth century, but in the early nineteenth they rapidly multiplied, either in the form of independent sets or as illustrations for the innumerable methods which appeared in response to the growing popularity of the piano and its conquest of the amateur market. Clementi was of the greatest importance in this respect. There are his *Preludes and Exercises in all the Keys* of 1790, his *Introduction to the Art of Playing the Piano* of 1803 (there are some original pieces among its fifty examples) and of course his *Gradus ad Parnassum* (1817–27), whose hundred pieces helped to lay the foundations for modern piano technique.[4] Already by then his pupil Cramer had produced two books of studies, in 1804 and 1810, and it is here that the term 'study' seems to have acquired its modern meaning. He also brought out a method, as did both Dussek and Czerny. As many an amateur pianist knows to his cost, the latter provided hundreds of studies in collections such as *The School of Velocity, Forty Daily Exercises, The School of the Virtuoso* and *The Art of Finger Dexterity*. The list is endless. Hummel, Moscheles and Kalkbrenner all produced methods as well as independent studies, Kalkbrenner's, like Clementi's, in all the keys. But by the late 1820s there were signs of new developments, as studies became less overtly didactic, increasingly 'mit geist'. Liszt's set of 1829 and Moscheles's Op.70 set of

1826 represented important steps towards the more musically interesting and ambitious concert studies of the 1830s, including Hummel's Op.125, Chopin's Op.10 and Op.25, Moscheles's Op.95 and of course the well-known later essays by Liszt and Schumann.

Unlike some of these later studies, Chopin's remain true to the didactic idea, addressing one principal technical problem in each piece and crystallising that problem in a single shape or figure.[5] Although he had not yet begun his teaching career when he started working on the studies, he was very soon about to do so, and it is of considerable interest to examine the range and nature of his teaching materials. His own music featured prominently of course, but he also used Beethoven, Mendelssohn, Weber and Hummel, and special attention was devoted to the Nocturnes of Field, the Suites, Preludes and Fugues of Bach and the Studies of Clementi, Cramer and Moscheles. The latter give us a useful clue as to the influences at work on his own early studies.

In turning to particular technical problems, Chopin inevitably covered some of the ground already trekked by Clementi, Cramer and Moscheles, though he had reservations about some of the premises underlying their approach to technique, notably on the equalisation of fingers. For Chopin the important thing was to use the hand according to its structure and to accept the varied power and characteristics of each finger, preserving its unique quality.[6] Detailed correspondences between his studies and those of his immediate predecessors have frequently attracted attention. Yet in every case Chopin transcends the model, as an examination of the first few studies from Op.10 will demonstrate. The C major Study, composed during the later months of 1830, is designed for the extension and contraction of the right hand, and its lay-out is similar to that of studies by Moscheles (Op.70 No.11) and Cramer. Cramer wrote two studies (D major and D minor) using sweeping arpeggiation for the lateral extension of the right and left hands respectively, and, as Gerald Abraham has pointed out, the D minor is very close in conception to Op.10 No.1.[7] Even in its technical demands, however, the Chopin represents a considerable advance, stretching Cramer's octaves to ninths and tenths and sweeping a four-octave span with every two-bar arpeggiation. The entire piece demands a compass of six and a half octaves, practically the whole range of the modern piano. And the pedal is now essential as a means of binding together the two-bar harmonic fields, even if its effect on an 1830 Broadwood or Pleyel would have been very different from that of the concert grand of today.

Setting aside technical parallels and differences, the important distinction between the Cramer and the Chopin is in the quality of the music. The extension of the arpeggiation to encompass the entire keyboard is not merely a technical advance. It results in a gesture of remarkable dramatic power, where huge waves of sound are driven with relentless momentum by strong underlying harmonic currents. And here it becomes more appropriate to consider the connection with Bach, much deeper than surface resemblances to Cramer or Clementi. The obvious comparison is with the first prelude of the *Wohltempiertes Klavier*, but the point can be generalised. The sense of harmonic flow in both Bach and Chopin is achieved by maintaining a dissonant tension over extended periods, and by long-range linear motions which emerge *through* the figuration, creating a strong counterpoint with the melodic bass. This 'dissonant counterpoint' with a melodic bass is in reality very similar in both composers and it is at least as important in propelling the music towards structural harmonies as are chord progressions dictated by diatonic hierarchies.[8] The final chromatic enhancement of a dominant pedal is also Bachian – a cadential 'organ point' underpinning sliding diminished sevenths, very similar to the closing bars of the D minor Prelude from Book 1 of the *Wohltempiertes Klavier*. It seems unhelpful to make a great deal of individual harmonic fingerprints and temporary tonicisations in such a context. We do better to grasp how the figurative pattern interacts with the bass to create long-range movement towards tonal goals, with the pacing of harmonic change carefully judged to sustain tension. By comparison the simple fifths cycles of Cramer's harmony in the D minor Study appear primitive and mechanical.

The Second and Fourth Studies from Op.10, with their semiquaver tracery over staccato chords, also suggest origins in Baroque procedure, particularly the *moto perpetuo* of some of Bach's Preludes. We might single out the D major and F minor Preludes from Book 1. For both studies, however, there is a more immediate and tempting parallel in the third of Moscheles's Op.70 Studies. Indeed Chopin's A minor, composed late in 1830, is close enough to the Moscheles to have led von Bülow to suggest that he may have used it as a model (Ex.7). Chopin may indeed have taken his cue from Moscheles, but technically the demands are very different. To begin with his dynamic indications and explicit fingering instructions are much more comprehen-

Moscheles, Op.70 No.3

Chopin, Op.10 No.2

Ex.7

sive than Moscheles's. And the fingering is crucial. Chopin's study is directed towards a facility in crossing fingers over each other and in developing independence of the third, fourth and fifth fingers. Accordingly he fingers the chromatic scale in the Baroque fashion (unorthodox for the time) of three over four and five, four over five and five under three and four, whereas Moscheles requires only one and two. Chopin also makes much greater demands of the performer in the right-hand chording which must be accommodated by the first two fingers without interrupting the flow of the semiquaver movement, whereas Moscheles uses only the fifth finger for this purpose.

Musically too there are major differences. Where Moscheles builds an element of contrast into the structure of his motive, with a perky diatonic consequent to the chromatic ascent, Chopin – Baroque-like – maintains the flow unbroken in a *tour de force* of whirling virtuosity. The line is drafted as a series of arcs, and the interest of the piece, in a context of rhythmic and textural uniformity, lies predominantly in the subtly varied contours of these arcs as they interact with harmony and phrase rhythm. As so often in Chopin the borderline between 'melody' and 'figure' is blurred. The 'basic shape' reaches its peak on a weak beat well before the halfway point of the four-bar phrase, necessitating minor undulations in the descending line, including written-out trills (bar 4) and changing-note patterns (bar 8). These undulations vary on repetition and their subsidiary peaks often 'throw' the phrasing off the beat, so that the effect is of a remarkable snake-like plasticity of line, held in check (as in Moscheles) by clear diatonic harmonies or chromatic substitutes. It is interesting, moreover, to compare the different methods used by both composers to achieve intensification in their middle sections. Moscheles relies upon textural diversification, involving the left hand in the chromatic scales and counterpointing the two elements in his original motive. Chopin, on the other hand, keeps the textural and rhythmic schemes intact and intensifies the argument through harmony and line, as Bach so often does. The arcs are reduced to one-bar periods or broken down altogether, and the harmony leaves its diatonic base to explore sequential patterns based on fifths cycles with a diminishing period of sequence. It is a conventional enough device, but Chopin gives it fresh interest, enlivening the approach to the dominant by disturbing the four- and two-bar symmetries at bar 29.

The first two studies cover some of the vital ground of Chopin's later right-hand technique, exploring both harmony (a widespread arpeggiation) and line (an intricate chromatic scalar movement). The Third Study, one of his most popular and one of the last to be composed (August 1832), offers a complete contrast in mood and structure. Here Chopin abandons the monothematic concept, whereby departure and return is effected through a single figure, and gives us instead a lyrical melody with contrasting middle section. The design is similar to the first of his Op.15 Nocturnes which had probably been composed by then. There can be little excuse, incidentally, for a lingering, self-indulgent performance of the E major Study. The earliest autograph (K.123) has the tempo marking *vivace*[9], later modified to *vivace ma non troppo* (K.124) and only with the published edition changed to *lento ma non troppo*: against this background we should clearly note carefully the *ma non troppo*.

The control of *legato* melody is just as much a matter of technique as rapid passage-work and Chopin had decided views on it, preferring to exploit rather than conceal a hierarchy of finger strengths and often using finger substitution to sustain line. Other composers had of course addressed *legato* melody in didactic pieces. Moscheles for one explored it in his C sharp minor Study from Op.70 and his melody has a similar rhythmic structure to Chopin's. But there the resemblance ends. Moscheles has composed a pleasing enough melody, but Chopin's is one of his most beautiful. He himself admitted his special affection for it to Adolf Gutman. It is impossible to give anything like an adequate explanation for the quality and beauty of a melody such as this, or even to go very far in identifying helpful contexts. Already in his early nocturnes Chopin had developed and refined early nineteenth-century traditions of lyrical pianism, especially the so-called 'London school', and some discussion of this will come in the following chapter. Certainly this seems a more useful association than the influence of Polish folk music, to which some commentators have attributed the irregular phrase structure of the melody.

Such irregularity is merely the surface of a much more thorough-going ambivalence in rhythmic structure which contributes to the fluid quality of the unfolding line. It will be enough to look at the opening five-bar phrase.[10] The anacrusic quaver encourages us to view the F sharp and G sharp of bars 1 and 2 respectively as anticipative as well as conclusive in function (Ex.8(i)), a tendency which is reinforced in bar 3, where the C sharp is perceived not as a goal but as a pivot in a longer-spanning motion to the F sharp in bar 4.[11] This has the further effect of weakening the sense of closure in bar 5 and of giving the final E of that bar an anticipative feeling which links it to the succeeding phrase.[12] There is further purposeful ambivalence when we look at contour and motive. It is easy to see how the overall shape is built cumulatively on a bar-by-bar basis through transformations of the opening motive. This indeed is typical of Chopin's melody. Yet this narrative unfolding, or through-composition, is counterpointed against an arch-like contour, with bar 3 as the peak and bars 4 and 5 a transformed reprise of 1 and 2 (Ex.8(i)). This interpretation is strengthened by the harmonic correspondences of the outer wings of the arch. We can retain an awareness of both interpretations simultaneously, the one time-dependent and dynamic, the other synoptic and inert, the one concerned with process, the other with design.

No single factor, then, makes for the hauntingly memorable quality of what seems on the surface like a simple, innocent tune. Rather we have a rich play on different levels of function and perception which sets Chopin

Op.10 No.3

Ex.8(i)

Ex.8(ii)

far above superficially similar essays by predecessors and contemporaries and which presents incidentally teasing questions for the performer. The sense of flow in the opening phrase of the melody persists through the succeeding three phrases, reaching its main goal at bar 17, the peak of an overall melodic arc which returns to base at bar 21.[13] The middle section of the study then takes up a phrase from the opening melody and inverts it to create a subsidiary study in parallel sixths and tritones. It is a texture familiar in general outline from earlier sets of studies (Clementi's E and D major from *Gradus ad Parnassum* are typical). But Chopin takes greater pains to free his textures from tonal constraints and to give them a more responsible role in the structure. The passage-work is still harmonically based, of course, often extending and elaborately decorating underlying dominant-quality harmonies, but at times it splinters into symmetrically mirrored patterns which slide in parallel motion, so that we tend to perceive it as much in textural as in harmonic terms. Such passage-work still functions essentially as harmonic prolongation, but it aspires towards a status independent of harmony. Much more than in any earlier work we sense harmony dissolving into colour.

Even when considered in purely harmonic terms, the sophistication of this middle section announces Chopin's new-found stylistic maturity. To some extent it embodies a further stage in an age-old opposition between diatonic hierarchies and non-tonal symmetries, between the principles of tonality and equidistance. Passages such as Ex.8(ii) are governed by symmetry, with diatonic functions suppressed and the total chromatic kept in play. Naturally any sense of local tonal attraction is weak in such progressions. But care is needed in their interpretation. Even on a foreground bar-by-bar level the harmony is still perceived as directional and it shares some important characteristics with diatonic progressions, notably semitonal connection and a tendency for chord successions to exhibit a 'complementary' pitch content.[14] Moreover the speed of the progressions – fast enough to blur individual impacts – and the effects of rhythm and accentuation influence the span-of-context within which we evaluate tonality-defining elements in the harmony. Subjective values will always play a significant role in our understanding of tonality, urging caution about too easy an acceptance of comprehensive theories of tonal structure.

However we understand such passages theoretically, there can be no doubt of the power of the climax in which they culminate, and of the skill with which tension is subsequently released in preparation for the return of the opening melody. The pacing of the musical argument is achieved here, as in the outer sections, with a perfection which already marks Chopin out as a master of the miniature. This can never be simply a matter of proportions – music *flows* through time – but it is intriguing all the same to notice the placing of the main tension points in the three sections of the study (A B A¹). In A the proportions (measured in crotchet beats) are 33–8, while in B they are 66–16, exactly twice those of A. The approach to the dominant harmony in B, a major structural downbeat, takes 41 beats, the exact length of A. In both A and B a head of tension is given little time to be released. To compensate and create a closing stability. Chopin varies his reprise so that the proportions are equalised to 17–16, making up the 33 of the first part of A.

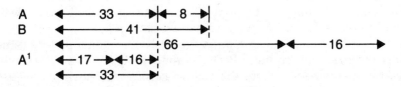

The Fifth and Sixth Studies, both dating from 1830, are sharply contrasting in character and in technical demands. Yet both are perfectly moulded to the needs and nature of the piano. The Fifth, the so-called 'Black-Key' Study, is a bravura exercise, with the right hand happily sporting its thumb on the black keys (Chopin's fingering on the autograph, K.135) while the left presents variants on a cheerful vamping accompaniment. As in the First Study lessons have been learnt from Bach, however dissimilar the surface of the music. Chopin's toccata-like motive expresses in nineteenth-century terms something of the same sentiments as Bach's in the F minor and B flat major Preludes from Book I and his long-range resolution of dissonances created across the figuration (often 'distributed' through four or five octaves) also echoes Bach. Throughout the mood is light. Von Bülow called it a 'salon piece' and Chopin himself thought of it as the least interesting of the set, especially if the listener is unaware of the black keys constraint.

The E flat minor Study is more ambitious, its intense, brooding quality far removed from anything previously characterised as a study. As so often there are surface resemblances to earlier didactic pieces. The harmonies invite comparison with Clementi's study in the same key from *Gradus ad Parnassum*, for example, despite the difference in mood and tempo. In both pieces the progression to the dominant is achieved in similar ways, as a summary of harmonic content demonstrates (Ex.9). There is nothing new

Ex.9

in this harmonic repertory. But Chopin goes well beyond Clementi and indeed beyond the harmonic norm of early nineteenth-century music generally in his expressive use of appoggiaturas to delay and obscure the underlying harmonic movement and in his reliance on stepwise, predominantly semitonal, part-movement as a source of continuity. It is an early glimpse of a world of painfully expressive chromaticism and dissonance which he was to take even further in later works and which culminated in Wagner's enharmonic continuum. But Chopin's chromaticism looks back as well as forward. Just as his chromatic symmetries have much in common with Bach's, so too his emancipation of an expressive semitonal part-movement against the triad calls to mind Bach's chromatic *Affekt*. In an aria such as 'Betrachte meine Seel' ', from the *St John Passion*, our attempts to justify individual harmonies in relation to a tonic have limited usefulness. The harmonic pillars which support the musical edifice are clear enough, but intervening material exploits tonal attraction through the fifth relationship only at the most immediate foreground level. Throughout the aria diatonic hierarchies form just one of several principles governing harmonic flow.

The middle section of the Sixth Study intensifies both the chromaticism and the dissonance of the opening and accelerates considerably the tonal and harmonic rhythm. Here Chopin employs sequential harmonies to swing the music far from its tonal base and permits only a single point of tonal clarification, the 'Neapolitan' E major of bar 21. It is a subtle gesture, for it reaches back to the opening harmonies and at the same time gives deeper meaning to the Neapolitan parenthesis in the closing bars.[15] Such 'tonal parentheses',[16] where Chopin will momentarily expand and prolong a chromatic harmony through the diatonic progressions pertaining to it, were to become very common in Chopin and if they have a source in any other single composer it would be Louis Spohr, whose music he knew and admired.

Technically the E flat minor Study may appear relatively straightforward, but like the others it reaches to the heart of the piano. The main requirement is a careful gradation of touch to control the four elements in the texture, a melody, a countermelody, a bass line and above all a semiquaver 'accompaniment', to use a wholly inadequate term. This latter winds its chromatically tortuous way through the texture, acting as a microcosm of the larger chromatic movement in the harmony and reinforcing the mood of introspective intensity. The whole presents an intricate counterpoint, entirely without harmonic or figurative 'padding', and it is a counterpoint as perfectly suited to the piano, with its capacity to shade and differentiate voices, as is Bach's to the uniform touch of the harpsichord or organ.

This kind of contrapuntal style, where fragments of melody emerge and recede from the texture, is also a feature of the Seventh Study, composed in the spring of 1832. The opening bars present us with an apparently simple texture, but the ear will tend to isolate and move around between several elements held in balance. It will be aware for instance of the pattern *qua* pattern. At the same time it will pick out a melodic strand through the on-beat repeated notes, a surface melody 'thrown' by Schumannesque syncopation and a melodic strand in the left hand whose metric grouping counterpoints three groups of two against the right hand's two groups of three. There is no real priority here; rather a mixture of components held in equilibrium, making up a composite, elusive texture which is given further interest through such articulative detail as the use of repeated notes against a legato line. As so often in Chopin a deceptively simple surface conceals a wealth of information.

Tonally the Seventh and Eighth Studies – in C major and F major – break the pattern of related pairs which was established in the first half of the cycle, though a pairing scheme returns in different form in the last four studies – F minor/A flat major and E flat major/C minor. The twelve studies were composed over a period of some three years and assembled into a cycle after the event. For all that they make a very satisfying whole and the tonal pairings suggest that Chopin may have increasingly thought of them as a unified cycle during the later stages of their composition. Even the Seventh Study, out of step with the tonal scheme, may be regarded as a central pillar strengthening the tonic region. The links between ends and beginnings are also strong and Chopin actually wrote at the end of the Third Study (K.124) *attaca il presto con fuoco*. As Jeffrey Kallberg has demonstrated,[17] there is much internal evidence to suggest that Chopin often

thought of multi-partite opuses as artistically unified or at least compatible
units, especially with mazurkas and nocturnes, though he was of course
very happy to follow the conventional practice of playing individual pieces
from the cycles. It has even been suggested[18] that, in view of the many
precedents, he may have intended to continue the cycle of studies to include
all twenty-four keys, sacrificing this scheme only in the interests of getting
the studies published and eventually transferring it to the preludes. In any
event the diversity of moods already evoked in the first half of Op.10 is
astonishingly wide, encompassing the drama and power of the First Study,
the skittishness of the Second, the sparkle of the Fifth and the brooding
intensity of the Sixth.

The Ninth Study in F minor extends this range of expression still further,
introducing another affective character and one which was to recur in
Chopin's music. It is perhaps best described as a suppressed passion which
breaks the surface intermittently with eloquent, urgent gestures, raising
the emotional temperature of the individual moment with impulsive and
seemingly spontaneous 'parlando' intensifications of the original material.
There are similar things in the 'Revolutionary' study, the most powerful as
well as the most popular of the cycle, and it may not be too fanciful to see
in it both an expression of the Slavonic temperament and a distant echo of
Italian operatic practice (Ex.10). On safer ground, we may observe that

Op.10 No.9

Op.10 No.12

Ex.10

technically the Ninth Study is directed mainly towards a control of widespread left-hand accompaniment patterns of the nocturne type. In itself this
is noteworthy, for until this point in Op.10 (as finally constituted) Chopin
had directed most of his attention towards the development of right-hand
virtuosity. Only in a few passages from the Third, Fourth and Eighth
Studies does the left hand become the focus of technical interest, and this

relative weighting of the two hands is a fair reflection of his music generally. The accompaniment pattern of the F minor Study, straightforward enough so far as the notes are concerned, must be performed smoothly and evenly and this requires a careful control of the three middle fingers in an extended hand position. The relevance to Chopin's later music is obvious.

By contrast the Tenth Study demands considerable technical dexterity from both hands and, more importantly, a capacity to co-ordinate the hands in cross-rhythms and shifting accents. In technique it is one of the most challenging of the cycle, fully justifying von Bülow's claim that 'anyone who can play this study in a real finished manner may congratulate himself on having climbed to the highest peak of the pianist's Parnassus. The whole repertoire of pianoforte music does not contain a study of perpetual motion so full of genius and fancy as this particular one is generally acknowledged to be, except perhaps Liszt's *Feux follets*.'[19] Chopin increases the difficulties by alternating legatissimo 'con pedale' and staccato articulations and by the wide leaps required of the left hand.

Arthur Hedley's remarks on the Eleventh Study echo von Bülow's claim for the Tenth. 'Nowhere in piano literature before 1830 is there to be found anything resembling the series of immense arpeggioed chords for both hands which this study presented.'[20] In fact it seems likely that once again Moscheles's Op.70 Studies provided a stimulus for Chopin, as Ex.11(i) suggests. The Second of the Moscheles Studies is an exercise 'pour les deux mains sur les accords dans leur différentes positions. Ils doivent tous être joués en arpège, c'est à dire que les notes dont ils a composent doivent être frappés l'une après l'autre, de la plus basse à la plus haute.' The instruction may have some bearing on the question of whether Chopin intended the same continuous arpeggio or the two simultaneous arpeggios which his and Moscheles's notation would seem to imply. As we might expect the Chopin makes much greater demands on the performer than the Moscheles. Its wide spacing requires 'stretching' in both hands, the melody must be phrased and evenly toned, although it changes from finger to finger, and the fragments of countermelody which emerge, characteristically enough, from the chording should have just the right prominence.

But the essential difference between the two studies lies in Chopin's refusal to admit any element of textural or rhythmic contrast. Indeed we noted precisely the same distinction in the earlier comparison of Chopin No.2 and Moscheles No.3. In the Chopin the interest and variety of the music, as well as its overall shape or 'intensity curve', has to be created through changing melodic contour, discreet wisps of counterpoint and, above all, harmony. The fluid, uniform textural surface conceals an harmonic language of considerable originality. The underlying harmonic movement is slow and simple, with no significant departure from the tonic region and only a momentary loss of tonal security at the beginning of the middle section. But the structural harmonies are connected by widely-ranging chromatic movement, including passages of sliding, unresolving

Moscheles, Op.70 No.2

Ex.11(i)

Chopin, Op.10 No.11

Ex.11(ii)

sevenths (Ex.11(ii)). Once more the harmonies in themselves are familiar enough, but the kaleidoscopic rapidity of their change was something new in 1830, and again it was in part a response to the acoustic qualities of an instrument whose potential had only been partly explored before Chopin. It was doubtless of just such a passage as Ex.11(ii) that Moscheles commented, 'The dilettantish harsh modulations which strike me so disagreeably when I am playing his compositions no longer shock me, because he glides over them in a fairy-like way with his delicate fingers.'

The Op.10 Studies offer an almost encyclopaedic compendium of the resources of the piano and in particular a workshop for the preparation of Chopin's own later music. But their significance within his output goes further than this. Above all they embody his suppression of the conventional. Even where the passage-work takes its origins in familiar keyboard textures, these are transformed utterly, given fresh meaning through novel interactions with harmony and phrase structure or through a discreet contrapuntal working. The differentiation within the textures of Op.10 and the intricacy and subtlety of their construction are remarkable. Far from an art of conformity, it amounts really to a thorough renovation of keyboard texture.

The Op.25 Studies and the *Trois Nouvelles Études* consolidate this achievement, exploring much of the same ground, but extending the paths a little and taking in some new scenery on the way. In particular the left hand is involved to a much greater extent than in Op.10. The last of the Op.25 Studies, for example, extends the basic scheme of Op.10 No.1, employing passage-work which is largely harmonic in impulse, but now both hands are included in the sweeping arpeggiation, so that linear elements (which had been the preserve of the left hand in Op.10 No.1) must emerge through the two-hand figuration. Again there are echoes of Bach – the prelude in the same key from Book 1, for instance – in the tolling 'chorale', against which subsidary material emerges in flexible rhythms.

In the Second and Fourth of the Op.10 Studies the figuration was melodically rather than harmonically conceived, and there are again numerous parallels in the later cycles. The F minor Op.25 No.2, for instance, presents a variation on the theme of Op.10 No.2. Once more there is a *moto perpetuo* in the right hand, a single line shaped in arcs of varying lengths and widths. The supporting chords of Op.10 No.2 have been replaced, however, by a single left-hand line which outlines the underlying harmonic scheme in triplets. It is a spare two-part texture and its delicate, elusive quality rests in the blurring of function between melody and figure in the right hand and between broken chord and contrapuntal line in the left. The same flowing two-part counterpoint is echoed in more plangent vein in the first of the *Trois Nouvelles Études*. The melodic shapes are also similar and the counterpoint is again given edge through a rhythmic tension between the voices. Such rhythmic counterpoint, common in Chopin's later music, is the principal technical feature of several studies, whether expressed through cross-rhythms, as in Op.10 No.10 and Op.25 No.2, or polyrhythms, as in the first and third of the *Trois Nouvelles Études*.

The melodic figuration of Op.10 No.2 is developed in a different way in the Sixth, Eighth and Tenth of the Op.25 Studies. Here the line is thickened into parallel thirds, sixths and octaves respectively, again in predominantly chromatic progressions. Inevitably these were already much exercised textures, but a comparison of Chopin's delicate thirds with Moscheles's (Op.70 No.13) or his explosive octaves with Clementi's (*Gradus ad Parnassum* Nos 44 and 65) only serves to highlight both the unparalleled virtuosity of the Op.25 Studies and their consummate artistry.

In most of the studies the basic figuration is evolutionary in character, itself shaping and modelling the form in a dynamic way. There are some, however, in which the pattern remains a static, gentle background, accompanimental in function, and here too we can trace an extension of technique from Op.10 to Op.25. The left-hand pattern of Op.10 No.9, for example is transformed in the first of the Op.25 Studies into a rippling arpeggiation for both hands, a texture which was to be overworked by many a later salon composer, but which is magical in effect in Chopin's hands, supporting a delicious melody, spawning discreet countermelodies and articulating an adventurous harmonic scheme. Schumann's description of Chopin's own performance of this study (the last of Op.25 to be composed) has been quoted often enough to require no complete repetition here, but it may be worth reminding ourselves of his reference to 'a deeper fundamental tone and a softly singing melody . . . a billowing of the chord of A flat, swelled here and there by the pedal . . . through the harmonies . . . in sustained tones a wonderful melody. . . .'[21]

In both Op.10 No.9 and Op.25 No.1 the accompaniment is harmonically conceived. In the Eighth of the Op.10 Studies, on the other hand, it moves beyond this role, assuming melodic as well as harmonic significance. Indeed its dynamic driving semiquavers are hardly an 'accompaniment' at all, but an independent counterpoint to the left-hand march theme. There is a similar texture in the Eleventh of the Op.25 Studies, the so-called 'Winter Wind'. Again the left hand has a march-like theme and again the right-hand 'accompaniment' combines harmonic and melodic functions in a uniquely formulated and strongly characterised pattern, sweeping across the registers to create a dramatic and powerful counterpoint to the principal theme. It is the most impassioned of the later set, recalling the 'revolutionary' study in its heroic tone and its structural breadth. Although Chopin uses a rather different means of achieving the heroic *Affekt*, it is difficult to resist comparisons with Beethoven.

Elsewhere in Op.25 the intricate counterpoint of fragmentary elements which characterises Op.10 No.7 is taken further. In Op.25 No.3 we have not one figurative pattern but a combination of four elements which nevertheless allow a melodic profile to emerge on the surface of the texture. Much of the point of the study rests in the detailed changes made by

Chopin on subsequent varied repetitions of the material, not only changes in the structure of the motives but in their dynamics and articulation. This raises an important issue. The smaller components of the structure are richer in detail – more *substantial* – in Chopin than in comparable essays by Clementi, Cramer and Moscheles, and in itself this is symptomatic of changing priorities in his musical language. Texture and sonority *per se* achieve a compositional significance in some of the studies which almost equals that of harmony and theme. Texture acquires unique value as an element of Chopin's mature style, and its characterisation through register, dynamics and articulation becomes all-important. This is true of many of the studies, but in some these non-pitched elements become the principal technical focus. The fourth and ninth of the Op.25 cycle are concerned principally with staccato articulation, for example, while the second of the *Trois Nouvelles Études* is a study in combining legato and staccato.

All in all the studies demonstrate a sensitivity to medium for which Chopin has no peers, but in which he has reasonably been compared to such pioneers of idiomatic harpsichord writing as Domenico Scarlatti and François Couperin.[22] Certainly there are affinities with Baroque procedures at various levels in Chopin's music. His love of Bach, grounded in early studies with Adalbert Żywny, persisted throughout his life and played no little part in shaping his mature style. The '48' and the suites were part of his repertory as well as providing him with some of his staple teaching material, and in later years he even corrected some of the Paris editions of the former. It is significant that he brought the Preludes and Fugues to Majorca, for it was there that he put the finishing touches to the cycle of 24 Preludes Op.28 which had occupied him intermittently since 1836. Already in his prelude in A flat major of 1834[23] the Bach connection was clearly established (its affinity to the D major Prelude from Book 1 has been demonstrated by Chomiński).[24] But with Op.28 the tribute is explicit. Like the '48', Chopin's preludes form a complete cycle of the major and minor keys, though the pairing is through tonal relatives (C major-A minor) rather than Bach's monotonality (C major-C minor). Bach's example had of course served other composers of didactic and contrapuntal pieces, including Clementi and Cramer. Indeed Chopin himself wrote to Wojciechowski in 1829 of a performance given by August Klengel of his 48 Canons and Fugues: 'One can say they are a continuation of Bach.'[25] But in Op.28 the affinities reach beyond externals and certainly beyond the cyclic tonal scheme which was in any case fairly common. Some of these affinities have already been examined in connection with the studies and it may be useful to summarise them at this stage with reference to the preludes.

First there is the nature of the bravura passage-work. In particular the *moto perpetuo* figuration of the B major (No.11), a kind of three-part invention, or of the E flat minor (No.14) and E flat major (No.16) has clear origins in Baroque keyboard music, the Fifth Prelude from Book 1, for instance, or the twenty-first from Book 2. Like Bach, moreover, Chopin was adept at the construction of figuration which generates a clear harmonic flow while at the same time permitting linear elements to emerge through the pattern. The First and Fifth of the Preludes, in C major and D major respectively, are typical, both of them elaborating a two-note 'trill' motive which grows out of the intricate pattern.[26] We might compare them with the Twelfth Prelude from Book 1.

It is also partly to his studies of Bach that we owe Chopin's highly personal contrapuntal style. Unlike preludes and studies by Clementi, Hummel and Moscheles, Chopin's do not contain fugal or canonic exercises. His Fugue in A minor and his canon at the octave are more in the nature of compositional exercises than finished pieces (this is especially so of the canon), and the imitative textures which abound in some of his early Warsaw pieces tend to sound self-conscious and laboured; only in later years was he able to absorb such gestures naturally into his musical thought. Yet, as our discussion of the studies has already demonstrated, a counterpoint of sorts is often at the kernel of the musical idea in Chopin, and usually a counterpoint which starts from the capacity of the piano to 'layer' voices through shaded dynamics, allowing voices to emerge and recede from the texture. Even the figure in the First Prelude (Ex.12(i)) is a subtle compound of discrete though interactive particles, a texture reminiscent of Op.25 No.3 and found again in the eighth prelude in F sharp minor (Ex.12(ii)). Like Bach, moreover, Chopin often enjoys a real polarity of melody and 'singing' bass, as in the E major Prelude (No.9), and he is good

Op.28 No.1

Ex.12(i)

Op.28 No.8

Ex.12(ii)

at devising a bass which can serve the dual function of harmonic support and polyphonic (melodic) line as in the B minor (No.6).[27]

These two areas of affinity – figuration and counterpoint – have further implications for harmony. In both Bach and Chopin consistency of figure and contrapuntal integrity will provide sufficient justification for severe and often highly unorthodox dissonance. The Second Prelude in A minor, for instance, allows its ostinato accompaniment to take in grating dissonances of a kind almost unknown among his immediate predcessors but not infrequent in Bach, as in the ostinato accompaniment to the florid aria which forms the slow movement of the *Italian* Concerto.[28] And in general the balance between linear and harmonic elements is similar in both composers and perceptibly different from the Viennese classical style. In Bach and Chopin an organic chromaticism often directs the music and dictates its chord connections so that foreground diatonic functions are emaciated and the span between structural harmonies lengthened. A case in point is the fourth prelude in E minor where semitonal part-movement prolongs the initial progression from tonic to dominant over a twelve-bar span. We might compare it to the A minor Prelude from Book 2. Often such semitonal part-movement is allied to sequential fifths cycles in the foreground harmony, creating just one form of those tonally evasive symmetries favoured by both composers.

It is perhaps to be expected that in the studies and preludes Classical tonal contrast should play only a limited role. Of their nature they tend to crystallise a single *Affekt* in a single pattern. Yet Chopin had already demonstrated in the Op.4 Sonata, the Piano Trio and the two Concertos that the dramatic potential of large-scale tonal tensions and the use of the dominant as a means of articulating formal divisions meant little to him, even in those genres where we might reasonably expect such features to be paramount. Rather than a dialectic of tonal contrast and synthesis he favoured a single impulse of departure from and return to tonal stability – a process of harmonic intensification and resolution. It is part and parcel of an essentially unitary conception of musical form, in itself closer to Baroque than to Classical prototypes. The musical argument in the Studies often unfolds within the context of simple ternary designs where the middle section functions either as contrast or intensification. The preludes are more often a simple statement and conflated response, with the final tonic delayed to create a stronger ending. Such designs were a norm of the Baroque period, but they were too static to accommodate the drives and tensions of Classical thought, and Chopin's adherence to them has often been criticised as evidence of an undeveloped, even primitive, sense of form.

Such a view will seem plausible only if we understand 'form' as synonymous with external pattern. In fact most of us experience (even if we do not analyse) music as a 'flowing state', shaping time through tension and release, growth and decline, intensifying and resolving impulses. These operate, moreover, on different structural levels, so that material which is unstable or 'dissonant' at the foreground (the level of the phrase, for example) may be stable or 'consonant' at the background (the level of the paragraph or of the entire piece). The relationship of such intensity curves to the static external pattern or design of a piece, in itself perceivable only after the event or, more precisely, gradually revealed as the music unfolds, may be one either of correlation or of counterpoint. In successful miniatures it is more likely to be the latter.[29] Viewed in such terms Chopin's formal sense is anything but primitive. In the preludes the simple binary or ternary designs act as necessary foils for dynamic, carefully paced intensity curves. Even where they present just a single impulse of mild intensification and resolution this is achieved through a subtle interaction of several parameters which influence the shape in different, often non-congruent, ways. Something of this may be demonstrated in a brief examination of four of the preludes.

Nothing seems simpler than the C major Prelude, but its construction is subtle. The figurative pattern itself is of some intricacy (Ex.12(i)), and it generates a basic shape, determined mainly by the interaction of melody and bass, which is counterpointed against a periodicity of four eight-bar phrases. As so often in Chopin an impression of perfect symmetry and balance is achieved through asymmetrical means. The melody of the first phrase defines an area of musical space (the major sixth G-E) through a simple melodic arc. The second and third phrases expand this, reaching towards two peaks whose phrasing is dislocated, encouraging an alternative reading of the macrorhythm as indicated in Ex.13, and contributing to an increase in tension in relation to the phrase structure. Resolution is then effected by the fourth phrase, which changes the nature of the melodic line, closing the gap between the original limits of G and E in a gesture of synthesis. Harmony supports the shape but at the same time sets up an independent bipartite structure. Characteristically the varied and active harmonic surface is underpinned by a diatonic middleground. The first phrase establishes the terms of reference, a simple I – IV – V – I progression, and this is expanded and prolonged in the last three phrases (Ex.13), creating two very different rhythms of harmonic change.

Harmonic rhythm is also a major structural feature of the Third Prelude, Op.28 No.1

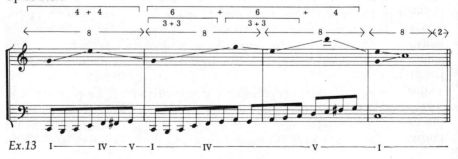

Ex.13   I————— IV —— V—I ————— IV ————————— V ———————— I ———

whose overall shape is similar to the first, again a statement with conflated response. The two-bar 'ornamental-figurative' pattern at the beginning outlines both harmonic space and melodic curve, and it introduces and accompanies a four-bar motive which gradually composes out a tonic triad (Ex.14). Although this achieves melodic closure, it nonetheless creates some feeling of anacrusis, due to the total absence of, and therefore expectation of, harmonic movement. Subsequent material answers our need for instability following this stasis, introducing calculated unpredictability in several ways, from disruption of the phrase structure at bar 11 to the unexpected outcome of the varied repetition, 'opening' the argument after four bars through a progression to the sub-dominant and reversing the direction of the melody. The effect is to create mild but sustained intensification throughout the conflated response until the resolution at bar 26. A synoptic view of the prelude reveals a perfectly shaped melodic arc, supported, as in the First Prelude, by a strong harmonic framework of primary functions (Ex.14). A special felicity allows the 'accompaniment' to take over the coda, reaching across the span of the work to the coda and confirming that it was always more than an accompaniment.

Op.28 No.3

Ex.14

The twelfth prelude in G sharp minor is a *moto perpetuo* movement whose flowing quavers articulate two related but distinct shapes. As we shall see, Chopin often associated what conventional theory would term tonal 'relatives' within a key signature as part of a single musical idea. Here the association is G sharp minor and B major and within their inclusive region shape A balances chromatic and diatonic material, creating a small-scale tension-release pattern, with skilfully differentiated rhythmic groupings (Ex.15). Shape B is approached by way of a cadential extension to A, altering the tension-release pattern from 4 + 4 to 4 + 8. The intensification which takes place from this point is partly due to a dislocation of phrasing – 3 + 4 + 1 against 4 + 4 – and partly to the more distant tonal region in which A returns, now widened diatonically (it 'puns' between C major and E minor), but without its stabilising descent. The melodic and harmonic instability here generates the main tension point of the piece, and the resolution comes with the tonal and thematic reprise at the precise midway point of the prelude. If we now look at the larger structure of the piece we find that shape B divides the first statement into two equal sections with the structural downbeat at bar 21.[30] In order to create a stronger ending, Chopin places the main tension point of the second statement some way *before* the midway point, allowing a much longer period for resolution and closure.

Ex.15 presents a diagram of both halves of the prelude, illustrating the counterpoint of shape and pattern.

Op.28 No.12

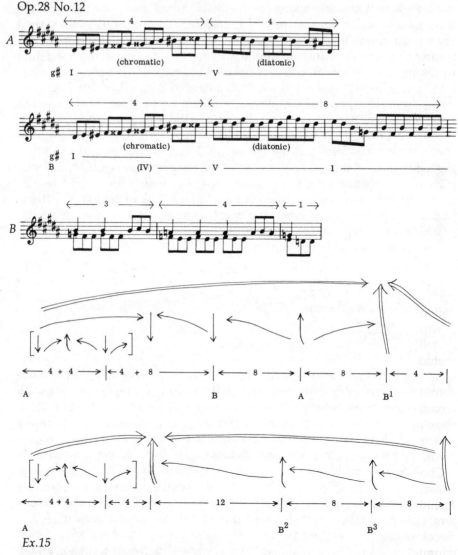

Ex.15

The Seventeenth Prelude in A flat major is more extended and its harmonic structure appropriately more sophisticated than that of the other three. The opening is of remarkable originality, a $^6_4 - ^5_3$ harmony where the melody flowers unexpectedly on the weak beat of the harmony, growing imperceptibly out of the repeated quaver movement of the opening two bars. The expected harmonic closure is denied us, however, both here and in the fuller restatement of the opening theme, and Chopin continues to postpone it until bar 18. Tonality is certainly stable, but it is achieved through dominant rather than tonic harmony. Following the closure of bar 18, enharmonic change takes us into an extended middle section where two episodes flank a central statement of the main theme (yet fuller in its scoring), again in the tonic, but again avoiding closure to the tonic triad. The episodes employ the sequential fifths with semitonal part-movement which is so characteristic of Chopin's harmony, extending or prolonging structural harmonies as indicated in Ex.16. The episodes are tension-

Op.28 No.17

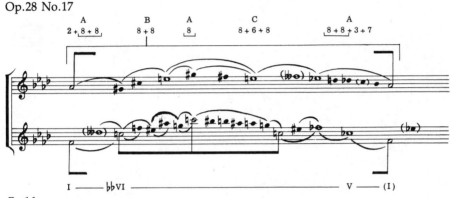

Ex.16

building and they both resolve on to statements of the main theme, the last of which finally satisfies our need for tonic affirmation and stability through its tolling pedal point. Since the texture and rhythmic movement of the prelude do not change significantly, stability is achieved primarily through tonal and thematic definition, and instability through the lack of such definition. Viewed in such terms the shape of the piece (intensity curve) is broadly synchronised with its external pattern, as we might expect of a more extended piece. A crude characterisation would be a five-section arch structure, with the second statement of the main theme acting as central pivot.

Chopin's genre titles are not always an infallible clue to the nature of his music, and it is not entirely clear why he described Op.28 as 'preludes'. Preluding was an integral part of the improviser's craft and several composers, notably Hummel and Kalkbrenner, had already offered composed-out pieces in all the keys which were intended to serve as literal preludes (Hummel's are no more than a few bars long). Chopin's Preludes are of a different order altogether, presenting a unified cycle of independent pieces which achieve something close to perfection of form within the framework of the miniature, expertly gauging the relationship of the musical substance to a restricted time-scale.[31] After these pieces the term 'prelude' gained widespread currency for short character pieces, but Chopin himself was to return to it on just one occasion. In 1841, two years after the publication of Op.28, he composed the C sharp minor Prelude, designated Op.45. It is a beautifully realised, hauntingly expressive piece, but even less a 'prelude' than the earlier pieces. With its recitative, sustained lyrical melody and intricate accompaniment, it has little in common either in texture or mood with the earlier cycle and we may well agree with Arthur Hedley[32] that it could just as easily have been grouped with the nocturnes.

5

Bel canto

By the time he composed the C sharp minor Prelude Chopin had already completed most of his nocturnes. He had of course borrowed the title, and to a large extent the manner also, from John Field and, like Field's, his nocturnes eschew any obvious virtuosity in favour of an expressive, reflective lyricism. The nocturnes are above all character pieces, exploring many nuances within a deliberately restricted affective range, most often nostalgic, languid, consolatory, the music of a sad smile.

From Schumann onwards it has become customary for commentators to ascribe much of the character of Chopin's lyricism to his love and knowledge of early nineteenth-century Italian opera. Certainly he had ample opportunity to steep himself in this music during his formative years in Warsaw and during his visits to Berlin and Vienna. In this respect the generous operatic repertory of Paris in the 1830s only served to consolidate an enthusiasm already well established. In broad stylistic terms his ornamental melody does indeed display a close affinity to the coloratura aria of Italian opera (Rossini in particular) and doubtless some of this was a direct result of his saturation with the medium. He maintained the closest contacts with singers, Sontag, Viardot and Lablache among them, and commented frequently on the special qualities of their performances. But in this he was merely subscribing to a general enthusiasm of the virtuoso pianist: there is scarcely a method which does not recommend using the voice as the principal model for legato piano style. Moreover the influence of operatic *bel canto* on late eighteenth and early nineteenth-century keyboard cantilena was so widespread that Chopin's response was certainly mediated through earlier piano music.

Mozart and Haydn, in the slow movements of their concertos and sonatas respectively, had already translated gestures from the opera-house into the language of the keyboard, as indeed had J. C. and C. P. E. Bach in their different ways before them. A younger generation, notably Hummel and Weber, went further in the development of an operatically inspired cantilena, characterized by a 'vocal' interval quality and by stylisations of vocal ornamentation. Much of Chopin's filigree ornamentation in his early music owes a great deal to Hummel in particular, extending a line of piano writing which we can trace back to Mozart. We need only compare the *fioriture* at the end of the slow movement of Hummel's B minor Concerto with the end of the slow introduction to Chopin's Op.2 to make the connection specific. Nor was the influence of opera on instrumental music confined to the world of the piano. The concertos, quartets and double quartets of Spohr often borrow their slow movements from the operatic aria, for instance, and the singular affective character of his melody, its sweet, rather plangent melancholy, is often close to Chopin's. A case in point is the slow movement of his Piano Quintet, which Chopin heard in 1829,[1] its atmosphere and indeed its melodic contour strikingly 'Chopinesque'.

Chopin's cantilena responded then to various musical stimuli, but its most obvious ancestry lies in a tradition of piano writing rather different from the Viennese style of Mozart and Hummel which so influenced his early bravura music. Categories are inevitably blurred, but we can detect a line of lyrical pianism originating with the English rather than the Viennese piano and stretching from Clementi through J. L. Dussek to John Field. It is this line in particular which bears upon the early Chopin nocturnes. For the earliest glimmerings of the nocturne style we must return to some of the music Dussek was composing just before 1800, in particular to passages such as Ex.17, from the C minor Sonata Op.35 No.3. Admittedly there were

Dussek, Op.35 No.3

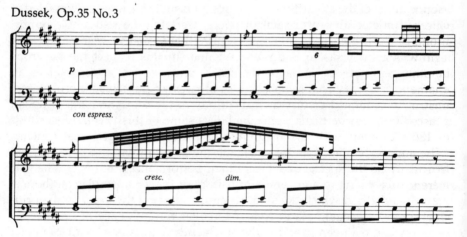

Ex.17

many facets to Dussek's musical personality, and in some works (the late A flat major Sonata, for instance) he foreshadows even more closely the rather different lyrical piano style of Voříšek and Schubert. Nonetheless the manner of Ex.17 was characteristic of several later works (the *Élégie harmonique* Op.61, for example) and it was this manner which was adopted at a very early stage of its development by G. F. Pinto and above all by John Field.[2] It fused with Field's experience of the vocal romance and the Italian aria during his years in Russia to create the piano style which most closely anticipates the basic texture of Chopin's nocturnes.

The style crystallised above all in the short character pieces which Field composed in the early 1800s, variously entitled romances, pastorales and serenades before he finally settled on 'nocturne' in 1814. His use of the term was in general rather looser than Chopin's. His nocturnes (even those initially conceived as such) adopt a variety of formal types and by no means always exhibit that floating melody with widened arpeggiation in the accompaniment, demanding the sustaining pedal, which we associate with the genre. Even the most 'Chopinesque' of them lack that built-in flexibility of rhythmic discourse and suppleness of melodic line which are so characteristic of the Chopin nocturne.

Nonetheless, Field's influence on the Chopin pieces is there for all to hear, even if its extent has been variously interpreted, from the serious underestimation of earlier commentators to more recent, hopelessly extravagant, claims.[3] It may even have reached a little below the surface of the nocturne conception. Field's ideal of a priority of expression over virtuosity may well have had some impact on Chopin's change of direction in the early Paris years, though it could only have been catalytic. The influence is at its strongest, predictably enough, in the early nocturnes. It is enough to compare the well-known E flat major, Op.9 No.2 with the two nocturnes in the same key by Field to see the connection. It is almost as though Chopin has combined elements of both. The waltz-like accompaniment pattern and the broad harmonic scheme of Op.9 No.2 are similar to the second of Field's E flat Nocturnes,[4] and the second themes of both pieces begin with an almost identical gesture. The cross-accents of the melody, on the other hand, echo the first of Field's nocturnes as do the characteristic ornamental run and the final cadential gesture. Other details of melodic construction are very similar in all three nocturnes – the turn followed by an ascending leap and the parlando repeated notes and their consequent (Ex.18(i)).

The ancestry of many of these details is of course operatic, with Rossini in particular frequently suggested. His *La Cenerentola* can serve as a convenient reference point for other operatic derivations, the cadenza preceding

Field, Nocturne No.8   Chopin, Op.9 No.2

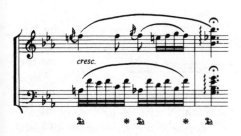
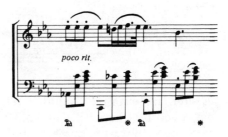

Ex.18(i)

Ex.18(ii)

Ex.18(iii)

closure, for example, found in Field's Sixth Nocturne and dramatically employed by Chopin in Op.9 No.3 (Ex.18(ii)). Or the stylisations of vocal techniques such as portamento and arc-shaped *fioriture* (Ex.18(iii)). Another Italianate feature is the tendency to sweeten the melody through the addition of thirds and sixths, a characteristic vocal duet texture, already

prominent in Dussek, which finds its way into Field's Divertissement
(H.13A) and the middle section of Chopin's Op.9 No.1

Such fingerprints of style – and several others could be cited – leave little
doubt that Chopin relied heavily upon Field for the external characteristics
of his early nocturnes, just as he had used Moscheles as a starting-point
for several of his Op.10 Studies. Once more, however, the model is transcended in almost every detail of construction. We need only glance again
at Op.9 No.2 and Field No.8 to note the greater formal and harmonic
richness of the Chopin, its more flexible and varied rhythmic flow and
above all its more supple ornamental melody.[5]

It is this latter which brings us to the heart of Chopin's achievement in
the nocturnes. In the successive statements of the principal melody of Op.9
No.2, separated as they are by other material, the ornamentation fulfils an
evolutionary, even developmental, function, borrowing from variation-form
a cumulative character which would find its most inspired expression in
later works such as the F minor Ballade. In his earlier music Chopin's
ornamentation, like that of other composers of the *stile brillante*, was essentially an expression of virtuosity, an opportunity to dress the melody in
elaborate finery. In the early nocturnes, however, his whole approach to
ornament changed. Bravura decoration, external to the character of the
original, gave way to an expressive enhancement and reinterpretation of
the melody, where variation is a natural outgrowth of melody, an intensification of its contour and itself part of the substance of the piece. There are
already signs of this in the E minor Nocturne, but it is carried further in
Op.9 No.2 and it was to reach full fruition in the F sharp major Nocturne
Op.15 No.2. Here the ornamentation, functioning as a source of energy as
well as a means of variation, is part of a single, continuously unfolding
line, characterised by those pliable rhythms – in effect a composed-out
rubato – which so characterise the mature nocturne style. There are
occasions when the descriptive talents of the creative writer penetrate to
the heart of music more tellingly than any amount of analytic dissection.
E. M. Forster's description of Beethoven in *Howard's End* comes to mind
and so too does Proust's account of Chopin's melody, those

> long sinuous phrases . . ., so free, so flexible, so tactile, which begin by
> reaching out and exploring far beyond the point which one might have
> expected their notes to reach, and which divert themselves in those byways
> of fantasy, only to return more deliberately – with a more premeditated
> reprise, with more precision, as on a crystal bowl that reverberates to the
> point of making you cry out – to strike at your heart.[6]

The refinement of ornamental melody in the early nocturnes makes as
important a contribution to the new stylistic individuality of Chopin's music
in the early 1830s as does the renovation of bravura textures in his early
studies. With these two achievements he was really bringing to fruition two
distinct, though increasingly interactive, lines of development within the

literature of the early piano, stemming from the English and Viennese intruments respectively. In doing so he set the compass reading for his own mature style. Both achievements are marked, moreover, by a suppression of the conventional gesture, as Romantic individualism triumphs over bravura conformity and the virtuoso becomes a poet. Even the piano textures of the nocturnes avoid any easy acceptance of received patterns, though inevitably they differ significantly from those of the studies. In *very* general terms they are characterised by lightness and clarity of sound, by a thinning out of density across the register (with a limitation of the role of the low register) and by an acute sensitivity to nuances of dynamics and articulation, aided by an unprecedented subtlety in the use of the pedal. These brief extracts from Op.15 No.2 convey something of the intricacy and variety which Chopin achieves within a prevailing melody and accompaniment framework (Ex.19).

Op.15 No.2

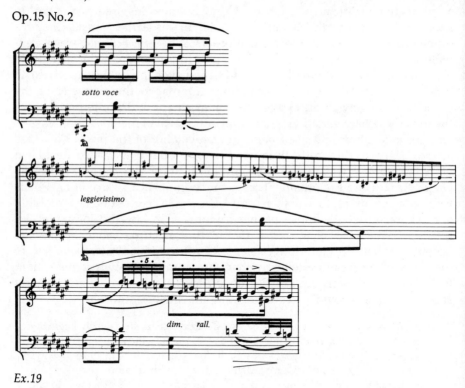

Ex.19

By no means all Chopin's early nocturnes employ the ornamental melody found in Op.72 No.1, Op.9 No.2 and Op.15 No.2. The first of the Op.15 pieces avoids it. So too does the third in G minor, whose function is at least partly, as Jeffrey Kallberg has convincingly demonstrated,[7] to synthesise the cycle as a whole through tonal cross-reference on both primary and secondary levels. Ornamental melody returns in the exquisite, if sweet-toothed, D flat major Nocturne, Op.27 No.2, composed in 1836. The D flat Nocturne seems in many ways to epitomise the most characteristic qualities of the genre. Even in its detailed interval structure the opening phrase typifies Chopin's melodic style, outlining one of the most prominent shapes underpinning his music, as Ex.20 suggests.[8] The continuation of the phrase

Ex.20

is also typical in the gentle undulation of its contour, describing a series of arcs of varying dimensions, and in the placing and weighting of its appoggiaturas, building into the substance of the melody the sort of expressive detail which is common in the 'galant' style and Mozart, but often displacing or altering the expected resolution. Even at the foreground level of melodic design it is this constant play on a network of probable outcomes which contributes to the richness of the music. While familiarity certainly dulls the effect of unpredictability, there is some level at which we remain surprised. The B flat of bar 6, for instance, comes half a bar later than we might reasonably expect, extending the phrase to 4½ bars and investing the A natural with a curiously stationary effect which is preserved even in later statements. When it is replaced by a C flat at bar 49 the gesture is charged with even greater potency. The G natural of bar 9 also resolves elliptically, moving to its expected A flat goal only fleetingly and progressing to a more stable but less predictable F (Ex.20). The rhythmic flexibility of this opening phrase is again a characteristic of many Chopin cantilenas. The eight-bar sentence may seem conventional enough, but it embodies a process of constant rhythmic transformation which, together with the avoidance of motivic repetition within the line, gives the impression of a spontaneous, seemingly artless flow of endless melody.

The second limb of the melody (B), thickening the line to thirds, alternates with this opening shape throughout the nocturne, its successive repetitions bringing ever more elaborate ornamentation. Although this second strain appears as a natural outgrowth of the first, its construction and the function of its later ornamentation are quite different, and this difference is crucial to the structure and *Affekt* of the nocturne. The second shape, unlike the through-composition of A, is a structure of symmetrical periodicity, its eight-bar sentence subdivided into two-bar units where a cell is followed immediately by its own variation. It is a technique which was to prove popular with later Russian composers and would eventually find its way into the music of Debussy and Ravel. Indeed the parallel can be extended. Chopin's ornamental melody, true to its operatic origins, lends itself more naturally to variation and decoration than to motivic dissection, and in this sense it has more in common with the thematicism of Russian (and later French) music than that of Austro-German composers. This in turn has implications for harmony and form which will be discussed in due course.

The difference in the construction of these two melodic shapes is reflected in their later ornamented repetitions. The ornamentation of B is directed towards greater intensification and it is B which sweeps the music towards its major climaxes. The ornamentation then is dynamic and evolutionary in character, a means of generating energy and motion. By contrast, the ornamentation of A is a form of expressive variation on a more-or-less unchanging 'aria', resulting at times in an almost breathtaking beauty of line where elaborate *fioriture* are incorporated within the unbroken lyrical flow. It is indicative of the respective functions of their ornamentation that, whereas the three statements of B vary in length from sixteen to twelve to eight bars, the three statements of A remain a constant eight bars. The intensity curve of the music actually reaches its peak at the end of the second statement of B and the extended sixteen-bar coda on a new cadential figure creates necessary stability and a stronger ending.

The basic distinction between the structures of A and B is between a continuously unfolding, non-repetitive line – a recitative type in the broadest sense – and a melody of symmetrical periodicity with internal repetitions, in effect a stanzaic type. Some of Chopin's finest melodies, including Op.10 No.3, Op.55 No.2 and Op.61, are of the former variety, but the stanzaic design is by far the most common in his music, in the nocturnes as elsewhere. Even with stanzaic melodies, however, the symmetrical phrases and patterns are more often than not disguised by rhythmic and melodic variation within the phrase, giving a fine balance between pattern (depending on retention and recognition) and evolution. There is, as it were, a continuous conquest of symmetry. The first of the Op.37 Nocturnes would serve as one example of this. Even more telling, however, is the opening melodic paragraph of Op.48 No.1, where melodic parallelism is qualified, both in an obvious way as at a^1, and more subtly as at b^1 (Ex.21). The rhythmic flexibility of the whole passage might be

Ex.21

noted. The later stages of this nocturne are interesting in that they achieve intensification not through ornamentation, but through a new textural background. The final statement of the melody is presented against a fully scored, pulsing quaver accompaniment whose rhythmic tensions with the melody do much to generate energy, sweeping the music inexorably towards the powerful structural downbeat of bar 74. The final bars of the piece are in the nature of an elaborated 'feminine ending', articulating the reactive final beat of an amphibrach grouping. This kind of apotheotic reprise was to be given its most powerful expression in the Polonaise-Fantasy and it later became an important element in the music of Skryabin.

The Nocturnes, perhaps more than any other works by Chopin, are mood pieces, reflecting a widespread tendency in early nineteenth-century music for the work to assume the quality of a personal poetic statement, in Dahlhaus's phrase a 'fragment of autobiography'. It was a period when the composer increasingly lived in and through his music, when he (along with others) was increasingly preoccupied with the capacity of instrumental music to affect the emotions powerfully. Hoffmann saw instrumental music as the most 'romantic' of all the arts, while Schilling claimed that no other art 'draws so heavily for its most beautiful and characteristic material from the profound depths of the emotions'.[9] For many it was precisely the non-referential character of music, its 'suggestive indefiniteness' which was valued. Thus Herder: 'Music rouses a series of intimate feelings true but not clear, not even perceptual.'[10] But for others it was all too tempting to translate the strong emotional responses evoked by music into more concrete terms, to give it referential meaning.

Chopin's music was granted a particularly generous allocation of such 'meanings' in nineteenth-century criticism, but he himself stopped short of the programmatic or denotative gesture. His mood-painting minimises stylisation and usually takes on powerfully subjective values. At the same time it inevitably relies upon the *con*notative gesture, drawing upon earlier affective conventions, as well as newly emerging conventions, often operatic in origin. The association of triple metre with tenderness or nostalgia, especially in Italian opera, and the 'discovery' of G flat major as a symbol of the remote and the profound are cases in point,[11] and neither association was lost on Chopin. Such symbols helped the listener to focus his affective response and no doubt encouraged commentators to pinpoint referential meaning in precise terms. Niecks, for instance, hears in the B flat minor Nocturne Op.9 No.1 'twilight, the stillness of the night, and thoughts engendered thereby', while Huneker remarks that the same piece is 'best heard on a grey day of the soul, when the times are out of joint: its silken tones will bring a triste content as they pour out upon one's hearing'. At times, moreover, the effect is more nearly referential – the 'religioso' of Op.15 No.3, for example, which is suggested again in the middle section of Op.37 No.1. And in some nocturnes the expressive (or in the deepest sense 'programmatic') detail actually seems to assume priority over structural integrity, with formal cohesion giving way to a 'law of feeling', an *Expressionslogik*. In the first of the Op.32 Nocturnes the notion of interruption is built into the argument by the hiatus in the main theme, but this can hardly prepare us for the coda, with its ominous drumbeat and dramatic recitative, elaborating a (misspelt) German sixth harmony to delay closure. The interruption of the song by this startling passage of instrumental recitative submits to no formal logic, but rather brings directly into the foreground Chopin's desire to make the music 'speak'.

Where the evocation of mood in music becomes a primary aim, it can unhappily lend itself all too readily to cliché and ultimately 'kitsch',[12] in which the poetic intention and its realisation are out of step and where the artifice is all too transparent. Chopin has suffered greatly through association with such kitsch. A vast amount of salon ephemera was produced in the nineteenth century by composers who were happy to adopt the external manner of Chopin's nocturne style, a manner which is all too easy to imitate. The result was often a form of attitudinising, where nostalgia would become easy sentiment, tragedy would become melodrama, religious feeling would become mawkish pretension. Criteria of value and quality in music are notoriously elusive,[13] and in the end our intuition will arbitrate between a Chopin nocturne and one by Heller, Jensen or Kirchner. Yet some observations can be made.

It is interesting to apply to such comparisons some of Meyer's criteria of value and greatness, based partly on information theory.[14] Using Meyer's terms of reference, we would conclude that, compared with a Chopin nocturne, the salon pieces by and large offer too little resistance to closure, too little purposeful uncertainty and hence too little information. Tendencies within the musical material will be gratified without obstacle or deviation and parametric relationships will be conformant. The Chopin nocturne by contrast makes us feel the 'uncertainty of the improbable while convincing us of its propriety'. It occupies a rich terrain of 'functional ambiguity', to use William Thomson's term.[15] Thomson has argued that such functional ambiguity, where contradictory potentials are embedded in the same structure, is a formidable condition of great music. In practice it tends to be achieved through parametric non-congruence on different hierarchical levels, whose simultaneously unfolding structures exist in a partial, but only partial, relationship to each other. Contradictory tendencies at local levels will then be subsumed into meaningful patterns at the next level up.

Something of this functional ambiguity will already have been conveyed by the discussion of rhythmic ambivalence in Op.10 No.3 (Ex.8(i)) and of melodic implication in Op.27 No.2 (Ex.20). Without embarking on further detailed analysis at this stage, it may be worth elaborating the point briefly by returning to the opening paragraph of Op.48 No.1 (Ex.21), a passage rich in both rhythmic and melodic subtleties. Harmony is not represented in Ex.21 but a glance at the score will show that the three eight-bar sentences (broadly A B A') are unified not only by melodic parallelism but by a stable C minor tonality, enhanced briefly by a Neapolitan inflection at the beginning of B. The regular tread of the harmony, directional motion of a strong bass line and eventual melodic closure of each sentence (implicit at bar 17) combine to create a firm underlying structure which subsumes irregularities on surface levels. Such irregularities include the alternative harmonisations of the same phrase at the beginning of a and a^1 with a third harmonisation following in A'. The continuation of A¹ (bars 20–24), despite its obvious derivation, is a flight of cadential fantasy which frustrates any reasonable estimate of probability based on the parallel passage in A. B introduces further unpredictabilities and uncertainties, breaking down the four-bar phrase structure of A and disguising the parallelism at b^1 not only through melodic variation but through a careful plotting of the bass line to ensure continuity and weaken the sense of closure at bar 12. More detailed analysis would explore the relationship between parameters, beginning with the non-congruence of rhythmic, harmonic and melodic 'downbeats'. Where harmonic and melodic closures coincide, as at bar 4, it is on an unaccented beat. Where rhythmic and harmonic accents are congruent, as at 17, we are denied full melodic closure. Only at the end of the paragraph (bar 24) does Chopin permit a completion of all tendencies.

Such subtleties and ambiguities are even more apparent in Chopin's last four nocturnes, the two of Op.55 (1843) and the two of Op.62 (1846). Many commentators have identified a third creative period in Chopin's development and the view has some justification. The most penetrating discussion is Jeffrey Kallberg's in his thesis and in a review of William Attwood's *The Lioness and the Little One*.[16] Kallberg begins with the often remarked drop in Chopin's output from 1842 onwards, adducing a variety of evidence to suggest that he found composition increasingly difficult in his later years. Not the least important is the evidence of the sources from the late period, where several manuscripts are rejected, others teem with corrections and extensive alterations are made on proofs. Kallberg concludes that, biographical considerations apart, the year 1842 marked nothing less than 'a complete critical assessment of the nature of his craft'.

No single factor provides compositional evidence of this assessment or re-assessment. For the most part it amounts to an extension of certain tendencies already present in his art but carried to the point at which changes becomes qualitative. We may remark here that where form and design are concerned the coda becomes all-important. It is often expanded into a lengthy, multisectional paragraph which can function either as a gesture of apotheosis or as a means of throwing new perspective on earlier material, even at times 'bending' the form in unexpected ways. A case in point is the F minor Nocturne Op.55 No.1. On the face of it this seems the least interesting of the last four nocturnes. Yet the seemingly endless repetitions of its indolent, rather cloying melody have a retrospective justification in that they contribute added piquancy to the unexpected flight of fancy in the reprise. Having resisted any temptation to ornament extensively in the first section, Chopin begins the reprise with yet another unadorned statement of the theme and we fully expect another series of repetitions. What follows is strikingly inventive. Chopin introduces a triplet ornamentation (already foreshadowed) which is transformed into a chromatic 'distance' pattern and this in turn glides imperceptibly into an accelerating coda figuration, so that the nocturne ends without further reference to its much-exercised main theme.

The E flat Nocturne Op.55 No.2 is in every way a richer and more adventurous piece than its predecessor, bringing to the service of its lyricism a contrapuntal edge and harmonic asperity which were given only restrained expression in the earlier nocturnes. During 1842 Chopin studied counterpoint treatises by Cherubini and Kastner and the later music is marked by a much greater emphasis on counterpoint.[17] Often Chopin will absorb elements of strict counterpoint, including canonic working, into the musical flow and, more importantly, he permits an independence of part-movement which is at times highly original and unorthodox. Right from the opening bars of the E flat Nocturne the accompaniment figure generates

Op.55 No.2

Ex.22

a 'dissonant counterpoint' with the melody, carefully placing the non-chordal notes in both voices to sustain harmonic tension (Ex.22) and in the process lending to the left-hand arpeggiation a linear value, even indeed a melodic character. The contrapuntal interest is increased by the entry of a third voice in bar 4 (Ex.22), creating an accompanied duet texture. As the three lines intertwine they are often in close position, occasionally overlapping and always carefully differentiated rhythmically. Indeed the rhythmic complexity is at times astonishing. Throughout there is a skilful balance between tendencies to blend and tendencies to stratify, and this in itself is a characteristic of a good deal of Chopin's later music. At times the part-movement seems designed to avoid at all costs any hints of conventional vertical alignment. The sense of underlying harmonic flow is still present, of course, but its momentum is greatly reduced and it carries on the surface a level of dissonance which must surely have seemed puzzling at the time (Ex.22). A familiar melody and accompaniment texture has here been rethought, shown in a quite new light.

The textural, rhythmic and harmonic complexity of parts of this nocturne, together with the shape of its motives, foreshadow closely some of the music Skryabin was to compose over sixty years later, and the parallel is strengthened by the sustained trills of bars 52–54. The same texture is taken even further by Chopin in the first of his Op.62 Nocturnes, where the reprise of the principal melody is presented entirely in trilled notes. The ornamentation of this reprise must surely be one of the most inspired moments in Chopin, and there is evidence in the autographs that he exercised great care to restrain and limit the ornamentation of the opening section so that it might make its point more effectively.[18] This again is typical of the later music, where ornamental melody is refined to an unprecedented degree. From the early nocturnes, which the composer himself would frequently embellish spontaneously in performance, to the scrupulously controlled, and above all structurally supportive, ornamentation of Op.62 No.1 is a considerable step, albeit within a fairly narrow frame of stylistic reference. The nocturne also shares with Op.55 No.2 the rhythmic motive x and much of its contrapuntal interest, to say nothing of the calculated unpredictability of its musical flow. The break in the continuity of the main theme when it returns at bar 27 is typical of this calculated unpredictability, resulting in a curious dislocation of phrasing. Moreover the presentation of the theme here and in the trilled reprise has a bearing on the very opening of the work, which began, we now realise, a little way into the complete theme, in mid-thought, so to speak. To one listener at least the impression created by the nocturne is of a carefully guarded private world, distanced from the immediacy of life, and this is reinforced by the strangely disembodied flowing semiquavers of the coda (derived from bar 11) where earlier material is transformed through chromatic-modal inflections, throwing into special relief the D sharp/E flat which has functioned referentially throughout and which brings the nocturne to a close.

It 'resolves' beautifully on to the tranquil E major of the Second Nocturne, whose warm consolatory melody provides a perfect complement to the B major and a fitting end to the entire cycle of nocturnes. The highest art is displayed in the presentation of the first section, an eight-bar melody followed by three 'variations', whose 'conquest of symmetry' involves a skilful balance between repetition and development, between unity and diversity. A(i) has no internal repetition, but neatly balances its rhythmic units to suggest statement, repetition, development and reprise (Ex.23). A(ii) begins as an ornamented repetition but departs from the source in its second half. A(iii) involves sequential working of the first part of A(i) but takes over some of the second half of A(ii). A(iv) fuses the decorative treatments of A(ii) and the sequential working of A(iii). Harmonically the variations gain in interest, the diatonicism of A(i) and A(ii) giving way to sequential harmony in A(iii) and a tonal parenthesis in A(iv).

The middle section B leaves such simple melody and accompaniment textures in favour of linear writing whose part-movement is again unorthodox, particularly with respect to the harmonic obligations of the bass line. Tension is maintained through a dissonant counterpoint which incorporates fragments of canonic working and through a propulsive rhythmic syncopation. The reprise of the first section is compressed into a twelve-

Op.62 No.2

Ex.23

bar elaboration of A(iv) and a twelve-bar restatement of B, incorporating an 'epilogue' theme.

Between the composition of Op.55 and Op.62 Chopin composed two pieces which, like the nocturnes, can be regarded as monuments to melody and ornamentation. The *Berceuse* Op.57 dates from 1844 and may well have been inspired by his happy relationship with Pauline Viardot's baby daughter, who stayed at Nohant in the summer of the previous year. Like the much earlier *Souvenir de Paganini*, the piece is really a set of sixteen short variations on an ostinato ground. Chopin spoke of them as his 'variations' and the sketch makes the conception very clear.[19] Unlike the *Souvenir*, however, the *Berceuse* is a work of rarest quality. The profusion of ornamentation is truly astonishing, carrying us across the 'seams' in a curve of complexity and exuberance which begins and ends with unadorned melodic presentation and reaches its apex at bar 43. Yet there is no matching increase in dynamic intensity and no change in harmony until the C flat at bar 55, a potent gesture in a context of harmonic uniformity, designed to strengthen the final tonicisation through a progression to the sub-dominant. The 'shape' of the piece then is carried almost entirely through an ever-changing ornamentation. In itself this ornamentation returns to many of the most familiar patterns of the *stile brillante*, but they have now gained new meaning precisely because of their divorce from harmonic progression, dynamic curve and even melody (the ornamentation is emancipated from the theme after the grace-note variation and regains obvious contact with it only in the closing bars). They thus acquire an independent status as objects in their own right. We hear them afresh.

'The finest of the nocturnes' was Arthur Hedley's description of the *Barcarolle* Op.60 (1846). The work was indeed among the last glorious flowerings of Chopin's lyricism, its Venetian setting, with the familiar rocking accompaniment and swaying melody in thirds and sixths, neatly symbolising that Italian strain which runs through so much of his melody. But Chopin's is no ordinary gondolier. His song is sweet and tuneful, untroubled by darker moods, but its innocence is deceptive. There is much sophistication in its gradually unfolding strains, some of which again employ an ostinato variation technique. They are linked by the subtlest of transitions, related by recurring cadence figures and ultimately directed towards unexpectedly powerful climaxes. Rather as in the Third Ballade, the process is one of rapid and accelerating intensification in the later stages, so that 'popular' materials become agents of apotheosis. Ex.24 is no more than a crude synopsis of the principal stages of the tonal and thematic argument, but it does at least show the weighting of the two main sections, bearing in mind that the power and energy are reserved for the second section where A and above all B(ii) are transformed into epic statements. There is even an element of sonata dialectic in the tonal synthesis of B(ii) and B(i) in the reprise. Much of the beauty of the piece, however, lies in those passages which would be relegated to 'transitions' in some textbooks.

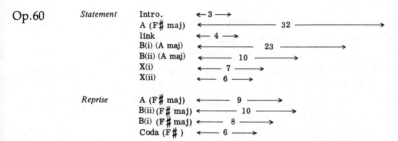

Ex.24

Often it comes down to tiny details – the reversal of dynamic intensities in bars 32 and 92, for instance, or the gradual insinuation of the rocking rhythm of B into bars 35–38. Elsewhere the links are more substantial. X(i) and X(ii) have the task of leading us from the A major of B(ii) to the tonic, but it would be wholly inadequate to call them 'transitions'. The mysteriously pulsing harmonies of the former create an upbeat to the exquisite *fioritura* of the latter, the more beautiful in that it is heard only once, and this in turn becomes an upbeat to the reprise of the main theme.

The ostinato variation technique found in the *Berceuse* and in parts of the *Barcarolle* is yet another distinctive property of Chopin's late style and Józef Chomiński rightly cites it as a link between these works and the F sharp major Impromptu of 1838.[20] The impromptu (Op.36) offers an early tentative exploration of this ostinato technique, where the stasis of the harmony throws out a challenge to other dimensions of the argument. In the impromptu it encourages expeditions to distant, if relatively stationary, tonal regions and a tendency to move from one to the other with a minimum of preparation. The opening melody, for instance, is presented as a chain of variants over a two-voiced harmonic ostinato in F sharp major, while the second theme expands a conventional V-flat VI cadence until there is a measure of harmonic stability in a D major region. Here the ostinato is even more rigid, anticipating such later glories as the trio of the A flat major Polonaise. The subsequent progression to F major for the return of the opening theme is even more of a tonal wrench.

The continuation of the theme from this point is most interesting and not unlike the procedure to be adopted in the later stages of Op.55 No.1. The accompaniment ostinato breaks into a triplet arpeggiation (bar 61) and this in turn influences the character of the melodic variation when the theme reverts to F sharp major. The variation is transformed into an astonishingly elaborate and extended arabesque in demisemiquaver arcs, losing all touch with the theme. The ornamental profusion of this final section (bar 82 ff.) is unexpected, but it is not entirely unprepared. Chopin has extended the *fioriture* which had been built into his earlier variants (cf. bars 17, 29 and 71) so that a familiar decorative treatment becomes part of the essence of the piece. Even so there is evidence that he was concerned at the abrupt change of movement at bar 82. In a sketch for the work (K.582) he has a second thought which is to reject such a rapid change to demisemiquavers in favour of a reading in triplet semiquavers, following the basic outline of the original arabesque. He may have rejected this in the end because the gain in continuity is achieved at the expense of elegance of line. The sketch indicates further difficulties with the coda, as so often in Chopin. His first instinct was to end with a straightforward cadence following the arabesque. Subsequently he decided that a better balance would be achieved by a reprise of the short 'codetta' following the first theme at bar 30. (There is, incidentally, a further sketch, K.581, showing an earlier version of this codetta where the progression to the second theme is even more abrupt than in the final form.) Chopin's first attempt at an epilogue abbreviated the codetta theme, but the resulting phrase structure is curiously unbalanced, and in the final form he reverted to the original form of the theme.

The F sharp Impromptu has been severely censured on formal grounds, and it is certainly arguable that its design scores more highly on novelty than coherence. Yet the work maintains a level of interest and variety which is barely approached in the other three impromptus, all of which fall into simpler tripartite schemes bringing together the worlds of the 'study' and the 'nocturne' rather in the manner of some of Schubert's better-known impromptus, and possibly inspired by them. The first is the so-called *Fantasy-impromptu* Op.66, composed in 1834 but never released for publication by Chopin himself.[21] It has become one of his more popular pieces, but its appeal is marred somewhat by unremitting and undisguised four-bar phrasing and by the unvaried repetition of its components. It lacks the enriching details of the A flat major Op.29, which Chopin composed three years later in 1837 and whose construction seems to have been modelled closely on Op.66; indeed it has often been noted that all four impromptus share very similar materials. The figuration in Op.29 adopts the same $1(a)$ + $1(a)$ + $2(b)$ scheme as Op.66 and the contours of a and b are similar in both works, but the bass line of Op.29 is much more directional and the pattern takes in some diverting harmonic parallelism. The central song is also richer, lavishly varied on repetition and enlivened by some intriguing tonal digressions.

The impromptus are not among Chopin's most significant works. He himself described the Third in G flat major as an 'occasional piece'. Yet their apparent spontaneity – 'as though born under the fingers of the performer'[22] – involved drafting and redrafting materials before arriving at a final form. The sketches for the Second Impromptu provide some evidence of this and the Third too exists in an earlier version, which differs in several respects from the final form. Chopin taught Carl Filtsch for some eighteen months, and there is a copy of this early version of the G flat Impromptu in Filtsch's hand among his papers. There is also an impromptu by Filtsch himself (then aged eleven) modelled on Chopin's piece, with the same key scheme and formal design and with annotations by Chopin. Ferdinand Gajewski has drawn attention to this isolated evidence of Chopin as a

teacher of composition, postulating that Chopin himself may have improvised the short coda to Filtsch's piece.[23] The early form of the G flat
Impromptu reveals no trace of the characteristic double note writing of the
final form, but this is a prominent feature of Filtsch's piece, and Gajewski
raises the intriguing, if tentative, possibility that Chopin's revisions may in
turn have been influenced by his pupil's youthful effort.

6

The spirit of Poland

Recent studies in the aesthetics of music have impressed upon us that nineteenth-century nationalism should be understood as much in terms of intention and receptive attitude as of musical substance.[1] Chopin was a Polish nationalist to the extent that he intended, and was heard, to be. The issue of folk music is of considerable importance, naturally, but its significance can easily be misunderstood. Whether or not one agrees with Zofia Lissa[2] that traditional Polish melodies for violin and flute were an important source for Chopin's lyricism (I for one am sceptical), there can be no doubt that folk music does at least play a prominent role in the mazurkas. It is the interpretation of that role which needs care. As Dahlhaus reminds us, the nineteenth century, by taking its stand on folk music, transformed the regional and social character of that music into a *national* character, an agent of the 'volksgeist hypothesis'.[3] Thus Polish folk elements had a nationalist significance in Chopin's mature music because they were heard, and intended to be heard, in this way, whereas they were merely a conventional exoticism in Weber and Hummel, or for that matter in Chopin's own early music. It does of course go a little deeper than this, for the more subtle effects of that new commitment were in due course to influence musical substance. As Dahlhaus remarks, the notion of 'authenticity', however dubious as an aesthetic category, was to change musical history to the extent that it led beyond conventional colouration of language towards its modification. Chopin went some way along that path, but only some way, and particularly in his mazurkas.

On a level below conscious intention the composer may of course reflect elements of a national, though not necessarily a nationalist, tradition. Issues concerning national character are notoriously treacherous,[4] but we are on reasonably firm ground in considering at least the influence of language. The implications for music of such obvious differences in spoken language as the open vowel sounds and liquid consonants of Italian and the (relatively) pinched vowel sounds and percussive consonants of German are a commonplace of criticism.[5] The Slavonic tongues too helped to determine certain continuities within Eastern European music, instrumental as well as vocal, ensuring some measure of independence of Western European traditions. Russia in particular developed a remarkably strong and individual musical voice in the nineteenth century, and one which was in due course to leave its mark on the most progressive Western styles. The Czech lands were closer to Western Europe, culturally as well as geographically, and their music reflects this, even if the tendency towards a 'marginal placement' results partly from a specific, and eminently challengeable, critical stance. The thread of Polish music was even less continuous, and its collective achievement certainly less coherent, than in the Czech lands. Poland's troubled political history impinged itself directly and powerfully upon the development of her musical life, so that periods of gathering strength, such as the late sixteenth and early seventeenth centuries, were prevented from reaching full fruition. The Swedish invasions of the mid-seventeenth century, together with growing political intrigues and disputes within Poland itself, resulted in a decline in the vitality of Polish music, and it is only towards the end of the eighteenth century that we find signs of renewal. During these years there was a growing preoccupation with national themes and a national style, a preoccupation symbolised in a way by Niemciewicz's *Historical Songs*, published in 1816 with settings by Kurpiński, Lessel, Szymanowska and others. Yet apart from their subject matter – a kind of 'lyrical history' of Poland – there is little of promise here for Polish nationalism. They were written for amateurs, and with a few exceptions (viz. Kurpiński's *Michał Korybut*) the words are much more important than the music.[6] For the most part they are even less musically interesting than those 'romances' and 'ballads', coloured by the rhythms of national dances, which were already popular in the aristocratic amateur music of the late eighteenth century.

This latter is the appropriate background to most of the songs composed by Chopin himself. It is pointless to compare them with the *Lieder* of Schubert or Schumann, for with a few exceptions they remain in intention and realisation within the sphere of the ephemeral, 'homely' ballad, usually strophic and often based on a national dance. For their unpretentious purposes the fairly lightweight verse of his friend Stefan Witwicki was much more suitable than the ambitious poetry of Mickiewicz. The fact is that Chopin was relatively indifferent to the literary ferment in Warsaw during the 1820s, a time when the spirit of early Romanticism was beginning to catch fire in the early poetry of Mickiewicz and Słowacki. It was that same spirit which gave birth to German *Lieder* and set composers on an anxious chase for some sort of fusion of word and note. Chopin gave little enough attention to such matters. He composed, and often improvised, songs to Polish texts throughout his life, but made little effort to preserve them for posterity. The surviving nineteen were published after his death, seventeen of them grouped together by Fontana as Op.74.[7]

Some knowledge of the repertory of songs in early nineteenth-century Poland helps us to see the Chopin pieces in perspective, for they relate in style and theme to certain fairly well-defined categories common in the salons.[8] The ten songs which survive from his early years reflect this Polish background particularly clearly. 'Hulanka' (Drinking Song) and 'Życzenie'

(The Wish), both settings of Witwicki, are really strophic dance songs, the former an oberek and the latter a mazur. Both employ *bourdons*, and 'Hulanka' also uses the characteristically sharpened fourth of Mazovian folk music. 'Hulanka' is a drinking song of a kind popular in Warsaw in the early nineteenth century and 'Życzenie' is a wistful love-song, its lyrics not unlike those of many a Schubert song, but its strictly syllabic setting and lively dance rhythm earthing it firmly in popular culture. There is nothing here of the Romantic's idealisation of folklore and folksong.

'Poseł' (The Messenger) and 'Czary' (Spells), again settings of Witwicki, are strophic 'dumkas' or rustic elegies, bemoaning an unrequited love in a krakowiak rhythm which seems inappropriately lively, complete with *bourdons* and touches of modality in the harmony. Again they belong to a familiar species of popular song in Poland, and in keeping with the type the strophic basis is taken as a purely musical convention, one never exploited to make the kinds of sophisticated points found in German *Lieder*. 'Gdzie lubi' (What she likes) and 'Piosnka litewska' (Lithuanian song) are romances somewhat in the manner of the vaudeville songs made popular in Poland by Jan Stefani. They are through-composed, the first a ternary setting of Witwicki with a brief moment of interest for the piano in the postlude, and the second (on a poem by Ludwik Ośinki) a charming dialogue between mother and daughter with an episode *à la mazur* as the girl recalls meetings with her lover.

Three of the early Witwicki settings are in the manner of the popular strophic ballad. 'Wojak' (The Warrior) is the best of them, similar to 'Erlkönig' in its equestrian motives, and building through the strophes to a fine, vigorous piano coda. 'Smutna Rzeka' (Sad River) is in the deliberately archaic style of older Polish songs, its mournful character finely and evocatively pointed by expressive appoggiaturas. 'Narzeczony' (The Bridegroom), by contrast, is a lively folksong stylisation, one of several to use elements of Ukrainian popular music (common in Polish songs at the time) and one of the only youthful songs to involve the accompaniment in anything other than a servile capacity. It is perhaps no coincidence that the finest of these early songs 'Precz z moich oczu!' (Out of my sight) should be a setting of Mickiewicz. Here Chopin responds to the intensity of expression in the poem to effect a more powerful musical statement. The declamatory introduction followed by two strophes is dictated directly by Mickiewicz's verse and in general Chopin's melodic line here is much more responsive to the text, its speech rhythms and inflections as well as its meaning, than in the other early songs. Harmonically too there is an added chromatic richness which looks ahead to some of Chopin's finest songs from later years.

Many of these later songs continue to rehearse the popular forms already discussed. 'Śliczny chłopiec' (Handsome Lad) and 'Pierścień' (The Ring) are dance songs (kujawiaks), setting Józef Zeleski and Witwicki respectively. 'Wiosna' (Spring), again Witwicki, is a dumka in pastoral vein, as are two settings of Zeleski, 'Dumka' and 'Dwojaki koniec' (Double ending), the latter again stylising Ukrainian elements. But four of the later songs transcend the limitations of the salon romance. 'Moja Pieszczotka' (My darling) is the most extended and ambitious of the dance songs, incorporating elements of both the mazurka and the waltz and bringing to Mickiewicz's cheerfully erotic love-song a warmth and tenderness which is enhanced by the chromaticisms at the end of each strophe, descending coyly in the first strophe and rising in the second as the lover's ardour increases. The elaboration of *'całować'* (kiss) from the climax of the second strophe to the final cadence is deftly achieved.

Very different in mood but no less impressive is the rhapsody *'Leci liście'* (Leaves are falling), a lengthy setting of narrative verse by the soldier-poet Wincenty Pol.[9] It is a passionate lament for Poland and the music takes us through a variety of moods, from the nostalgic mazurka of the opening to the krakowiak which evokes the devastation of Poland's countryside through war, the slow march in the tonic major depicting the defence of Warsaw and the funeral chant on a single pitch recounting the collapse of the Polish forces. The song ends with a reprise of the krakowiak and mazurka respectively. 'Nie ma czego trzeba' (There is no need), a setting of Zeleski, is a strophic elegy whose eloquent simplicity of line is enhanced by modal archaisms in the harmony and by an expressive melisma at the end of each strophe, though there are problems of underlay here in the third stanza. Perhaps the finest of all the songs is the last to be composed, 'Melodia' (Melody), a setting of Zygmunt Krasiński dating from 1847. The opening phrase in the piano is incorporated into a lengthy harmonic progression which acts with the melodic arc in the voice to delay closure until bar 13. It is a beautifully shaped and carefully paced paragraph. The subsequent material explores harmonic avenues which are uncharacteristically adventurous for Chopin's songs, and these combine with a declamatory vocal style to create a most evocative closing section, drawing the piano's opening phrase into the final vocal statement.

While these few late songs clearly come from the same stable as the folk-inspired ballads and romances composed in large numbers by late eighteenth and early nineteenth-century Polish composers, they bring to the style an elegance, refinement and at times depth of feeling which places them almost on a par with the *Lieder* of Schubert and Schumann. Yet for all that the songs have always, and rightly, been regarded as peripheral to Chopin's output. Vocal styles certainly played a part in shaping his lyrical pianism, but the voice itself was not his natural medium. None of the songs evokes the spirit of Poland with the authority and poignancy of the mazurkas and the mature polonaises.

When Chopin returned to the polonaise in the early 1830s with the C sharp minor Op.26 No.1 his whole approach to the genre had changed radically. The dance form became for the nostalgic exile a potent symbol of Poland, and specifically a Poland oppressed. The familiar rhythmic and melodic formulae were transformed into agents of a proud, even aggressive, evocation of Poland's past splendour. No longer a conventional means of creating Polish colour, the polonaise became an expression and affirmation, in turn defiant and tender, of national identity. It was certainly received in this spirit by Poles, both at home and abroad, throughout the nineteenth century, symbolising the national struggle and helping to cement the Polish spirit at a time when the country was without political status. For many the mature polonaises were viewed as a pianistic expression of Polish history, evoking glorious incidents from that history such as the battle of the Hussards of Subieski (Op.40 No.1) or the battle of Grochów (Op.44), and there are references in Chopin's correspondence which suggest that for the composer too the works had specific historical associations. Yet we need no such associations to see that the popular national dance has here acquired a quite new status, drawing upon elements from several earlier prototypes but transforming them into an expression of the monumental and heroic.

Much of the heroic character is a product of Chopin's search for an increased strength and volume of piano sonority, a far cry from the gentle lyricism of the nocturnes. Full chordal textures in rhythmic unison alternate with powerful octave passages, while grace-notes, wide leaps and of course the pedal are all employed to unite metallic octaves at registral extremes with chordal writing in the middle register. Like much of Weber's piano writing the effect is at times orchestral, but much more than Weber Chopin translates the power of the orchestra into perfectly idiomatic pianistic terms. It is significant that the polonaises do not orchestrate well. More crucial to the heroic *Affekt* is a deliberate rhetoric which overlays bold simple outlines – scale and arpeggio motives, simple diatonic harmonies – with inflated 'theatrical' gestures in which ornament and substance are clearly differentiated, unlike the nocturnes where they are ideally blurred or fused. Many of these gestures are rhythmic in impulse, a terse rhythmic characterisation of the individual moment which throws it into sharp relief against the broader sweep of the music. Others involve a melodic ornamentation directed towards energy and power rather than display or expression. Others are characterised almost entirely by a dramatic and substantive contrast of dynamic levels or a directional use of graduated dynamics. The rhetorical element can take other forms – obsessive repetitions of the main theme, for instance, and a tendency towards deceptive closure within the phrase, the strong cadence *formula* which is not in fact a cadence. And more telling than any of these as an agent of drama and energy is the resource of harmony, employed in the polonaises in powerfully dynamic fashion.

Many of these features can be examined in the first of the mature polonaises, the C sharp minor Op.26 No.1. The rhythmic design of the opening motive and its presentation in blunt octaves are typical of the arresting, forceful gestures, almost violent in character, which are favoured in the polonaises, thrusting the individual moment into the foreground of the argument. The answering phrase, a full chordal statement of a conventional cadence, further underlines Chopin's inflation of the simple gesture into a powerful rhetoric and his desire to extract the maximum strength of sonority from the keyboard. Although the four-bar phrase is a clear tonic affirmation, its role is anacrusic to the main theme. Stylised introductory 'upbeats' of this kind are again characteristic of the late polonaises, present in all but two. They are of course a legacy of the court dance, but Chopin elevates them into a tension-building anticipatory gesture and usually incorporates them into later restatements of the theme. 'Introduction' and 'preparation' thus become unusually important structural functions in the polonaises. Also characteristic is the contrast in dynamics between the two statements of the main eight-bar theme, building an effect of echo or response into its presentation. The theme itself is strongly directional, partly due to its melodic contour – three rising shapes generating an upbeat to the final descent – but mainly because of its harmonic setting.

Invariably in Chopin rapid, seemingly wayward harmonic movement is the surface prolongation of deeper structures governed by clear diatonic functions. Conventional, Rameau-based harmonic analysis often obscures this by interpreting primarily at a foreground level of tonal reference and thus failing to differentiate between structural and linear-derived or contrapuntal harmonies. The series of chords underlying this opening theme, employing dominant functions at the most immediate foreground level, has been described by one commentator as 'startlingly original'.[10] It is hardly so, or at least not in the sense intended. The essential point is that closure is postponed through a secondary emphasis on sub-dominant harmony and a 'Neapolitan' resolution which causes a metrical dislocation of the final cadence (Ex. 25(i)). The intention is once more to generate energy and momentum. That energy and momentum is preserved, moreover, in the second limb of the opening section, though it is now achieved through rhythmic syncopation, a gradual increase in dynamic intensity and a racing, upward-leaping ornamental figure, forceful and commanding in character. Such figures, whether scalar or arpeggiated, are present in almost all the mature polonaises, a more dynamic version in a way of the trusty 'Mannheim rocket'.

It would be pointless to expect in the polonaises the textural intricacies of the studies and preludes or the sophisticated ornamental melody of the nocturnes. Like other dance pieces by Chopin, they preserve for the most part the uniform textures, regular phrases and literal repetitions of their dance origins. In the C sharp minor Polonaise there are eight unvaried statements of the opening eight-bar sentence in the first section alone. Such literal repetitions have the effect of heightening the contrast afforded by the middle section in D flat major, a lyrical episode where both ornamentation and harmony are expressive in character. It is worth looking at some of this harmony more closely here as it exemplifies again Chopin's fusion of an organic chromaticism in the part-movement with rapidly moving fifths cycles in the harmony, a flurry of movement on the surface over tonal stasis

Op.26

Ex.25(i)

Ex.25(ii)

in the depths (Ex.25(ii)). The expressive quality of this middle section is intensified by the contrapuntal character of its second part, where the left hand functions both as an harmonic bass and a melodic 'accompaniment' to the main theme.

Formally the C sharp minor adopts the traditional 'da capo' scheme common in stylised dances and favoured again in the two Op.40 Polonaises, though the internal repetition plans differ.[11] With Op.26 No.2 in E flat minor, on the other hand, there are hints of that formal expansion of the genre which was later to culminate in the *Polonaise-fantasy* Op.61. There are certainly elements of ternary or arch structure in the E flat minor, but it is really closer to a rondo. And once again the repetitions are literal and the sense of upbeat all-important. The main theme is preceded by a lengthy preparation in two distinct stages, achieved by methods already familiar from Op.26 No.1. The first phase, preparing the dominant harmony, is characterised rhythmically – an alternation of contrasting cells whose rhetorical point is reinforced by *rit. . . . a tempo* markings. The second phase, preparing the tonic, superimposes on the familiar dance rhythm a dynamic melodic ornamentation – a trill followed by another 'rocket' *con forza* – driving through the upper register to fall back on the structural downbeat of bar 12. The whole cumulative paragraph is further propelled by a gradual crescendo from *pp* to *fff*.

As in Op.26 No.1 the energy generated by the introduction is sustained through the main theme itself, with short-breathed phrases building to a tension point over a full seven of the eight bars, leaving a single bar for the traditional 'polacca' cadence. The tension is maintained partly by melodic contour and dynamics, but mainly by a dissonant linear counterpoint between the outer parts, where references to the tonic harmony appear, but are confined to the weak beats. The entire section is an immensely subtle balance of contrasting elements with, as Paul Hamburger points out,[12] motivic correspondence underlying the surface contrasts. Such correspondences extend moreover to the rest of the work. The two episodes of the rondo structure are related by rhythm and melodic contour and Chopin takes care to distance them from the main theme, particularly through tonality. The second, in B major, presents a contrasting tonal colour which nonetheless has clear enharmonic links with the E flat minor tonic, but the first is in the more remote D flat major and it follows the tonic cadence without transition. The tonal distance is mediated in both cases by skilfully graduated returns to the rondo theme and the tonic region. In Chopin, as in Tchaikowsky, such transitional material, however skilfully contrived, usually lacks the sense of inevitability which attends the mediation of ideas in Beethoven and Brahms. This is partly a matter of differences in structural function. In Chopin, particularly in the dance pieces, transitional material is literally that, a bridge between relatively self-contained themes and/or stable tonal regions. In Beethoven and Brahms the term is often misapplied to passages which are really integral links in an organic chain of events which may or may not have thematic and tonal definition.

Of the two polonaises Op.40, dedicated to Fontana and composed in 1838 and 1839 respectively, the first in A major breaks no new ground formally or stylistically. It might almost be taken as the most 'typical' of the six, preserving the rhythmic and melodic fingerprints, the cadential gestures and the *da capo* formal plan of the traditional dance, but investing them with that note of power and heroism which so marks the later polonaises. Indeed the heroic *Affekt* is such that at times Schumann's guns seem close enough, with a fanfare theme in the trio, rumbling trills in the bass, an almost orchestral strength of sonority and a studied overstatement of the most familiar diatonic relationships. The C minor achieves its effects by subtler means. Harmonically it is one of the richest and at times its wisps of concealed counterpoint, non-thematic figuration and rhythmic and melodic elisions all but lose sight of the dance origins.

The F sharp minor Op.44, composed in 1841, evokes the spirit of Poland through a synthesis of its two principal dances, the polonaise and the mazurka. The practice was not entirely without precedent in Poland, but on the epic scale effected here it amounts to a new conception of the dance piece. Once more there is an extended upbeat – an almost Lisztian crescendo of double octaves outlining a dominant area with extraordinary power. This sets the tone of the Polonaise. In a way it is similar in mood, though more powerful in realisation, to the A major. Like the A major, it keeps its materials close to the dance archetype, both in rhythmic structure and in the simple harmonic rhythm underlying the main theme. The theme itself achieves maximum strength of sound through a leaping left hand, an accompaniment shared between the two hands and an ornamentation which extends to bass grace-notes and trills. Especially powerful is the presentation of the theme in deep left-hand octaves with a new counter-subject in the right hand. Later repetitions are varied, moreover, in the

direction of still greater power, incorporating the familiar 'rocket' ornamentation in the left hand.

The short scalar subsidiary theme is distanced by an abrupt harmonic
change which creates a strong surface contrast but effects no real tonal shift,
sliding smoothly back to the tonic by way of a sequence of descending
whole-tone steps and mirroring in the process the opening of the main
theme (Ex.26). Indeed we can see retrospectively that an important function

Op.44

Ex.26

of this subsidiary theme is to act as anacrusic to the tonic region, and it
fulfils the same role in relation to the new material in the relative major, as
Ex.26 suggests. This new material, rather as at the comparable stage of the
A major Polonaise, is non-thematic in character and it is daring in the
extreme in its relentless repetitions of a terse rhythmic motive followed by
bald V – I affirmations. Here the rhetoric makes its point through an almost
brutal removal of inessentials to uncover and drive home with dogged
insistence the bare skeletal framework of the dance. The rigidity of the
pedal A is reinforced by its refusal to respond to the gradual twisting of
the harmony away from its initial Lydian quality.

Unlike the narrative unfolding of ideas which characterises other
extended works by Chopin – the ballades and fantasies, for instance – the
big polonaises retain the relatively crisp sectionalisation of the dance piece,
though pains are taken to achieve a balance between contrast and continuity
in the succession of materials and between diversity and unity in their
characterisation. The first part of the F sharp minor Polonaise offers no
fewer than eight more-or-less discrete and sharply defined sections, based
on three distinct themes. But the most striking character contrast of all
comes in the A major trio, for here Chopin abandons the polonaise in
favour of a mazurka, albeit *doppio movimento*, transforming the heroic energy
of the one into the wistful charm of the other. In context the mazurka takes
on something of the character of a dream-like parenthesis. For all the
contrast, however, the gentle thirds and sixths of the trio can be related
easily enough not only to the main polonaise theme but also to the bravura
introduction, and it is this latter link which takes us back to the polonaise
in a most deftly achieved transition. The rhythmic shape of the mazurka
theme takes on the *intervallic* shape of the introduction and a brief passage in
which old and new intercut introduces once more the whirling semiquaver
octaves of the opening bars. It is typical of Chopin's extended ternary

designs that the reprise is compressed, to the extent here (and elsewhere) of omitting thematic substance. Abraham describes it as 'perspective foreshortening'.[13]

The same procedure is adopted in the reprise of the A flat major Polonaise Op.53, composed in 1842 and sometimes known as the 'Heroic'. It is the last and greatest of the polonaises. The sixteen-bar introduction is in itself a masterpiece. Two types of upbeat alternate – the 'dynamic' (*a* bars 1–2), where harmony and rhythm drive the music, and the 'temporal' (*b* bars 3–4), which is initially a release mechanism from the former, but whose lack of change and movement becomes in itself anticipative. As the main theme approaches the intensity is increased by a disturbance of the sequence of two-bar units thus:

$$a \quad b \quad a \quad b \quad a \quad a \quad \left\{ \begin{matrix} a \quad b \\ + \\ b \end{matrix} \right.$$

The sense of propulsion is electric and it is strengthened by the curve of dynamics and by harmony, with semitonal movement over a dominant pedal generating a head of tension which invests the tonic resolution with monumental power. The main theme itself is the most concentrated exemplar of polonaise rhetoric, essentially variants on a $^6_4 - ^5_3$ formula supported in the first three bars by no fewer than nine statements of a V – I progression in the bass. The 'rocket' ornamentation is there too, expanding *a* from the introduction and now involving both hands as it drives through four octaves, while the widely leaping bass and right-hand trills and mordents contribute to a full 'orchestral' sonority.

As so often the trio has a fanfare theme, but here it is superimposed on a remarkable ostinato of a kind already characterised as belonging to Chopin's late style.[14] The motive (this time suggesting *b* from the introduction) endures no less than forty-two repetitions before the unchanging E major harmony abruptly shifts to E flat major. The potential of this as a means of returning to the tonic is just as abruptly thwarted, however, as Chopin repeats the entire E major section. This time the flatwards progression leads into the second part of the trio, whose special charm lies in its relaxation of the stern diatonicism of the rest of the work. Its flowing semiquaver movement emerges as a wistful episode, a brief respite from the surrounding energy. The final bars are especially strong, drawing the trio's ostinato into their progression and enhancing the final cadence through sub-mediant harmony.

The Op.44 and Op.53 Polonaises expand the framework of the genre so much that they almost lose touch with the traditional type of dance piece. They are more like tone poems based on the dance, grander in conception and more powerful in realisation than any of the earlier essays. Chopin was only to return to the polonaise once more, four years after the completion of Op.53, and it is significant that he composed then a *Polonaise-fantasy*, rather than a polonaise. Where Op.44 and Op.53 retain the basic ternary framework and gestures of the dance, Op.61 moves far beyond both and it seems likely that this is how his involvement with the polonaise would have continued, had he lived longer. In almost all editions and studies the *Polonaise-fantasy* is grouped with the polonaises, and there is of course every reason for doing so, just as the later mazurkas, which have moved well beyond simple dance pieces, are grouped with the earlier. Yet Op.61 has departed sufficiently from Op.44 and Op.53 to merit separate treatment. It is more 'fantasy' than 'polonaise', and discussion of it will be deferred until the final chapter.

A very different dimension of the spirit of Poland is evoked in the mazurkas. The polonaise had a lengthy history both as a national dance and a stylised dance piece, but it was only in the late eighteenth and early nineteenth centuries that the mazurka acquired either status. As a national dance the mazurka subsumed but did not totally destroy the distinctive characteristics of those regional dances from central Europe which fed it, the powislak, światowska (round dance) and above all mazur, oberek and kujawiak. As the mazurka gained in popularity in the salons and indeed the streets of the cities, its music lost some of the more vital qualities of those peasant origins, and the urban accommodation naturally influenced the many early nineteenth-century attempts of stylisation, resulting at times in a rather sentimental approach to popular materials. By contrast Chopin, the only composer of significance to attempt stylisation until much later in the century, responded both to the town mazurka and to its rural predecessors, preserving the unique qualities of the former as a source of energy for an art-form of some sophistication, and one which he was to make very much his own. Rural models already flavour the mazurkas composed during the Warsaw period. The three main regional dances are clearly distinguishable in the different tempi and gestures of the first three Op.68 Mazurkas, for instance, and also in their *dudy* drones, Lydian modality, characteristic rhythmic accentuation, melodic shapes and ornamentation.

It was with the Op.6 Mazurkas, however, that he arrived at a fully mature formulation of the mazurka as a self-contained, stylised dance piece, and these were written not in Poland but in Vienna during 1830. Most early nineteenth-century stylisations would have been intended either for dancing or listening, but Chopin made it very clear that Op.6 was *not* for dancing. From these and the five of Op.7 (1830–31) onwards, he reserved for the mazurkas some of his most deeply felt and poignant music, and also some of his most original. Much of the originality stems of course from just this use of folkloristic materials as transforming agents. It matters not a whit that many of the characteristic mazurka fingerprints are shared by folk musics far afield from Poland. They are no less capable of modifying substantially the diatonic and rhythmic norms of received practice. Chopin was obviously not the first composer to turn to popular songs and dances as a source of renovation, but his involvement with long-established traditions was less total, and permitted more thorough-going renovation, than we find in Western European mainstreams. His mazurkas helped to set the tone for later nineteenth-century nationalist 'schools'.

Folkloristic elements obviously play a major role in the mazurkas, but their significance can be over emphasised. No less crucial is what Chopin himself brought to the dance form. Here we might note that many of the more distinctive features of the mazurkas have their origins not in folk-loristic idioms at all, but in a boldly innovative extension of the most sophisticated strands of Western European harmonic practice. Chopin reserved for the mazurkas some of his most astonishing harmonic adventures, at times almost to the point of iconoclasm. It is in the perfect mating of these worlds to their mutual enrichment that the true originality of the mazurkas lies. Indeed it is difficult to think of a comparable cross-fertilis-ation of vital peasant music (with its own powers to reshape existing prac-tice) and the most advanced contemporary techniques until the music of Bartók.[15]

The nature of this cross-fertilisation can be examined in the Mazurkas of Op.6, Op.7 and Op.17, all composed between 1830 and 1833. The first of the Op.6 cycle is a mazur stylisation taking its starting-point from one of the common rhythmic shapes of the folk dance

Chopin's enjoyment of the second or third beat stress (often coinciding with foot stamping in the dance) is obvious throughout the mazurkas, and he occasionally pointed its disruptive effect in performance to such an extent that listeners lost touch with the underlying triple metre.[16] The cross-accents and rhythmic variations written into the mazurkas inject the music with a primitive energy and dynamism which again challenges aspects of conventional language at the time. The open fifths at the beginning of Op.6 No.3 are stressed as follows:

while in the trio of Op.17 No.1 we have a similar disagreement between accent and stress (cf. bars 49–52). The short-breathed motivic working of Op.6 No.1 – constant repetitions of one- and two-bar cells – is also character-istic of the mazurkas (it is especially pronounced in Op.17 No.3) and again it takes its cue directly from the folk model, as do the appoggiaturas and *bourdons* of the third section. But the harmonic setting distances these models in its balanced juxtaposition of a diatonic affirmation of the F sharp minor tonality and its chromatic evasion. The diatonic presentation in itself suggests Chopin's later practice in the mazurkas in its alternation of minor and 'relative' major (cf. Op.33 No.3, Op.41 No.4, Op.50 No.2, Op.59 No.1). The chromatic material too is prophetic. No longer a bridge between more stable areas, as in the Warsaw mazurkas, it has become integral to the melody and harmony. As Ex.27 indicates it is conditioned totally by a

Op.6 No.1

diatonic   chromatic

Ex.27

semitonal descent in all voices, whose symmetry, based on 'notes equally related among themselves', suspends local tonal commitment and preserves the seventh chord as a norm of harmony (cf. Op. 6 No.3 bars 59–62 and Op.7 No.2 bars 21–4). It is above all the regular phrase structure which mitigates this and which strengthens the return to diatonic harmony at bar 9.

A similar balanced relationship between diatonic and chromatic material obtains in the opening theme of Op.17 No.4. But there the chromatic material exhibits that curiously unorthodox part-movement (exposed octaves in bars 9 and 10) which contributes to the distinctive quality of several of the mazurkas (cf. Op.7 No.2 bars 10–12) and again emphasises their distance from Western European norms. Viewed in a longer span of context the harmonic language of this mazurka is audacious in other respects. The goal of the opening theme is A minor, though tonal definition is achieved through dominant rather than tonic harmony (bars 12–13) and it is only at the end of the varied repetition that full closure is achieved (bar 20). Against this background the introduction studiously avoids both tonic *and* dominant harmonies of A minor, leaning rather towards the sub-dominant D minor, though the ear might well perceive this as having a tonic function, albeit unsupported by *its* sub-dominant or dominant. It is just as likely to hear F major as a tonic, for Chopin has built into his opening bars an ambiguity of harmony (and also of metric scansion) which prepares the later vacillations of both melody and harmony.[17] The ambiguity is compounded by the modality (Aeolian on A?, Dorian on D?) and by an initial chord progression whose part-movement over a pedal point is only later shown to have a motivic significance which 'justifies' the initial dissonance (Ex.28). The coda incidentally returns to this opening ambiguity, with the important difference of course that a tonal reference point has by then been established.

The mazurka is in the expressive kujawiak manner, and its theme is close to certain kujawiak archetypes, though its subsequent elaboration employs an expressive *fioritura* which belongs more naturally to the nocturne, once

Op.17 No.4

Ex.28

more drawing together two very different worlds. In general kujawiak melodic shapes – violin and flute melodies – predominate in the mazurkas, even where the tempo is that of the mazur or oberek. Correspondences to folk models are often close, and Polish studies make them abundantly clear.[18] Mazur shapes are also common, and especially the scalar models found, for example, in Op.7 Nos 1 and 3, the latter also using the most popular of all the mazur rhythmic patterns. Folkloristic influences are also strong in the trio of Op.17 No.4, notably in the use of an open fifth *bourdon*, stylising the *dudy* or *gagdy* drone which often accompanied folk dancing. This kind of *bourdon* is a familiar device in the mazurkas, particularly in trios, and it often supports melodies of an almost oriental interval quality. The trio of Op.7 No.1 is typical, with a sharpened fourth creating a tritone against the *bourdon* and a sharpened sixth giving an augmented second with the fifth degree (D flat – E natural).[19] Often, too, Chopin employs variable notes within a mode, alternating natural and chromatically altered degrees, as in Op.7 No.2. Again there are many precedents for this in original mazur and kujawiak melodies and it lends to some of the mazurkas a very special quirky character, entirely without echo in the remainder of Chopin's output.

The modality of these early mazurkas and the occasional ambiguity of harmony which results are confirmed by the Op.24 cycle, composed in 1834–5, notably in the augmented seconds of the first piece and the Aeolian character of the second. Once again there are clear folkloristic origins for both these mazurkas, as Ex.29(i) indicates. Tonal definition is weakened in the second by the absence of a dominant harmony and of a sharpened seventh and also by the tendency to touch equivocally on C major as a secondary, but ultimately conclusive, emphasis within the prevailing A minor tonality of the main theme. The ambivalence is heightened by the alternation of these modal statements on A with material on C in which the *bourdon* technique is drawn right into the harmonic orbit of the piece, resulting in archaic-sounding consecutive fifths (Ex.29(ii)). Even tiny details of part-movement and melodic inflection often have their origins in modal properties as in the dissonant Lydian B natural which colours the F major cadence at bar 27. The Lydian mode is by far the most common in Polish folk music, and it appears again in Op.24 No.4, the one mazurka to make use of a genuine folk melody. It is especially haunting and beautiful when it appears in unharmonized octaves (bars 54–61), and Chopin was to return

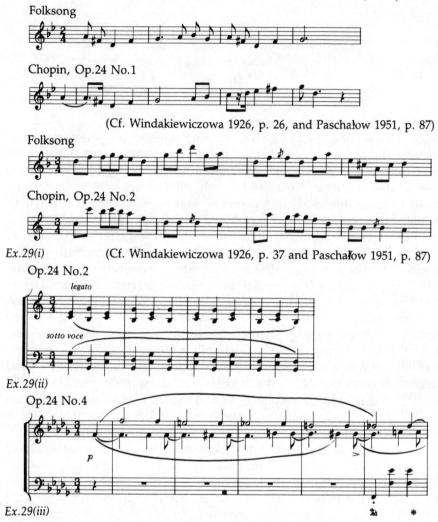

Folksong

Chopin, Op.24 No.1

(Cf. Windakiewiczowa 1926, p. 26, and Paschałow 1951, p. 87)

Folksong

Chopin, Op.24 No.2

Ex.29(i)   (Cf. Windakiewiczowa 1926, p. 37 and Paschałow 1951, p. 87)

Op.24 No.2

legato

sotto voce

Ex.29(ii)

Op.24 No.4

p

Ex.29(iii)

to this evocative soundscape in later mazurkas, Op.50 No.1, for example, and Op.56 No.3.

From the Op.17 set onwards, the last mazurka in an opus tends to be more extended and more ambitious structurally than the other three, so that it may act as an effective conclusion if they are to be performed as a cycle.[20] This is certainly true of Op.24 No.4, whose design might be represented crudely as X A B A (B A) C D A A'. Some hint of this structural weight is already offered by the tone of the four-bar introduction, which closes in on the tonic by means of a semitonal 'wedge' of somewhat arcane sophistry (Ex.29(iii)). The formal subtlety is by no means simply a matter of thematic patterning, but it is worth noting all the same Chopin's charac-teristic compression of the reprise in favour of an extended coda, based on the main theme but transforming it utterly. Already we catch a glimpse of the extended 'epilogues' to later cycles. The energy of the main theme itself derives from a simple model and sequence technique whose ascending pattern creates three 'incomplete' and only one 'complete' statement. Its alternation of dominant and tonic harmonies in both the major and minor keys is again typical of later mazurkas (Op.30 No.4) and it has even been suggested (Paschalow) that this feature has direct origins in folk music. The coda's thematic inversion and descending sequence reverses the process found in the main theme, giving one 'incomplete' and three 'complete' statements. The resulting stability is then reinforced by a shift to the major for a closing variant, though the major harmony is exquisitely coloured modally by the retention of the flattened sixth from the minor key. The entire paragraph presents us with a period of calm lyricism and its length is justified by the tonal volatility of the material in section D, where four-bar blocks are dislocated tonally rather in the manner of Spohr (cf. Op.7 No.4 bars 33–6).

The lively exoticism of these early mazurkas is less pronounced in the Op.30 and Op.33 cycles, composed between 1836 and 1838. Modality and *bourdon* pedal points have by no means disappeared, but they are less in evidence, for the folkloristic influence is now expressed more through procedural parallels than surface detail. In particular these cycles explore the call and response patterns of popular dance music, enhancing their repetition schemes with layered dynamics and subtle variations in the detail of harmonic and textural backgrounds. In the third of the Op.30 mazurkas,[21] for example, the main theme is 'echoed' in reharmonized form, contrasting diatonic and modal presentations, as Ex.30(i) illustrates. This suggests

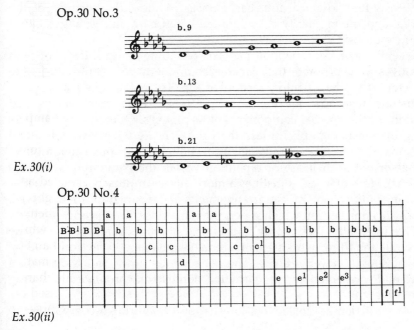

Op.30 No.3

b.9

b.13

b.21

Ex.30(i)

Op.30 No.4

Ex.30(ii)

striking parallels with later developments in Russian music, where folksong-
based material is repeated against changing harmonic and orchestral backgrounds rather than dissected motivically.

The first two mazurkas of Op.30, sharply contrasting in character, present
similar alternations of solo and chorus in their outer sections, while in
the middle section of No.2 Chopin transforms popular repetition into an
unchanging melodic ostinato, comprising eight statements of the same two-
bar phrase with four alternative harmonisations. In both mazurkas there
are delightful unpredictabilities in the detailed working of material. The
second treats the sub-dominant and dominant degrees in the final three
notes of its two-bar motive as chromatically variable, while the first juggles
with the mediant and supertonic pitches at the identical cadential point,
and contradicts the melodic closure of bar 8 by an opening of harmony and
part-movement to create elision with the next phrase. Much of the fascination of the mazurkas lies in such tiny subtleties of harmony and melody,
investing the deceptive simplicity of the music's surface with fresh meaning.

And often too with an added depth of feeling. In Op.30 No.1 in particular
the raw vitality of the folk dance has been left far behind, sublimated into
an expression of reflective, nostalgic melancholy, where the reprise of the
opening material takes on a new and even more poignant character after
the events of the middle section. By contrast, the repetition schemes of
Op.33 No.2[22] are designed to bring the folk model right into the foreground,
the only one of the eight pieces to do so. Here the incessant and unvaried
repetitions, together with the vamping diatonic harmonies, capture something of the whirling, foot-stamping energy of the oberek. There are no less
than twenty-four identical four-bar phrases in the outer sections of the
mazurka, and the regularity is underlined by an harmonic arrangement of
the phrase into six groups of four.

In several mazurkas repetition patterns penetrate beneath the surface of
the motives to incorporate their smaller components. Ex.30(ii) reduces the
architectonics of the opening section of Op.30 No.4 to one-bar units to
demonstrate just how far the structure relies upon exact and varied
repetitions of the one-bar components of its motives. Of the thirty-two bars
making up the paragraph no less than thirteen are taken up with literal
repetitions of *b*, itself, as Windakiewiczowa shows, a popular folk motive.
Whether or not such insistent repetition within the paragraph is a direct
reflection of folk practice, it justifies a more diffuse approach to the broader
structuring of the mazurka, the arrangements of the paragraphs themselves.
It is only this first section which is permitted a reprise. The second, similarly
repetitive internally, recurs only in the form of a brief reminiscence in the
coda, while the third, working its material sequentially in tension-building
waves of sound, never returns. The coda winds down to a stop with a
variant of *b* presented in an harmonic context of chromatically sliding
parallel sevenths.

The construction of Op.30 No.4 foreshadows the through-composition of some of the later mazurkas, where simple dance symmetries are subordinated to broader structural concerns incorporating developmental processes. Arthur Hedley, with perhaps just a little overstatement, dubs some of these later pieces 'tone-poems'.[23] The last of the Op.33 mazurkas takes a further step along this path. It is the most extended of the mazurkas thus far and its broader paragraphing is proportioned in precise sixteen-bar lengths as indicated in Ex.31, with linking material incorporated within

Op.33 No.4

Ex.31

the scheme. The tonal structure is the major unifying influence, anchoring the music firmly in B minor/major, and balancing the two semitonal descents to B flat major with a Neapolitan tendency within the B minor harmony, a tendency most completely realised in the final bars (Ex.31).

The Op.41 cycle, composed in 1838, draws together the harmonic variation of Op.30 and many of the more explicit folkloristic elements of the earlier mazurkas. All four of the pieces incorporate *bourdon* pedals and two of them play with the alternating diatonic and modal presentations found in Op.30. The new departure is the quality of the modality. In both cases the mode is Phrygian, its first appearance in the mazurkas. In No.1, the so-called 'Palma mazurka', the approach to an E minor tonic is initially diatonic, then Phrygian, while in No.4 the process is reversed as Phrygian material in C sharp is succeeded by diatonic material in the relative major. Rather as in Op.30 No.1 a later statement of the Phrygian material in No.4 alters the mode to create an augmented second between the second and third degrees. Elsewhere in the cycle we find those whimsical details which colour the earlier mazurkas, from the tonal dislocations of No.2 to the unexpected 'mid-thought' ending of No.3.

With Op.50, Op.56 and Op.59 we can detect a major change in the tone of Chopin's mazurkas, as popular elements are subordinated to greater formal sophistication and wider expressive range. On the most superficial level this is revealed in the preponderance of expressive kujawiak models, but it goes much deeper than this, as the mazurkas register something of that more general change of direction in Chopin's music of the early 1840s. The third and last of the Op.50 Mazurkas (1841–42) is a powerful rhapsody whose textural intricacy and intensity of expression are only lightly earthed by folk elements. At times indeed we need to remind ourselves that this is a dance piece. Chopin's growing interest in contrapuntal methods in the 1840s has been noted, but strict counterpoint is the last thing we might reasonably expect of a mazurka. The opening theme of Op.50 No.3 is presented as an imitative point whose spare linear texture immediately takes us beyond the sphere of the dance, though it gives rise to a brighter consequent. This principal theme alternates with more popular materials, Lydian tinged, in a pattern which gives every appearance of developing into the extended ternary design characteristic of the dance piece, though elisions are subtle and the pivotal D section answers the probing questions of A with a moment of unexpected and very beautiful consolatory lyricism. At the point where we expect closure of the ternary arch structure, however, the music leads imperceptibly to an opening of the form as Chopin begins to work the material of A into an extended and impassioned development section. Harmonically the intensity is built up by means of a modal and sequence technique whose chromatic part-movement within an enharmonic continuum strikingly pre-echoes Wagner. Ex.32 indicates the symmetrical

Op.50 No.3

Ex.32

basis of much of this harmony, with the interval of sequence a minor third and much of the harmonic quality made up of minor, diminished and augmented triads. The closed symmetry of the dance has here been diverted into a goal-directed momentum of astonishing power, reaching its compelling climax at bar 173.[24]

The Op.56 and Op.59 cycles (1843 and 1845 respectively) do not set out to match Op.50 No.3 in power and intensity. Rather they evoke a more introspective, private world where the carefree mazurka takes on a wistful, regretful character, its sprightly rhythms and exotic modality recollected less in tranquillity than in nostalgia. Right from the opening of Op.56 No.1 this introverted quality emerges from the drooping sequence at the major second, based on a 'pendulum' model in the left hand. The phrase structure is carefully ambivalent in its overlap of the left hand's six bars and the right hand's four, and the attempt to 'lift' the music with a lively ascending consequent over a *bourdon* fifth proves short-lived, frustrated by a cadential foreshortening which ushers in the opening material again. Tonality supports the gloom, for the opening idea takes some time to home in on the B major tonic, beginning rather with a suggestion of C sharp minor. Only the waltz-like flowing quavers of the episodes, enhanced by their tonal distance a major third on either side of the tonic, achieve a contrasting lightness of mood. It is a sequence of events which returns in later mazurkas. Op.56 No.2 has a middle section built again on a descending sequence at the major second and answered by a flowing quaver figure, discreetly canonic and playing, like the very opening of the mazurka, on the contrast between diatonic and Lydian fourths. Then there is Op.68 No.4, whose falling chromatic sequence in F minor gives way to a consolatory flowing quaver passage in A major.

The structural breadth of Op.56 No.1, with its long developmental coda, is matched by the third and final piece in the cycle. Here the sheer fecundity of new, albeit related, material is unprecedented in the mazurkas, to say nothing of the remarkable phrasing of the B flat minor episode (bars 89–121) – 4 + 3/2 + 3/2 + 3/4 + 4/4 + 3 – or the intricate polyphony of the extended coda. There is a similar richness in the Op.59 cycle, in the concealed counterpoint of No.2, which contains one of the most tortuous of Chopin's sliding chains of chromatic harmonies, and in the glorious canonic bridge to the reprise of No.3, with its eloquent, harmonically so subtle, coda. With these late mazurkas Chopin has moved a very long way from the colour and vigour of Op.6 and Op.7. Something of the meticulous care which he exercised in their construction has been demonstrated by Jeffrey Kallberg in his analysis of the rejected public manuscripts of Op.59.[25] Kallberg has examined in close detail Chopin's three different attempts at a sectional coda for Op.59 No.2 in relation to both tonality and proportions, eventually leading to the rejection of an exemplar which had been reasonably tidy until then. He also shows how Chopin rejected a manuscript of Op.59 No.3 solely in the interests of cyclic unity, transposing the entire piece from G minor to the final F sharp minor in order to forge strong tonal links between the three pieces in the set.

Compared with Op.50, Op.56 and Op.59, Chopin's subsequent mazurkas – the three of Op.63, the second and fourth of Op.67 and the last of Op.68 – are much less ambitious. On the surface they appear to represent a deliberate return to the manner of the early mazurkas, but details of style, such as the canonic writing in Op.63 No.3, invariably betray their chronology. Op.68 No.4 deserves a special word. Fontana thought (erroneously) that it was Chopin's last composition, and it survives only in a sketch which was reconstructed by Franchomme in the first instance and later (including the F major middle section at the bottom of the sketch) by Hedley, Ekier and others. All the gestures are familiar, the balance of chromatic and diatonic material in the first phrase, the flowing waltz-like *moto perpetuo* of the A major episode, the elision in the phrase structure as the A major arrives two bars 'too soon', and the chromatic symmetries of bars 32–39. But the elegiac tone of this mazurka has a very special poignancy. For all that we are grateful to Wojciech Nowik and especially Jeffrey Kallberg for their revelation that it was not indeed 'the last mazurka', the discovery carries with it a certain sense of loss.

7

Salons

Apart from the polonaise and the mazurka, the one dance piece which attracted Chopin repeatedly was the waltz. It is not surprising that his earliest attempts should have followed hard on the heels of the youthful polonaises, for the waltz craze swept across Europe at an astonishing rate in the early nineteenth century. The composers who laid its musical foundations, Josef Lanner and Johann Strauss the elder, became the idols in turn of Vienna, the Austrian Empire and the wider world, and very soon their waltzes were mimicked by other composers of functional dance music. Stylisations began early in the century, with Schubert in particular composing piano pieces specifically designated as waltzes, even if they are barely distinguishable from his Ländler and other species of 'German Dance'. A major impetus came from Weber's *Aufforderung zum Tanze* of 1819, the work which, more than any other, created the model for later stylisations. Weber captured to perfection the characteristic movements of the dance, its smooth gliding, or alternatively giddy whirling motions, and he instigated the typical design of the salon waltz – a pot-pourri of contrasting sections preceded by a formal introduction or 'announcement' and followed by a synthesising or developmental coda. Other major composers quickly turned their attention to the waltz, both as a self-contained piano piece (Schumann) and as a component of orchestral symphonism (Berlioz).

The dance reached Warsaw early in the century, and piano stylisations – waltzes 'for listening' – very soon began to rival the polonaise as a popular salon genre. Already in the second decade Maria Szymanowska composed waltzes for piano duet, and there are examples by other leading composers of the pre-Chopin era, Kurpiński, Dobrzyński and Stefani among them. Moreover in some of these early pieces we note already the tendency for the Polish waltz to take on at times the flavour of the mazurka. Occasionally indeed the borderline between the two is blurred, as typical rhythmic and melodic motives from the mazurka invade the more urbane realm of the waltz. On the surface, of course, the two dances have a good deal in common, and their origins and early developments are not dissimilar. Both emerged into the halls and salons of the city at around the same time, with the important difference that while the town mazurka remained fairly close to its rural origins, the urbanisation of the waltz took it much further from its prototypes in Southern Germany and Austria, the Dreher and Ländler among them.

Chopin was not without models, then, when he set about composing the six waltzes which precede Op.18. There are hints of the future in these early waltzes, as we noted with the early A flat major, but in general they are rather different in character from those which the composer himself decided to publish, simpler in form and usually slower in tempo. The E flat major (1829–30) has all the heady vigour of a stately minuet, while the B minor (published by Fontana as Op.69 No.2) leans towards the gentle expressive lilt of a kujawiak. The D flat major Op.70 No.3, written for Konstancja Gladkowska, and the curiously Schumannesque E major have more of the authentic flavour of the waltz, but it is above all the E minor of 1830, with its introduction, repeated note motive and bravura coda, which comes close to the mature manner.

With the E flat major Op.18, composed in 1831, Chopin crystallised the essential tone of the later waltzes, a tone markedly different from that of the mazurkas, though it occasionally looks in their direction. Light and airy in mood and usually, though not always, 'up-tempo', the waltzes are as extraverted as the mazurkas are private. They may be sparkling and brilliant, suave and graceful, coy, even coquettish, but always their aim is immediate appeal, capturing for domestic music-making something of the lightness and elegance of the ballet. It is significant that Op.18 and the three waltzes of Op.34 should have been dedicated to wealthy society ladies. They were first and foremost music for the salons.

The salon was an institution in Paris. Weber counts as many as 850 with such a substantial musical interlude that they could be called private concerts during 1846 alone, and he goes on to characterise them as 'the cocktail parties of the time'.[1] There were of course salons and salons, from the dazzling gatherings at the Rothschilds, where the most famous artists of the day would assemble and where there would be a high degree of musical expertise among the guests, to the soirées of well-to-do citizens eager to ape their social betters and be seen to lend their support to the arts. The general trend was for the organisation and presentation of the salons to be taken over by bourgeois rather than aristocratic families, and it was the bourgeois salon which provided the stronger musical impulse. This in turn was part of a broader movement, whereby the middle classes increasingly dominated the cultural as well as the social and economic life of Europe, their values, rooted in the capitalist mode of production, becoming the leading ones. Ironically it was those very values which produced the notion of a critical, self-examining *avant-garde* in the early nineteenth century, something far removed in spirit from aristocratic art. Yet this central development needs to be viewed against a background of the more popular dimensions of bourgeois taste, its love of the spectacular, answered by Grand Opera and the virtuosity of the benefit concert, and its need for the homely, the solidly domestic, answered by simple songs, often *im volkston*, and *Biedermeier* piano pieces.

It is easy to have too cut-and-dried a view of these developments. The social history of early nineteenth-century music is complex, with many interweaving strands. We find, for instance, that the tastes of the middle-class home very soon invaded the most fashionable of salons so that repertoires tended to blend and cross. As the century progressed, moreover, we find the aristocracy turning increasingly to the emerging world of 'professional' light music, while the bourgeoisie, anxious to support, and be seen to support, the more serious endeavours of the day, patronised progressive, 'avant-garde' music. As Proust remarked when describing M. de Marsantes, an aristocrat who liked Offenbach: 'Had he been a bourgeois he would have liked Wagner.'

Yet despite the nuances the general pattern of change remains clear and one manifestation of it was a rapid growth of music-making centred on the piano in the middle-class home. Indeed the pianistic revolution played as great a part here as in the public concert, encouraging the development of accessible music for amateurs, arrangements for two and four hands, dance pieces, pot-pourris,· songs-without-words and lyric 'character pieces'. Vast quantities of this music were produced by composers such as Heller, Henselt, Döhler and many others, to the delight and profit of music publishers. This *Biedermeier* art, prone to easy sentiment, ephemeral charm and homely *cliché* touched the major composers too, for 'Trade' and 'Art' were not consistently viewed as the 'mortal enemies' of Berlioz's slogan. Mendelssohn's 'songs without words' are cases in point, as are some of the more trivial character pieces by Schumann. All were written for an expanding amateur market located in the middle classes. And this was also the market at which Chopin aimed his waltzes. With Chopin, however, there is a subtle difference in approach, if not in function. He wrote 'light music' in a new spirit, or rather in a much older spirit, approaching the materials of the functional dance more in the manner of Bach than that of the Classical composers, or for that matter the later Romantics. Mozart and Schubert wrote their dance pieces as an easy spin-off from more serious work, rather as Beethoven did his folksong arrangements. Chopin was capable of this attitude too, especially in his earlier years. Indeed other national dance pieces such as the three *écossaises* reveal it clearly enough. Even his later sorties to Spain and Italy (*Bolero* 1833, *Tarantella* 1841) are *Trivialmusik*, not without quirky points of interest, but on a much lower level of invention than the mature waltzes. By contrast Chopin agonised almost as much over the waltzes as over the ballades. They cannot be dismissed as hackwork, even the hackwork of genius. They are beautifully finished miniatures which accept the atmosphere of the salon and the conventions of the society dance and elevate both into a sophisticated art-form.

The E flat major Waltz, Op.18 was the first authorised for publication by

Chopin himself. He described it as a *valse brillante*, but we should not be misled by such titles. The waltzes have little in common with the *stile brillante*. They prune redundant ornamentation and direct any virtuosity towards the natural exuberance of the dance itself. To describe the A minor Waltz Op.34 No.2 as *brillante* is clearly no more than a passing nod in the direction of conventional practice. Op.18 sets out very clearly the bone structure of dance conventions supporting Chopin's mature stylisations. There is an 'announcement', followed by a parade of contrasting tunes, alternating lyrical and figurative types, and an exciting coda with an acceler-ando or 'stretto' effect. The rigid four-bar phrasing preserved from the functional dance is common to most of the waltzes. Other characteristic features include the flowing quaver movement of section B, giving a special lightness to the mood and texture and pointing up the contrast with the spiky dotted rhythms of the mazurka. Then there are the suave Italianate thirds and sixths of section C, their swaying motion given added charm by the gentle appoggiaturas. Also typical are the piquant cross-rhythms of section D and the shower of sparkling acciaccaturas on a chromatic descent in section F. All these gestures recur in the later waltzes. The reprise of the opening material follows a sequence of no less than seven separate ideas in the arrangement ABA CDC EFE G ABA Coda, establishing the pot-pourri design favoured in most, though not all, of the later essays. Certainly the result in Op.18 is sectional, but continuity is aided by rhythmic links between A and B, motivic links between B and D, textural links between C and E and again between D and F. Section G, the last theme to appear, is an extension, moreover, of an anacrusic phrase already implanted in D, while the extended coda, introduced by a calculated break in continuity, draws together elements of A, B, D and F.

The first and third of the Op.34 waltzes, composed respectively in 1835 and 1838, rework many of the gestures of Op.18. The announcement of the A flat major Op.34 No.1 uses the same rhythmic pattern (bar 1) as in Op.18 and its continuation (bar 2) has a motive almost identical to Op.18(B). Two of its themes (bar 17 and bar 81) return to the swaying thirds and sixths of Op.18 (C), while the flowing quaver movement of Op.18 (B) appears at bar 33 of the later waltz. This *moto perpetuo* is a principal feature of the F major Waltz Op.34 No.3, which also takes up the cross-rhythms of Op.18 (D), arranging its quavers into three groups of four across a two-bar span. We also find again those chains of acciaccaturas from Op.18(F), this time forming part of an arpeggiated figure. Op.34 No.3 is relatively concise in structure, though it retains the concept of a chain or sequence of independent ideas, arranged as Introduction A B C A Coda. Again the coda ties the loose ends together while at the same time introducing elements of novelty. Material from the introduction and from A gradually drifts into rhythmic discontinuity and silence, before a rousing cadential reference to C.

Op.34 No.1 is more ambitious. Like Op.18 it is an extended piece with a fecundity of melodic ideas, but it is more subtly unified and more weighty in substance than the earlier piece. The announcement is arresting and portentous in character, and the principal theme A skilfully ambivalent in its phrase structure, as Paul Hamburger points out.[2] Hamburger goes on to describe the succeeding material as a 'refrain' which 'ties together the sections of a straggling pot-pourri'. It is difficult to see the basis for this judgment, since, after its initial repetition, the idea appears just once more (bar 193) as part of a reprise of A and in the same sequence, i.e. as an extension of the second limb of the main theme. More to the point is the close-knit variation and development which takes place in the intervening sections. The 'new' material of bar 49 (B), strongly characterised by its mazurka-like accentuation on the third beat, is a variant of the opening two-bar motive, and it is immediately followed (bar 65) by an ornamented variation of the same idea, B flat, employing scalar 'rockets' of the kind familiar from the mature polonaises. The next section (C) begins with a further variation of the opening of B, but this time the continuation in parallel sixths recalls the main theme A. Links are strengthened by the use of a similar firmly conclusive dotted rhythm figure to achieve closure in both B and C. At the heart of C is a thirty-two bar phrase (C^1) – statement and variation – in which the feeling deepens and there are unmistakable hints of Slavonic sentiment. On a first reading of the external pattern this section might be taken as the fulcrum of the waltz around which other material describes an arch. Yet, rather as in Op.50 No.3, Chopin unexpectedly opens the form as the arch reaches closure. The reprise of A initiates a more extended response to the 'exposition' of the waltz in which the most remarkable feature is the opening out of the dotted rhythm figure, strongly cadential on its earlier appearances, into the new *moto perpetuo* of D and the coda. The design, and the ambivalence at its heart, might be represented as

It is anything but a 'straggling pot-pourri'.

The fleeting glimpses of mazurka characteristics in Op.34 No.1 are extended in several waltzes, quite apart from the E flat major piece of 1840 (marked 'Sostenuto') which is conventionally grouped with the waltzes, but which was not so described by Chopin, and could equally plausibly be claimed for the mazurkas. Waltz and mazurka characteristics coexist in the popular A flat major Waltz Op.69 No.1 (1835), for example, and again in the G flat major Op.70 No.1 (1833). It is intriguing that neither of these are among the waltzes approved for publication by Chopin himself. Nor was the F minor Op.70 No.2 (1841) and the A minor without opus number (1847–9), which are similarly on the borderline between waltz and mazurka.

This is also true of Op.34 No.2, Chopin's own favourite among the waltzes. Right from its opening bars the A minor has more than a passing resemblance to the kujawiak, in its slow tempo with written-out rubato, its pedal points and its melodic contour. Later sections confirm and strengthen the connection. The material of bars 37–52 alternates A minor and C major very much in the manner of the mazurkas, playing on an alternation of Lydian and diatonic fourths in both regions. Even more striking is the harmonic variation in the restatement of the A major theme of bar 53, translating the melody into A minor with elements of the Phrygian mode, a process common in the mazurkas of Op.30 and Op.33 in particular. In general this waltz presents a striking contrast to its companions in Op.34, offsetting their diatonic revelries with darker harmonic colours and an expressive lyricism embodying a wealth of subtlety in its detail. A case in point is the way that Chopin preserves an element of the right hand's 'off-beat' entry when its function changes from accompaniment to melody. The slightly halting effect which this produces in the melody and the ambiguity of phrasing are powerfully expressive. Even more telling is the flowering of the left-hand melody into a consolatory quaver line in the coda, the more affecting for its warm dominant major harmony and its counter subject in the right hand. Here the nocturne invades the waltz.

Op.42 (1839–40) returns to that special lightness which Chopin reserves for the waltzes. It is not the glitter of the ballroom but the intimacy of its shadowy corners which is evoked here. The announcement is enticing rather than commanding in tone, and it leads to a main theme which plays lightly on its simultaneous duple and triple metre and also on an ambiguity in the larger phrasing (which is the downbeat?). The waltz is a lengthy one, and here there *is* a refrain, a *moto perpetuo* quaver figure which links successive sections as indicated: AXBXCXDXAXCX. The character contrasts of the main sections are nicely judged, from the suavity and delicacy of A, to the more earthy, folk-like vigour of B, the lively, skipping rhythm of C and the deeper feeling of the central section D, whose warmer lyricism is supported by a richer harmonic vocabulary. Much of the interest of the waltz lies in a sense of potential growth or development held in check or interrupted. In the first statement of C the dotted rhythms intrude *ff* in portentous fashion, but the sense of drama is abruptly stifled by the refrain. Equally in D the period structure breaks down towards the end as sequential working seems to be building into development, only to be cut short again by the refrain. The restatement of A is similarly interrupted two bars before completion and linked mysteriously to a statement of the refrain which itself begins to develop for the first time. The outcome of these portents is the second statement of C. Here the unpredictable reigns. First the music corkscrews towards A major, briefly realising an implication of those earlier intruding chords, but with closure preceded by an extraordinary ascending scale reaching across more than three octaves. As the music is wrested back to the main theme the tonal direction again shifts, leading us back to the closing accelerating refrain by a progression typical of Chopin in its drastic compression of remote, tonally evocative harmonies to the point at which their tonal attraction is all but neutralised.

The three waltzes of Op.64 are the collective high points of Chopin's contribution to the waltz, presenting contrasting and complementary views of the dance while at the same time reiterating and refining the gestures of the earlier pieces. The giddy momentum of the so-called 'Minute Waltz', dedicated to Delfina Potocka, is carried through a *moto perpetuo* which, like Op.34 No.3, builds a hemiola pattern into its rhythmic design. The C sharp minor returns in its bitter-sweet main theme to the thirds and sixths of Op.34 No.1 and incorporates a flowing quaver refrain akin to that of Op.42. Again the central section in D flat major touches that more expressive, nocturne-like note so often associated with this key in Chopin, rich in harmony, delicious in the curve of its ornamental melody. The A flat major is more restrained in tone and notably less generous in thematic elements than most of the mature waltzes. Points are made with subtlety and reticence in this waltz. The main theme is subtly varied, for instance, both in its contour and its harmonic setting, while the transition to the left-hand melody of the middle section is masterly, carefully balancing the residue of the old and the insinuation of the new. Harmonically too the journey is full of interest, not just for its local colour, but for its unexpected glimpses of more distant areas which disappear from view before we have fully registered them.

In these late waltzes Chopin's art is at its most urbane. He took some pains over their composition, as a study of the sketches reveals,[3] bringing to them the same refinement of detail, the same polish, as to ostensibly more ambitious works. There is a corollary to this. Just as the 'light music' is unusually sophisticated, so the 'serious music' turns repeatedly to the idiom of light music, and especially the popular dance. In itself this is clearly nothing new, but it *is* unusual to find popular dance rhythms drawn right into the centre of a sophisticated argument, to the point at which any contradictions melt away. Again one thinks of Bach rather than the Classical masters. Bach not only stylised popular dances with the utmost refinement, but also based some of his major (including sacred) works on the idiom of the dance. For Chopin the waltz provided a source of energy for more complex thoughts, and any examination of his involvement with it must extend beyond the waltzes themselves. Extended works such as the scherzos and ballades and mood pieces such as the nocturnes draw much of their sustenance from the waltz. Its familiar left-hand accompaniment pattern fulfils a role in his music which might reasonably be compared with that of the Alberti bass figure in Classical keyboard writing, articulating the harmonic background to thematic material in diverse contexts. The main themes of the Second Scherzo and Fourth Ballade might be taken as just two of many examples. The permeation of waltz elements into other genres goes further than this, however, extending to the use of more detailed phraseology, notably the *moto perpetuo* quavers which we have identified as a prevailing characteristic of the Chopin waltz. Episodes such as bars 138–150 of the G minor Ballade, bars 162–178 of the D flat major Scherzo and bars 124–131 of the A flat major Ballade are typical. At times indeed the correspondences between waltz-like episodes and actual waltzes are very close indeed, as Andrzej Koszewski has demonstrated.[4] This tendency for the waltz to slide imperceptibly in and out of more ambitious contexts is an important feature of Chopin's music, almost indeed a discreet stylistic counterpoint, yet employed without a trace of irony.

It amounts to a dialogue between the cultivated and the vernacular which is at times close enough to constitute a fusion, and it was notably out of step with the tendencies of the age. Much of the special quality of Chopin's achievement lies in the delicacy with which it interleaves two layers of music-making which were rapidly becoming incompatible, as the world of light music increasingly took its own path and developed its own language, its separateness reflecting a schism within middle-class culture.[5] Relative to that development Chopin was neither one thing nor the other, but both. It was perhaps a peculiarly Slavonic achievement to demonstrate again in the nineteenth century that there need be no contradiction between the accessible and the sophisticated, even if the position could not be maintained for long against the flow of things. Tchaikowsky was to follow Chopin in this respect, and he too paid a certain penalty for his popularity.

8

German dialogues

The bulk of Chopin's mature output admits no contradiction between the popular and the significant. His waltzes, designed for the salon, lose little in sophistication to the more ambitious ballades and scherzos, too profound for the salon, yet drawing much of their energy from the waltz. There are, however, works which stand a little way outside this integrated world, with its constant mediation between the cultivated and the vernacular. On the one hand we have works such as the *Bolero*, the *Tarantella* and the Op.12 Variations which meet the demands of the salon on its own fairly shallow terms. At the other end of the spectrum lie the sonatas, where popular materials play only a modest role, subordinated to the demands of the historical archetype. The sonatas are Chopin's most direct response to the achievements of the German Classical tradition.

In the wake of the high Classical style the sonata was cultivated with greatest energy in Austro-Germany. The point is made graphically by William Newman in his magisterial *The Sonata since Beethoven*,[1] and Newman's chart reminds us that the 'German hegemony', as he describes it, went some way beyond the familiar handful of major figures. Early attempts to codify the elusive principles of sonata-form also emanated from Germany, with implications for pedagogy, criticism and indeed creative process which were not always beneficial. In particular such attempts strengthened a tendency to criticise the non-German sonata or symphony in the light of certain *a priori* assumptions about what the sonata is or should be. This critical stance – and it remains with us in many quarters – would view the nineteenth-century Russian symphony, for example, as an unhappy deviation from, rather than a potentially exciting collaboration with, German symphonism. Such a collaboration, really a kind of dialogue between indigenous thematic and formal treatments (developed in the concert overture and tone poem as well as opera) and aspects of the symphonic tradition, is admittedly precarious, and it did on occasion lead to uncomfortable results, but the music should at least be judged in relation to its premises and aims. And the dialogue was often fruitful, generating a creative friction which was to find its ultimate expression in the twentieth century in some of the music of Stravinsky.

Like the Russian nationalists, but a generation before them, Chopin approached the sonata from a distance. His student efforts, the Sonata Op.4 and the Trio Op.8, indicate all too clearly that in his early years at least this was not the air he breathed most naturally. When he returned to the sonata in 1839, adding three movements to the funeral march composed two years earlier, he had already proved himself a master of other lines of thought, musically speaking. The *Sonata funèbre*, to use the descriptive title which Chopin himself (unusually) approved, is a dialogue between these lines of thought and the German sonata principle. Like the Russian symphony, it has been criticised often and vigorously for failing to achieve a result which it never sought.

Schumann set the ball rolling with his remark about 'four of Chopin's most unruly children under the same roof', since which commentators have felt obliged to take a view on the unity or otherwise of the work. The traditional criticism in the nineteenth century was that the sonata is split in two, that the last two movements have little to do with the first two. Twentieth-century writers responded by demonstrating no end of thematic links between the two halves. Both Hugo Leichtentritt[2] and Józef Chomiński[3] draw attention to a connection between the 'trio' of the scherzo and the ostinato accompaniment to the Funeral March. Alan Walker[4] goes much further, uncovering a common intervallic source for the *grave* of the first movement and the *moto perpetuo* of the finale, and demonstrating a relationship between the first subject of the first movement and the opening of the funeral march. Such observations on a unity of thematic substance are obviously pertinent, but their significance should be gauged according to the structural weight of thematicism relative to other aspects of the work's musical language. The merits of Walker's approach will be discussed in due course. It will suffice to remark here that 'unity', often glibly discussed, is a highly problematical notion in music, certainly not susceptible to any single investigative approach, and that in any case we must begin with more down-to-earth matters, such as the broad shape of the piece. And here it is Chomiński[5] who comes close to the essential point in his perception that the work is in reality a synthesis of Chopin's earlier achievements within the framework of the four-movement sonata. The four-movement scheme provides in short a context within which the figurative patterns of the studies and preludes, the *cantilene* of the nocturnes and even the periodicity of the dance pieces may be drawn together.

The finale, for instance, has the unitary form and figurative consistency of a study or prelude. Several parallels suggest themselves. There is the E flat minor Prelude (Op.28 No.14), for example, or the E flat major Prelude (Op.28 No.19) suggested by Chomiński himself. Both Op.28 No.19 and Op.35 (iv) have a similar texture, tracing a single line in triplet octaves; they are almost identical in length (seventy-one and seventy-five bars respectively); and they both end with a sudden *fortissimo* chord. Once the connection with a Baroque-inspired study or prelude has been established, the finale seems less 'futuristically athematic . . . without precedent in the

history of the keyboard'.[6] Admittedly it does differ from the E flat major
Prelude in some important respects. The prelude's triplets are more clearly
focused harmonically and, related to this, their function is partly to provide
harmonic support for a top-voice melody. In the sonata finale harmonic
and linear functions are less easily differentiated. We are presented rather
with a speeded-up version of those figurative melodies found in the studies,
in Op.10 No.2 and Op.25 No.2, for example, or in the first of the *Trois
Nouvelles Études*.

The construction of this snake-like single line is of extraordinary subtlety,
both of phrasing and of implied harmonic background. The harmonic implications of the line may be projected on to a longer span through trans-
position, as in bars 1–4, or they may be neutralised through sequential
repetition at the major second, as in bars 5–8. Or, as in bars 9–10, the line
itself may be tonally disruptive, a series of semitonally sliding triads. The
effect is rather like a film sequence coming in and out of focus, with
moments of relative diatonic clarity – the opening, bars 24–30 (stabilised
through literal repetition), the reprise at bar 34 and the final bars – under-
mined by the shifting, seemingly directionless activity surrounding them.
This elusive quality is increased, moreover, by the constantly changing
spans of melodic sequence and by the overlaps between them, so that
recognisable (i.e. repeated) shapes emerge only fleetingly and tentatively
from the continuous stream of sound. As a finale it is certainly a remarkable
movement, its length and character spelling irony in relation to the funeral
march which precedes it. Schumann meant something of the sort with his
description of a 'sphinx with a mocking smile'.

The second movement is a scherzo in name and character, taking its cue
from the muscular rhythmic energy of Beethoven, but its middle section,
unlike the Beethoven trio, seems to belong to another world. It is a gentle
song in the relative major enclosed within an aggressive dance, rather as
the impromptus enclose a nocturne within a study. Many of the gestures
in the outer sections suggest reference points in Chopin's polonaises and
independent scherzos, the repeated note idea, for instance, the chordal
movement sweeping across the registers and the rapid passages of $^6_3$ chords.
It is not so much a 'theme' as a series of rhythmically articulated scale
passages. The middle section, on the other hand, abandons such rhetorical
gestures in favour of accompanied melody. It is a lyrical episode, closer to
a berceuse than a nocturne (there are indeed affinities with Op.57), and its
central part is remarkable for the delicate balance between an intricate
contrapuntal part-movement and prevailing melody and accompaniment
textures. Thematic links aside, the coherence of the movement relies upon
a skilful control of a tonal argument whose premises are established in the
opening bars. Here the voice-leading and characterisation create a
progression from a stern E flat minor to a lighter G flat major (Ex.33(i)).
This is the overall progression of the movement, but the route is interesting.
The varied repetition of the opening changes the progression enharmonic-

ally to arrive at F sharp *minor*, and this in turn directs the music sharpwards towards a new area of drama and rhetoric. Ex.33(i) outlines the process and

Op.35

Ex.33(i)

Ex.33(ii)

its sequel, showing how the lyrical middle section is integrated within the tonal scheme, fulfilling the expressive leanings of the G flat major region. The diagram also indicates that the return of the melody in the closing bars is more than a thematic reminiscence. It represents a tonal synthesis in which the conflicting tendencies of E flat minor to move to both G flat major and F sharp minor are reconciled.

Like the Scherzo, the Funeral March encloses a nocturne in the relative major, so sharply contrasting in character that it led Ehlert to a quaint conceit: 'After so much black crêpe drapery one should not at least at once display white lingerie.'[7] This is the consolatory tone so typical of the nocturnes, and the rhythmic structure and accompaniment pattern relate it specifically to the B major Op.32 No.1. 'A rapturous gaze into the beatic regions of a beyond', cries Niecks, 'a vision of reunion of what for the time is severed.'[8] Although the tempo remains unchanged, the effect of this middle section is not one of natural growth from, or even complementarity to, the funeral march. The distance is as great in a way as that between the scherzo and its 'trio' and the remoteness is underlined by Chopin's denial of any but the most fragile tonal or thematic bridge between the two sections. If we broaden our view, moreover, and consider the last three movements as a whole, the impression of a juxtaposition of contrasting, relatively self-contained musical worlds is strengthened – dance and berceuse; funeral march and nocturne; study. Schumann was certainly right in his observation that it is no conventional sonata, though not in the conclusions he went on to draw from this.

And what of the first movement, where the shadow of tradition looms largest? Apart from the avoidance of a 'double reprise' (tonal and thematic), the external pattern of the movement respects the main sonata-form outlines, but its dynamic is subtly different from the classical sonata. Four bars of majestic slow introduction lead into one of Chopin's most powerful conceptions – a breathless, passionate theme comprising curt, insistent two- and three-note motives which gain a whole new dimension on repetition through the simple expedient of shifting the accents. Phrase symmetries have been subordinated here to a motive working which drives the music towards a powerful climax, with the head of tension released through a flowing 'second subject' in the relative major. The contrast in characteris- ation between the stormy motive of the first subject and the 'beautiful theme' of the second is marked, intensifying such propensities of the classical sonata until they take precedence over tonal dialectic. The result is a sense of 'romantic' distance between the two groups rather than a classical polarity which would demand an ultimate resolution or synthesis. Like the first theme, the second gains in intensity on repetition, with a new accompaniment pattern and a new continuation, building a climax which is in turn resolved on to a third, concluding, paragraph. This too is tension- building, its repeated-note motives winding a tight spring which is only uncoiled by the two chords at the end of the exposition.

These three main sections exhibit, then, three strikingly different textural and rhythmic façades, loosely identifiable as motivic-figurative, lyrical and motivic-chordal. Having presented them end-to-end in this manner, Chopin closes the form by means of a conflated response to each in turn. The 'development' is a response to the introduction and first subject, with the necessary instability created partly through shifting tonality, but much more immediately through breaks in continuity. Where the three paragraphs of the exposition, each tension-building, were relatively self-contained and homogeneous, the development alternates fragments of motivic and lyrical material and then superimposes them in a dramatic intensification of the original statement. The power of the main climax is all the greater in that the strength of sonority is achieved not through rhetorical passage-work, but through a concentration of motive working and a deployment of the keyboard in a three-tier stratification of texture (Ex.33(ii)).

A 'double reprise', with the first subject in the tonic, would perhaps have overworked the first subject material which so dominates the development. This is the explanation usually afforded for Chopin's breach of normal canon here, though by the same token many a Mozart movement would be damned for thematic redundancy. There is perhaps a more compelling reason. In the classical exposition contrasting materials are held in a condition of tension and equilibrium, achieved above all through tonality, and synthesis is effected when the initial tonal contrast is resolved, i.e. when the 'second subject' is brought into the tonic region in the reprise. Chopin has conceived his movement differently. Rather than a tonal dialectic, we have sharply contrasting, relatively self-contained thematic characters, where it is the function of the lyrical second theme to resolve the tension and drama of the agitated first theme. The response to this exposition – the development and reprise – preserves the relationship. It heightens the drama and energy of the one through motivic development and increases the stability and calm of the other through tonality, a return to the tonic region. This is the essential shape of the movement and it invests the reprise of the second subject with special privilege. This theme is indeed the heart of the movement, a nocturne-like melody embedded in the more impassioned material of the first subject and development. Moreover the alternation here of motivic-figurative and lyrical materials becomes a model for the later movements, so that the entire work can be heard in these terms. In effect three 'nocturnes' are embedded in its substance.

It seems important to grasp the unique shape of this sonata before any considerations of thematic unity are broached, particularly as it differs importantly from the historical archetype. Inevitably Chopin's model results in a slackening of the formal and tonal bonds of the classical sonata, and the surface motivic and thematic links which abound within and between the movements (many of them no doubt conscious) have a largely compensatory role, quite different from their integral function in the organicism of Beethoven and Brahms. Thematic links abound, too, in the B minor Sonata Op.58, which Chopin completed five years later in 1844. Yet in this work they have a rather different significance. Having come to terms with the four-movement sonata in Op.35, approaching it obliquely by way of his unique achievements in the study, nocturne and dance piece, Chopin now felt able to tackle the genre on its own terms, so to speak. The difference in approach is clear when we examine the first movements of the two works. In the B minor the thematic shapes are less self-contained, and their presentation less sharply sectional, than in Op.35. There is a gain in organicism (*pace* Niecks[9]), though arguably a loss in the striking, distinctive quality of the idea *per se*. Thematic links then are not only a means of unifying contrasts as in Op.35. They also contribute to a process of continuous development and transformation within the bar-by-bar progression of the movement, an unbroken thread spun of related ideas. The process is supported, moreover, by a much closer integration of melody and accompaniment than in the earlier work. The texture is spare and close-knit, with intricate motivic-contrapuntal play and only fleeting returns to an harmonically motivated nocturne-style accompaniment. It is a view of the sonata which accords well with general tendencies in Chopin's later music.

Any attempt to demonstrate the nature of this bar-by-bar evolutionary process will inevitably appear clumsy. Yet it may be worth giving some hint of the subtle, minutely detailed motivic, harmonic and rhythmic cross-references which ensure continuity of thought, many of them, it need hardly be added, a by-product of the composer's intuitive sense of flow and balance rather than the result of any conscious manipulation. Reference

Ex.34

will be made to the score and to the thematic inventory of Ex.34. The opening four-bar phrase, constructed motivically from the two principal shapes (i) and (ii), is a closed form, harmonically, thematically and rhythmically. The varied repetition of the phrase opens the structure a little harmonically, arriving at a conventional half-close on the dominant but giving this an 'enhanced' dominant function which leads to a restatement of the opening phrase in the sub-dominant region. The addition of a new accompaniment detail – an inversion of (i) – is trivial enough in itself, but it does create the necessary propulsion to prepare a departure from the closed thematic statement by way of a sequential working of (i), together with its inversion. Again closure is postponed, as the 'dominant seventh' of bar 16 functions as an augmented sixth and introduces a new shape (iii) in bar 17. The link is strengthened by the scalar basis and by the rising top-voice motion of bars 12–16 of which the opening note of (iii) is a fulfilment. The melody comprises three elements which are important for later developments, the two rhythmic cells (x) – the first appearance of a triplet rhythm – and (y), and the hints of imitative working in its presentation. The tonal deflection at this point (towards G minor harmony) remains only partially realised, as cadential close is frustrated by an interruption at bar 19 – a 'buffer' of arc-shaped figuration (bars 19–20) whose primary function is to re-establish the semiquaver momentum. This semiquaver movement also provides a link, through the left-hand accompaniment, with the 'new' theme (iv) of bar 23, its presentation realising fully earlier canonic implications. The goal of this theme is the cadence of bar 29, though here, as at bar 19, a G minor closure is thwarted by an interrupted cadence and another 'buffer' of arc-shaped figuration. A new figurative pattern prepares the second group, its syncopated thematic character established at bar 31 and its tonal function two bars later. Tonally the entire passage from bar 17 to bar 33 has been an extended flatwards 'scenic route' from tonic to relative major. It is only with the second subject at bar 41 that tonality is stabilised and there is a real sense of structural downbeat.

The second subject melody (v) perfectly exhibits that 'conquest of symmetry' which pertains to Chopin's finest lyrical moments. Its quality resides in a delicate poise between latent periodicity and continuity, between pattern and growth, recurrence and variation. Different ways of proposing the same question and answer are essayed (bars 41–48), there are subtle rhythmic elisions, supported by harmony (bar 48), there is a concealed counterpoint in the left hand – all the nuances in short of Chopin melody, where the microscope can reveal a wealth of subtlety under the simplest surface. The overall effect of course is of a continuously unfolding melody whose necessary distance from earlier material is partly a matter of texture (the nocturne-like accompaniment replacing more close-knit motivic working) and partly of rhythm (the triplet arpeggiation replacing earlier semiquaver movement). The distance is considerable, but it is mediated by a carefully staged return journey, reintroducing semiquaver movement as an accompaniment to the second limb of the second subject (vi) and reverting to a more sectional model and variation construction. By the final stages of the process (bars 63–65) there is only a short step to the figurative material of the third group (vii and viii) and continuity is strengthened by cross-references such as bars 58 and 79. As in many a Classical sonata, the closing material proposes new thoughts (ix) which form a link to the early stages of the development section.

The construction of this development section is interesting in itself. There is an even greater concentration of information, with contrapuntal working generating at times an almost totally thematic texture (bars 94–98). This in turn can give rise to fresh associations such as the combination of (ii) and (iii) to form a self-contained shape (bars 110–117), itself then susceptible to sequential treatment. Chopin avoids any reference to the second subject (v) in the development section so that, as in the B flat minor Sonata, it may open the reprise. But the second limb of the second subject (vi) does appear, developed through tonal distance, motivic expansion and a short section of canonic writing of a kind typical in late Chopin. The canonic material works well, but the earlier 'development' of (vi) weakens the sense of flow. It is the only unsure step in a masterly presentation.[10]

Compared with Op.35, the opening movement of Op.58 takes a step closer to the German tradition, and this is confirmed by the other three movements. It is less obvious in the outer sections of the E flat minor Scherzo, a light-fingered *moto perpetuo* reminiscent of some of the studies, and employing a familiar Chopin device to achieve closure – a strong linear descent emerging hemiola-like from the pattern. But the warm sonorous thirds and interweaving part-movement of the B major middle section suggests a new character, distinctly less 'Chopinesque'. To generalise wildly, there is something of the heavy, brooding quality of North German lyricism in this passage, more of Brahms than Field, we might say, though in view of the date we are thinking of affinity rather than influence. Certain turns of phrase (bars 66ff, for example) unavoidably register the parallel.

There are German resonances in the slow movement too, though here the reference point is earlier than Brahms. It has as much to do with the accompaniment as with the melody itself. The flowing arpeggiation or alternatively slow waltz pattern so familiar in Chopin accompaniments has here been replaced by a stately, measured tread, whose dotted rhythm acts as a form of steady, gentle propulsion, lending to the melody something of the Classical poise of a late Beethoven or late Schubert slow movement. It is perfectly offset by the gloriously long, limpid central section, 'rather a reverie than a composition',[11] its flowing quaver movement pausing now and again to ask a persistent three-note question.

It would be difficult to imagine a greater contrast than the two finales of the mature piano sonatas, irony and understatement giving way to affirmation and apotheosis. Chopin was of course no stranger to the affirmative, even heroic, gesture, but the rondo finale of Op.58 is goal-directed music of a kind not altogether characteristic of his work as a whole, and once more it leans somewhat in the direction of the German tradition. This is especially noticeable in the rondo theme itself. Here Chopin risks crudity in the interests of a relentless, driving momentum, one-dimensional in presentation. The subsidiary material is of a more familiar cast, a sparkling right-hand virtuosity which alternates with the rondo theme throughout and dominates the exciting coda.

It is difficult to make much sense of the frequent criticisms of these sonatas. Three themes recur. One holds that Chopin was essentially a miniaturist and incapable of working in extended forms, another that the rigid constraints of sonata-form in some sense inhibited or misdirected his creativity, and a third that Chopin's deviations from conventional practice demonstrate a failure to understand the essence of the form. Since the first would presumably dismiss the scherzos, ballades and fantasies as well as the sonatas, it is perhaps over-conscientious in its censure. The other two neatly cancel each other out. The fact is that Chopin approached the sonata principle with considerable ingenuity in his later years, adapting it subtly to his own requirements in the B flat minor and moving from that secure base towards a closer accommodation with the historical archetype in the B minor, a process which continues with his last major work, the Cello Sonata Op.65.

The cello was the only instrument apart from the piano for which Chopin wrote significant music. He had already collaborated with the cellist Auguste Franchomme on a *Grand Duo Concertant*, and Franchomme it was who played the last three movements of the sonata with Chopin at his last Paris concert. Few compositions gave him greater trouble. He worked on it through 1845 and completed it, after many drafts, the following year. 'I write a little and cross out a lot,' he wrote to his sister. 'Sometimes I am pleased with it, sometimes not. I throw it into a corner and then pick it up again.'[12] One result of these labours is an unusually extensive body of sketches.

A detailed study of the Cello Sonata sketches would itself fill a book, and in a sense has already done so.[13] It will be enough here to remark that they are unlike any other Chopin 'continuity drafts' in the extent of their *dis*continuity. A great deal of the material proved to be redundant to the final version, much of it was drafted in many different forms before it was considered acceptable, and ideas are given several different continuations. We may take as a brief example the impassioned piano statement of the second theme of the first group at bar 36 and consider its context. The sketch is K.870 and page numbers are those pencilled on the sketch. They are not Chopin's.

Page 9 Bars 24–28 close to final form. Another continuation suggested, then rejected in favour of the final form of 29–33, though with details of the piano part different. There is then (without link) a first draft of the theme (as 36–39), but with a different continuation at 40–41.

Page 11 An approach to the theme, later rejected. This version aligns with the final form at 34, but precedes this with six bars presenting the theme on piano in G minor accompanied by cello arpeggiations (as at 36). This would have weakened the impact of 36. A (later rejected) continuation from 40 to 44 where the sketch realigns with the final form, though it is not taken further at this stage.

Page 12 Another approach to the theme, preserving a form of the G minor cello arpeggiation, this time realigning at 35.

Page 13 An attempt at a continuation of the theme. Recognisable at 39, an alternative continuation for 40–41, an attempt at the piano semiquaver passage in 42, then a final form of those semiquavers, but with a different cello part.

Page 18 Another attempt at a continuation 40–44, preserving the triplet pattern as on page 11. Again the final form effects a direct link of

> the scale passage on page 13 (42–43) and the return of the opening theme at 44.

This discussion in no sense parades as an analysis of even this small corner of the extensive sketches for the sonata, a task well beyond the scope of the present volume. It is offered in order to give the reader some concrete sense of Chopin's difficulties in arriving at a final form of the work. It is clear from the sketch, moreover, that these difficulties hinged particularly on the approaches to, and links between, clearly defined thematic shapes, as at bars 36 and 44. As we might expect, other parts of the sketches hint at Chopin's difficulties in achieving a satisfactory relationship between the two instruments. Often he drafted the cello part first, obliging the piano to adapt itself to that. For a composer soaked in a single medium such problems had to be thought through from first principles, and it involved curbing certain tendencies in his piano writing which were by then second nature.[14] The end-product more than justified the labour, even if it results in a piano style curiously un-Chopinesque in parts. It is arguable indeed that Chopin finds a more satisfactory blend of stringed instrument and piano than such later masters as Brahms and César Franck, both of whom accepted without difficulty the *concertante* conventions of Classical chamber music, even where the nature of their material rendered those conventions increasingly dubious. Chopin too shares his material between the instruments, but he is sensitive to the contexts in which this may be achieved successfully. The variety of textures in the presentation of the two themes making up the first group alone is considerable, ranging from piano solo, lightly accompanied cello, cello with piano countersubject, piano solo with cello accompaniment to a contrapuntal interchange of equals, including some quasi-canonic working. The second group is no less inventive, beginning as a true *gesangperiod* for both instruments and developing into a three-part invention in invertible counterpoint.

If the Cello Sonata demonstrates Chopin's capacity to learn new skills in the closing years of a short life, it also shows his ability to consolidate some of the skills he had already acquired in the two mature piano sonatas. Formally the first movement of Op.65 takes a further step in the direction of a closely integrated sonata structure, growing organically from a small repertory of related motives. Not even Brahms's Second Symphony owes more to its opening bars than does this work. Ex.35(i) shows a few derivations and transformations in the exposition section, but the motivic saturation is extensive, with (x) achieving very special prominence as the first entry of the cello, preceding its statement of the main theme. Economy is the key-note. Even the trivial link between the first and second themes in the first group (bars 20–23) is put to later use in the second group, both in its opening theme and at bar 81, and it turns up again in the development section at bar 141. In a similar fashion the arresting arc-shaped 'buffer' (bars 5–8), a device familiar from Op.58, is drawn into the later argument. It is

Op.65

Ex.35(i)

Ex.35(ii)

expanded at the beginning of the development section and again before the second subject reprise, serving in both cases to highlight motive (x).

This latter moment is the more powerful because of the elliptical approach to the tonic major, reflecting the harmonic structure of the second subject as it appeared in the exposition. Ex.35(ii) summarises that harmonic structure, showing how the melody takes an unexpected route from the dominant preparation of the G minor tonic through a chain of seventh harmonies to arrive at the relative major only with its second limb. There are similar harmonic subtleties in the earlier approach to the theme at bar 24, and it may be worth looking more closely at that point to show the careful balance between the need for punctuation and the need for continuity. We may note first that the melodic closure which releases tension at bar 20 is not supported harmonically, in that there is a deflection one step flatwards before the full harmonic closure of bar 24. And here the continuity is provided by the melody, for the three-note anacrusis to the theme agrees sequentially with notes 2–4 of the theme itself, ensuring a seamless flow across the cadence. As Ex.35(iii) indicates, there is in both cases a non-congruence of melodic and harmonic closures, and this is characteristic of the first group as a whole. It contributes to the sense of continuously evolving, organically growing shapes which is so marked in this music. The

Op.65

Ex.35(iii)

very opening of the sonata establishes the symmetrical periodicity of the main theme itself, a four-bar unit comprising two balanced phrases. But as the cello develops the material it loses sight of the four-bar phrase, spinning a constantly changing line out of the same basic shapes. This is also true of the second limb of the first subject (bar 24), which involves no significant internal repetition within the cello melody. It is partly because of this continuously unfolding quality that the second subject, with its clear periodicity and sequential repetition, is so beautiful in context.

Józef Chomiński has convincingly demonstrated that Chopin was consciously relating the four movements of this sonata in a cyclic fashion.[15] The *Ur-motif* (x) initiates the folk-inspired scherzo as well as the delicately Romantic slow movement and the final tarantella. This in itself suggests a German bias which is confirmed by other stylistic features in the later movements and which is at times far from comfortable. The slow movement, with its discreet alternations of cello and piano phrases, has its own magic, but the finale is less happy. Certainly it is the least characteristic of the four movements, and at times its gestures sound like unmuted responses to Mendelssohn and even Schumann, for all Chopin's professed dislike of their music. Such affinities emphasise the unique character of this work, unlike anything else in Chopin. It seems dangerous to generalise on the basis of the Cello Sonata about later directions in Chopin's music, as some have done.[16] It remains a work apart, posing its own special set of problems for Chopin. Certainly new directions are suggested in late Chopin, but if we are to risk speculation about them we must also take into account the very different clues afforded by other late works, notably the *Polonaise-fantasy*.

9

The preludes revisited

There are many facets to Chopin's art and the discussion in preceding chapters has tried to reflect that variety while at the same time broaching on occasion more elusive questions concerning quality (perhaps the most important thing about a work) and structure. The analysis of his music then has taken several different forms, according to the needs of the moment, but its starting-point has invariably been an approach loosely defined by David Epstein as 'historical-stylistic'.[1] Its thrust has been to illuminate musical processes by comparative methods, relating Chopin's music to relevant stylistic backgrounds and to certain norms of structure and language, with the aim of pinpointing (through similarity) the sources of his style and (through dissimilarity) its defining characteristics in maturity. By and large this is the way of the past, both in its preoccupation with style and in its historical dimension, its sensitivity to context, its reflection of 'la race, le milieu et le moment'.[2]

While such an approach must make room for the more searching and systematic lines of investigation into musical structure which have developed since Schenker, it remains a defensible starting-point, and much more than that. At the very least we might argue that an analysis of Chopin's music which ignored such extra-opus factors as the different repertoires of the benefit concert and the *réunion* or the widespread practice and influence of improvisation in the early nineteenth century would fly in the face of history.[3] Historical sympathy would further urge caution as to the nature of the thing analysed, given the inherent flexibility of the composer-performer relationship in early nineteenth-century piano music (even or especially when composer and performer were one and the same). Any notion of a final, once-and-for-all version of a Chopin piece has been rendered questionable both by text-critical studies and by research into performance practice. Moreover the history of performance practice raises even more basic questions concerning the dual identity of the work as a written score and an auditory performance. This has been the subject of several studies in aesthetics, notably by Ingarden,[4] who refers to score and performance as 'basic being' and 'historical being' respectively and distinguishes the work-in-itself from both as a kind of neo-Platonic 'ideal aesthetic object'.[5]

Studies in the history of reception have further encouraged a more fluid view of the work – a tendency to see it less in terms of a fixed object than as a set of interactions between more-or-less unchanging materials – the symbols on the score – and constantly changing receptive attitudes, determined by intersubjective factors. It is clear in the nineteenth century alone, for instance, that the German view of Chopin was rather different from the French view, which in turn was very different from the Polish and Russian views. Needless-to-add that within such determinate *receptive* frameworks individual *perception* is infinitely variable, a truism which constantly frustrates any aspiration of the analyst towards the objectivity of the natural sciences. Even the scientist cannot eliminate himself as an experiencing subject from the picture. The musical analyst not only cannot, but arguably should not. As Meyer persuasively reasons, 'Because rules do not determine strategies, common-sense reasons are necessary to explain specific musical events. . . . And because common-sense reasons are necessarily *ad hoc*, criticism is, and always will be, an art – not a science.'[6]

In practice most analytical work seems to assume a 'deeper layer of receptional insight'[7] which survives changing receptive attitudes and multiple individual responses. Yet it is clear that the analysis takes its cue from an act of perception and the meeting-point between the two is notoriously elusive. As Jonathan Dunsby puts it, 'Just how perception underlies analysis is never so clearly spelled out as are theories of perception and theories of analysis.'[8] An older style of criticism recognised no difficulty in this, regarding it as axiomatic that the critic's job was not to formulate theories, but to convey his experience of a work directly to his readers. This is the approach of early style analysts of Chopin such as Frederick Niecks, whose book still has much to teach us.[9] Technical comment is reduced to a minimum here and the evaluative element relies on no clear criteria other than an intuitive musicality and common sense. We are fortunate that Niecks was well endowed with both, but inevitably there are assessments which make strange reading today, especially of the concertos and sonatas. Niecks's principal tool was the metaphor. For him the middle section of the Fifteenth Prelude evokes the image of a monastery with monks processing in a funeral march. 'Terrors and phantoms' and 'aggressive dreams' are the stuff of the C sharp minor section, to be wiped clear by the 'smiling freshness of dear familiar nature'.[10] The descriptive language model was taken further by James Huneker, who complains that the Second Prelude is 'ugly, forlorn, despairing, almost grotesque and discordant . . .', seeing the 'deepest depression in its sluggish, snake-like progression', even indeed an 'aversion to life'.[11] It was a view of the A minor Prelude shared by many in the nineteenth century. Again there is little technical comment, beyond a reference to the 'vague tonality, beginning in E minor', and to 'the use of thematic parallelism'.

Gerald Abraham, on the other hand, is less concerned to 'feel his pulse', as Tovey would have it, preferring to discuss the same two preludes in technical terms. No.15 is viewed in relation to Chopin's formal process, that characteristic 'perspective foreshortening' of the reprise and the compensating appearance of a new idea in the coda.[12] There are further comments on its evasion of symmetries and its integral use of ornamentation. On No.2 he goes much further than Huneker's 'vague tonality', remarking that not even the prelude to *Tristan* avoids the tonic more persistently than Chopin's prelude and developing the parallel by suggesting that both establish a 'subconsciousness of the tonic key' by the same means, a sort of polarisation in dominant and sub-dominant regions. It is a tempting analogy, but perhaps misleading. The opening of *Tristan* establishes more than a 'subconsciousness' of the tonic. It leaves no doubt at all as to the identity of the tonic key, though it establishes it through dominant rather than tonic harmony. Chopin, on the other hand, opens outside his tonic. If the E minor harmony is to be given a *dominant* function it can only be assigned retrospectively. In general Abraham's book is characteristic of much English writing on music – even today – in its attempt to describe and 'place' the composer's style through an identification of individual fingerpoints of harmony, melody, texture, etc. on the assumption that, as Arnold Whittall puts it, such 'particular stylistic procedures can be collectively held to comprise the composer's "language" '[13] As with Niecks's metaphors the many perceptive and illuminating insights in Abraham's book remain wholly uncontaminated by any systematically formulated theory about the nature or indeed the value of the musical work. Abraham would probably reject the need or advisibality of any such theory.

Both the descriptive language model and the style-analytic approaches have been taken further by other commentators. The expressionist view of Derek Cooke[14] and, more recently, Peter Kivy[15] that music is expressive not only of generalised but of specifiable emotions, and even of determinable degrees of mood elevation and depression, has been pursued in experiments which borrow some of the tools of empirical sociology, and these experiments occasionally extend to an examination of music's denotative powers. Marion A. Guck used the sixth of Chopin's preludes (in particular bars 11–12 and their immediate context) to explore the relationship between metaphoric and analytic structures, using a group of nine students in a practical test.[16] From the initial collection of metaphors three 'organising metaphors' were developed by agreement, each conveying similar conceptions. Of these the image of a 'breathing labourer' was considered the most useful and it was analysed in depth in relation to the structure of the prelude. The counterpoint of melodic contour and recurring chords was related to the counterpoint of breathing and heartbeat and within this basic image a refinement and elaboration of the metaphor in relation to the musical language revealed remarkably detailed correlations, as though indeed 'structure and response are fused'.

Similar experiments were carried out in Lwów in Poland by Zofia Lissa, who was trained in psychology as well as music, in keeping with Marxist convictions that music not only has a direct relationship to the world of social and political reality, but that it embodies concrete meanings, even if these will assume different forms in different cultures. Lissa worked mainly on aesthetics, and her studies of Chopin include a powerful essay on the nature of his nationalism. A great deal of Polish writing on Chopin has been of the style-analytic variety, however. Two books from the 1930s – *Melodyka Chopina* by Bronisława Wójcik-Keuprulian[17] and *Harmonik Chopina* by the Polish-born Swiss musicologist Ludwik Bronarski[18] – stand at the head of an impressive list of analytical studies. Wójcik-Keuprulian offers a schematic account of melodic types in Chopin, drawing her terms of reference from earlier German theorists such as Ernst Toch and Hans Mersmann. She identifies the major type as 'ornamental melody' (Mersmann's term)[19] and accordingly spends much of the book on the nature of ornaments. Within this general category she finds several sub-divisions such as 'ornamental-cantabile' (the D flat major Prelude) and 'ornamental-figurative' (the G major Prelude) and goes on to discuss the ornamental basis of many of the motives in Chopin, the 'trill' motive and 'chord' motive which are blended in the First Prelude, for example. Throughout the book there is no attempt to discuss the *context* – rhythmic, textural and harmonic – for melodic activity.

Bronarski's study takes as its starting-point the once influential harmony textbook by Louis and Thuille[20] which brings together Rameau's theory of fundamental progressions and Riemann's view of functional harmonic relationships. The very layout of Bronarski's book, with sections on diatonic, chromatic (chaper 17) and enharmonic (chapter 18) progressions follows Louis and Thuille closely. Whatever its pioneering importance, however, the book is limited as a means of penetrating the significance of Chopin's harmony, exhaustively classifying his chromatic chords without reference to voice-leading and context. In his comments on Prelude No.21, for example, Bronarski laboriously pares the first four bars of all 'inessential' notes to reveal a complex chord sequence, and he goes on to identify individual chromatic harmonies such as the 'altered subdominant seventh' of bar 32 and a version of the so-called 'Chopin chord'. In a simple harmonic reduction he reveals this lurking beneath the voice-leading of bars 13–16, and explains its tonal function as of sub-dominant quality. The strands of the argument are tortuous, but the conclusions are reasonable within terms of reference which interpret solely in the vertical dimension and restrict the span of context to the most immediate chord succession.

It is easy to see the shadow of Riemann's harmonic theories, in particular his 'parallel-klangs', looming over this kind of interpretation. And this is characteristic of the widespread inclination of Polish scholarship – even today – to borrow its methodology from Germany. Józef Chomiński, one of the most perceptive of all Polish musicologists, has himself pointed out that his harmonic analysis and symbology derives from Riemann, and more particularly Erpf,[21] and to that extent it remains fairly traditional in its thrust. Unlike Bronarski, however, Chomiński has been sensitive to the need to relate individual insights, harmonic or otherwise, to the totality of a work. He has stressed the interdependence of all parameters and the danger of isolating any one for investigation at the expense of others. Chomiński has made a major contribution to our understanding not only of how melody, harmony and rhythm act together to model the form of a Chopin piece, but also, and most importantly, how they relate to piano texture. He was not of course the first to explore this arena. Ernst Kurth discusses the F major prelude in relation to the competing claims of harmony and texture,[22] and Hugo Leichtentritt even uses visual graphs to demonstrate melodic contour and texture-space in the fourth prelude.[23] But Chomiński goes much further. His *Harmonika a faktura fortepianowa Chopina* is one of several studies in which he has investigated the structural role of texture and sonority.[24]

Chomiński's interparametric approach comes over clearly in his analysis of the Fifth Prelude in D major,[25] where he shows how, in a context of uniform semiquaver figuration, the form is controlled by subtle interactions and contrasts within the motivic, harmonic and rhythmic processes. Thus in the first sixteen bars, before the reprise, motivic working suggests a tripartite structure as follows: 1–4, 5–12, 12–16. Chomiński demonstrates the elements of contrast (in turn providing *energy*) between, for example, the first two sections – not only contrast of motive but also of rhythm and metre. The opening section might be viewed in a $\frac{2}{4}$ metre with three anacrusic semiquavers, an interpretation which is strengthened by the 'Alberti' pattern of the accompaniment but which cannot be sustained through Chomiński's second section and which therefore creates an initial element of contrast.[26] There is further contrast in the harmonic structure between the stable platforms of sections one and three and the restless movement of the central section. Chomiński goes on to argue that, while texture and figuration play a less critical role here than in other preludes, they still act not only as a binding force, but as a means of demarcating the structure (cf. bars 14–16 and 30–32), and he strengthens the argument through comparison with the earlier A flat major Prelude. His analysis of the Second Prelude begins by attempting two alternative Erpf-derived readings of the harmonic structure in order to point up the inadequacies of functional harmonic analysis as a means of penetrating the structure of this elusive piece. He goes on to look at melodic tonality and modality, and finally to examine the 'emancipation' of pure sound values.

This is also the approach taken by Zofia Lissa in a study which looks at those aspects of Chopin's harmony – parallelism, ostinati, organic chromaticism – which departed from the norm of his own historical period and proved prophetic of twentieth-century techniques.[27] She too begins by discussing the Second Prelude in terms of traditional harmonic functions, demonstrating the multiple interpretations possible within that approach. She points out the difference in our present-day perceptions of such tonal relationships compared to an early nineteenth-century audience, and argues that where there is a 'vacuum' in traditional tonal functions other elements emerge to fill it, notably the autonomy of particular (dissonant) interval colours, thrown into relief by sparse textures, slow tempo, registral separation and the deliberate monotony of the accompaniment figure. Lissa refers to the quite different effect of similar textures and gestures where traditional tonal functions are respected. She goes on to generalise on the nature of stylistic change, where the departure from the norms germane to some historical styles leads to the crystallisation of future stylistic norms.

In recent years there have been numerous attempts to render such style analysis more systematic, ranging from the pragmatic approach of Jan LaRue (who makes little reference to Chopin) to various types of feature and distributional analysis. Chopin's harmony has been the subject of some prototypes of feature analysis at the Eastman School of Music, based largely on the work of Allen Irvine McHose, an ultimate extension – one might say *ad absurdum* – of Rameau's inversion theory. At the cost of totally isolating harmony from voice-leading principles and other contextual influences, Betty-Jean Thomas has undertaken a vast study of harmonic and non-harmonic materials in Chopin,[28] establishing four classifications of root movements and three basic types of chord progressions. By counting the 'beats' in a piece (the unit determined by time signature and tempo marking) she arrives at percentage figures for the frequency of usage of chord-types and progressions, and, by making comparisons with Bach, Handel, Scarlatti and others, she arrives at certain generalisations concerning Chopin's harmonic style. There are (apparently) 30 per cent fewer diatonic triads in Chopin than Bach; 9th, 11th and 13th chords form over 3 per cent of his harmonic materials. And so forth. Stylistic differences between Chopin and Bach, Thomas concludes, are the result of new tertiary sounds, of a redistribution of chord types and of changes in the relative importance of functions *within* a classification, though there is little difference in the frequencies of the classifications themselves. She also identifies harmonic progressions not controlled by chord classification, including 112 passages of parallelism, and deals statistically with dissonance treatment and to a limited extent with texture (3 per cent of total beats are 1- and 2-voiced passages). At the end she tabulates the total chord usage of Chopin's complete piano music, an astonishing feat of misdirected industry which tells us virtually nothing of significance about his style. As Eugene Narmour has remarked, 'the distributional effect of a quantitative attribute makes for trivial information'.[29] Just how trivial is demonstrated by the analysis of the Fourth Prelude in E minor in her chapter on chord classification by root movement (Ex.36). Here Thomas is describing progressions with roots a third apart (representing 12.8 per cent of the total root movement in Chopin) and the prelude is used to illustrate a passage of ten consecutive chords with roots descending in a circle of diatonic thirds, starting on II[7] and ending on VII[7] Bars 3–8). It is an analysis which fights shy of interpretation,

Op.28 No.4

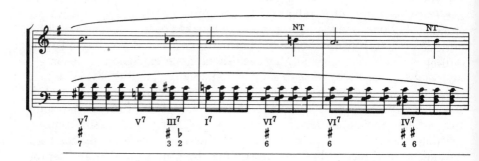

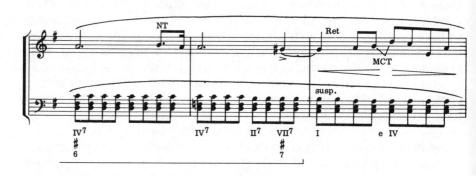

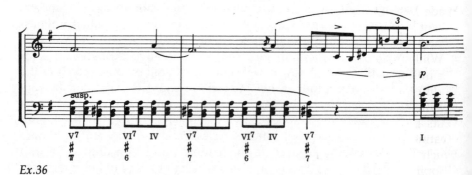

Ex.36

offering no criteria of harmonic priority, ignoring linear elements and (surprising in view of her terms of reference) drawing no inferences from the changing rates of harmonic change.

The analytical approaches outlined so far in this chapter have been concerned primarily with either metaphor or style description. Attempts to clarify the structure of complete pieces are of course made in several of these studies, but, Chomiński apart, the method is usually a schematic 'formal analysis' which, by ignoring time-dependency and treating the components of a work rather like static entities, tells us little about how the elements of a structure function in relation to each other. Gerald Abraham, for example, has presented tabulated analyses of several works, including the *Polonaise-fantasy*. As a rough-and-ready guide to the order of thematic events in a piece this can be useful, but it is worrying to find the composer criticised for structural weakness on the basis of an approach which is entirely one-dimensional, incapable of accounting for the hierarchies, the embedded or 'nested'[30] structures which are at the heart of tonal music.

As a branch of theory such *Formenlehre* has of course a lengthy history, but as a tool of analysis it came into its own with Riemann and Leichtentritt. Riemann's understanding of form is inseparable from his anacrusic theory of rhythm and phrasing. Even where a piece appears to begin with a downbeat, an upbeat will either have been *implied* before the beginning or the downbeat will immediately give way to an upbeat scheme. The large-scale rhythmic structure will then consist of weak-strong patterns which combine additively to form successions of 8-bar periods. This forms a model at the background of the musical structure, modified in the foreground in that the upbeat may be suppressed and the eight-bar module contracted or extended, often by cadential repetition. In addition to his analyses Riemann produced several 'phrased editions' while he was a piano teacher in Hamburg in the early 1890s, including several pieces by Chopin. These editions are *de facto* analyses, outlining the main components of the form by means of numbers written below the barlines. Elisions and contractions are clear from the irregularities in the numbering and various 'reading signs' are used to give greater detail on articulation. Other signs have the usual meanings but are treated with greater critical strictness, and distinctions are made between dynamic and agogic accents, in effect between stress and accent. Here, for instance, is part of Riemann's 'phrased edition' of the Fourth Prelude, demonstrating all the above points (Ex.37).

While Riemann's premise that there is a latent schematic model of eight-bar units poses serious difficulties in some music (not least where bars are of different lengths!) it is often a realistic starting-point for Chopin analysis. It suffers at deeper levels, however, in its assumption of an equivalence of units based primarily on length and in its one-dimensional linearity, its treatment of all components as on a single level of formal significance. Much the same is true of Leichtentritt, who has written extensively on Chopin and whose ideas are based largely on Riemann. His understanding

Op.28 No.4

p espress.

(2)   *sempre legato e senza sordino*   (4)

poco cresc.   (6)   (8)

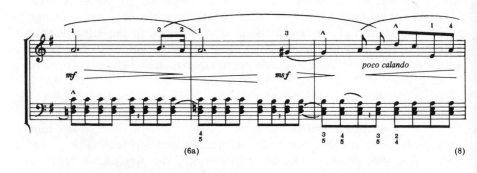

mf   *msf*   *poco calando*

(6a)   (8)

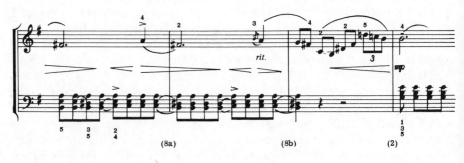

rit.   *mp*

(8a)   (8b)   (2)

Ex.37

of phrase structure is also anacrusic and he borrows Riemann's punctuation analogy and eight-bar model, with the same drawbacks. 'The eight- or sixteen-measure phrase underlies all musical structure. More extended pieces are simply composed of a series of such phrases.'[31] In the Third Prelude, for instance, he perceives a background symmetry of three eight-bar units, with a two-bar introduction, a one-bar extension to the first unit and a final six-bar coda. His understanding of the extension to the first unit is of interest, moreover, in its reversal of the strong-weak pattern of bars 3–4 and 5–6 into the weak-strong pattern of bars 7–8 and 9–10, leaving an anacrusic bar 11 before the repetition.[32] Often Leichtentritt underlines the schematic symmetries by using simple diagrams, as in his analyses of the Fifth and Eleventh Preludes.[33]

Analysis of external pattern and phrase lengths has been taken much further in recent years in a body of writing which investigates proportions in very close detail. Primary significance is often assigned in this writing to the Golden Section, which formalises so neatly some natural tendencies of music. There have been major studies of Mozart,[34] Bartók[35] and Debussy,[36] but Chopin too has submitted to the slide-rule. Michael R. Rodgers proposes a Golden Section proportion underlying the overall melodic descent and the principal tonal division of the second prelude and two sub-level golden sections within the two minor seventh descents.[37] Such an approach begs the question of compositional process. Even a cursory glance at Chopin's sketches reveals that he frequently added or subtracted passages for purely contextual reasons, suggesting that as part of the conscious manipulation of material such considerations can have played very little, if any, part. Moreover an analysis based on lengths and proportions, however sophisticated, is susceptible to the same criticisms as the formal analysis of Riemann and Leichtentritt, quantifying kinetic elements as though they were spatial and static.

To be fair, both Riemann and Leichtentritt paid lip service to a broader concept of form and phrasing which would understand the 'motif' as a source of energy. Thus Riemann describes the motif as an impulse of 'growth and decay' and Leichtentritt remarks that 'motion' is 'an important attribute of style'. In practice, however, their analyses do not take such notions very far and it remained for later theories of rhythm to explore them more fully. Cooper and Meyer, in their book on rhythm,[38] identify rhythmic structures through the ways in which unaccented beats are grouped in relation to an accented beat, describing the resulting patterns by means of poetic feet and applying the concept to broad structural levels, as well as to the level of the phrase. Neither the poetic feet model nor the concept of structural levels was new, of course, but their synthesis in Cooper and Meyer marked an important milestone in rhythmic theory. The basic concept is shown in their analyses of the first and fourth of the preludes, where the same melodic motion is interpreted as trochaic in one instance and iambic in the other, illustrating well how rhythm can bear upon melody

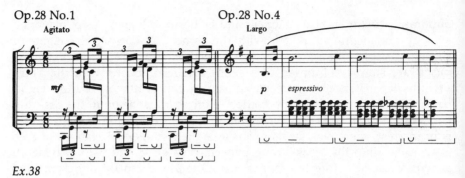

Ex.38

(Ex.38) In their analysis of the Nineteenth Prelude the concept is projected to four architectural levels, and there is an attempt to relate rhythmic functions not only to melody and harmony but also to 'mobility and tension'. The analysis also demonstrates the relationship between rhythmic groups and morphological lengths (phrase structure in Riemann's sense), thus permitting useful generalisations about the structure of the prelude resulting from the 'interconnections among form, rhythm and continuity'.

For all its insights, the dualistic character (accent, non-accent) of the poetic feet model can lead to oversimplified and misleading interpretations, particularly in dealing with the relationships between constituent rhythmic levels.[39] In a later study, Edward T. Cone takes a broader view of rhythm, identifying *three* types of strong beat, the initial, medial and terminal, which again he projects to several structural levels. His discussion of the Seventh Prelude illustrates clearly how metre must yield to a more organic rhythmic impulse which controls both the melodic line and the harmony to give the prelude its overall shape.[40] Clearly Cone's approach has come a long way from traditional formal analysis. The emphasis has shifted decisively from *pattern* to *process*, concerned with progressive-recessive textures, tension and release at every level. Central to the approach is the concept of musical 'motion' through change within different parameters, relating to a basic dialectic of growth and decline, intensifying and resolving tendencies.

The clearest ancestry of this concept of 'wave', 'shape' or 'intensity curve' is in the work of Ernst Kurth, who referred to form as the control of energy through time and space and described 'motion' as the generating force in music. He objected to any rigid classification of music into external formal patterns, perceiving its essence – the 'soul' of the art – as a 'flowing state'.[41] A more recent study which views musical form in a similar way is Wallace Berry's *Structural Functions in Music*,[42] and Berry discusses some of Chopin's preludes at some length, examining the contribution of harmony, rhythm and texture to the overall intensity curve of the music. Like Cooper and Meyer, and also Cone, he regards the notion of structural levels as central, and he uses the Ninth Prelude to illustrate his view of tonal order as an 'inflation' of harmonic order. Ex.39(i) analyses the first five bars of the prelude as an elaboration of a single tonic harmony. The reductive process

Op.28 No.9

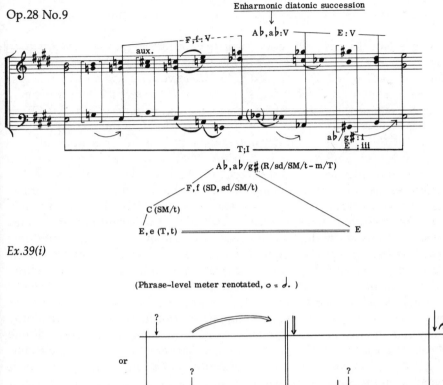

Ex.39(i)

(Phrase-level meter renotated, o = ♩.)

Ex.39(ii)

in Berry doubtless took its cue from Schenker, but there are crucial differences, notably in Berry's assumption of a kind of 'level invariance' (foreground as an inflation, rather than a prolongation or interruption, of background), an approach which can lead to an evasion of interpretative decisions concerning the priority of harmonic events. The same prelude is later examined by Berry in rhythmic terms and in particular to demonstrate the non-congruity of broad metric structure and higher-level accents. Ex.39(ii) reveals a multi-dimensional formal process in the prelude – a counterpoint of metre and phraseology which is common in Chopin and which in this instance generates the more dynamic points in the intensity curve.

Obviously the intensity curve will have affective as well as structural significance, and in this sense it forms a part of Leonard Meyer's powerful theory of 'embodied', as opposed to 'designative', musical meaning. Meyer works from the fundamental *Gestalt* laws of *Prägnanz* (the 'normalisation' process where the mind, in its search for completeness and stability of shapes, will seek to regularise the irregular, complete the incomplete and select the 'best' of several interpretations) and Closure. In relation to tonal melody Meyer understands by Closure such tendencies as gap-fill, triad continuation and descent to the tonic, and he uses these to build an implication-realisation model, relying on his poetic feet theory of rhythm to determine structural notes. Such ideas were first formulated in an early book *Emotion and Meaning in Music*,[43] and Chopin's Second Prelude is used there to demonstrate the 'law of good continuation', which encourages the mind to arrange separate stimuli into a continuous motion or shape. He describes the prelude in terms of the establishment of a process, its continuation, a disturbance (bars 12–16) and the re-establishment of the original process. Much of the value of Meyer's analysis here is that it shifts the emphasis from the customary harmonic approach to this prelude to an examination of its melodic structure. In relation to the 'disturbance', Meyer demonstrates, for example, that the same harmonic goal would have been reached had the sequence continued in the normal manner, so that, as he puts it, 'any technical explanation of m.12–16 purely in terms of harmonic goals and such must be inadequate . . . the explanation lies in the importance of doubt and uncertainty in the shaping of aesthetic affective experience.'[44]

While Meyer uses *Gestalt* theories as a starting-point for his work, his conception of musical structure is essentially a dynamic, time-dependent one, rather different from the view of structure which emerges from the organicist approaches of Schoenberg and Schenker. Indeed Meyer's objections to these approaches could not be spelled out more clearly. 'Unity is not a matter of employing a single tonality or a single melodic kernel as the basis of all the themes of a piece.'[45] Schoenberg and Schenker are gestaltist in the sense that they assume a unified whole which can be assigned conceptual priority over the parts and which at some level determines the meaning of those parts. Something of this fundamental difference in approach is evoked by Cone's reference to two modes of aesthetic perception, the time-dependent 'immediate apprehension' and the gestaltist 'synoptic comprehension'.[46] David Epstein too has referred to analytical systems which 'view the work in its already-composed, fully laid-out structure' as opposed to systems concerned with the 'inner motion of compositional growth . . . the internal mechanisms by which a work unfolds in time'.[47]

Schoenberg's strongly organicist approach to thematic substance[48] has been developed by several analysts, Rudolph Réti, for example,[49] and in England Hans Keller and Alan Walker.[50] Walker, a pupil of Keller, has worked extensively on Chopin and has attempted to demonstrate the structural coherence of his music by relating apparently contrasting thematic elements to underlying *Grundgestalten*. Occasionally this results in interesting and ingeniously traced relationships, though the extent to which they demonstrate the 'unity' of a work remains highly questionable, especially as Walker confines his investigations to theme and motive. But often the relationships are difficult to justify, foundering on a reductive process whose terms of reference are far from clear. At times indeed it is difficult to identify any criterion for reduction other than analytical convenience.[51] In the nature of things Walker devotes most of his attention to more extended and ambitious structures than the preludes. He is after all concerned to demonstrate the background unity underlying contrasting foregrounds. Józef Chomiński, on the other hand, has adopted a similar approach to the preludes *as a whole*, adducing musical support apart from the tonal scheme for their conception as a unified variation cycle, both in terms of the formal archetypes embodied in larger groupings (1–6, 7–12, 13–17, 18–24) and an overall motivic integration.[52] As Chomiński sees it, the two-note motivic shape which emerges from the first bar of No.1 runs like a linking thread through later preludes in various transformations. Since the shape is a scalar step, the case is not difficult to make.

By far the most compelling and certainly the most influential body of analytical studies of Chopin is to be found in the writings of Heinrich Schenker.[53] Indeed Schenker's pioneering work has left its mark on more than one of the analytical approaches cited in previous pages, even where the ultimate conclusions may be radically different. His concept of the *Stufe* as the means by which diatonic frameworks in strict counterpoint are 'composed out' in the foreground of a work has become sufficiently well known to require no explication here. It embodies powerful insights, in particular a separation of structure and prolongation which enables us to penetrate to the structural core of a work. We can recognise the immense value of this, while at the same time maintaining reasonable doubts about some of Schenker's higher claims, notably on the capacity of his reductive method to establish the unity and ultimately the *value* of a work.

One certainty is that Schenker's methods work better for some compositions than for others. Even Eugene Narmour, who has written a well-known critique,[54] recognises the usefulness of the approach in styles where harmonic flow is the dominating element of structure and progression, even if other dimensions of structure will tend to suffer in a Schenker analysis, and implicative functions will be suppressed. Chopin's music, like Beethoven's, responds to Schenker's methods with peculiar aptness. Not only is harmony one of the principal shaping elements in much of his music, but a distinction between structural and 'contrapuntal' harmonies is central to his musical thought. The distinction has of course been drawn

by many other commentators in one form or another,[55] usually as part of
a discussion of stylistic traits, but Schenker offers some framework within
which we may explore its structural implications. Moreover, his particular
assessment of the balance between the vertical and the horizontal in tonal
music makes supreme sense of those long-range linear motions which are
so prominent in Chopin, functioning both as goal-directing and tonality-
defining mechanisms.

Schenker's analyses are impressive not just because of any special potency
attributable to the graphic method in itself, but because of the exceptional
blend of intellectual rigour and musicianship with which he exercises it.
His foreground graph of the Third Prelude is a case in point.[56] Here there
is a division by interruption of a $\hat{3} - \hat{1}$ Fundamental Line, producing a
familiar $\hat{2}$ 'divider' before the resumption of the linear progression and bass
arpeggiation, with a neighbour note prolongation of the regained headtone
and a register transfer (Ex.40). As an analysis of the tonal events of the

Op.28 No.3

Ex.40

prelude this is exemplary, clarifying and illuminating our aural perception
of the underlying structure. It is true to the way the music sounds.
Occasionally, however, Schenker's reductions are less convincing, either
because the divergence of background 'structure' and surface formal realities is uncomfortably wide, or because the requisite of a Fundamental Line
seems to lead to prescriptive readings. His graph of the second prelude is
problematical in several ways[57]. Here Chopin permits a $\hat{5} - \hat{1}$ Fundamental
Line over a V – I form only. Among the uneasy aspects of this reading is
the derivation of $\hat{3}$ from the only C natural in the melodic line, changing the
meaning of the 4th step as previously registered motivically. This divorce
between 'structure' and 'form' (as established by foreground motivic parallelism) is a frequent adverse criticism, though to be sure Schenkerians have
their answers. The selection of $\hat{3}$ is also worrying because of the discrepancy
it reveals between 'structural' notes and notes which the composer himself
has emphasised through the phraseology of the music, its rhythm in the
broadest sense. Schenker does not ignore rhythm and phrasing, but he
subordinates them drastically to harmony and voice-leading. This is another
frequent criticism.

Chopin has figured largely in the extensive body of American writing
inspired by Schenker, ranging from straightforward applications, such as

Oswald Jonas's discussion of the F major Prelude,[58] to such adaptations as Felix Salzer's graph of the First Prelude.[59] Some analysts have explored particular implications arising from Schenker's voice-leading graphs. Charles Burkhart, for example, has looked at some of the special problems and felicities which arise from the dual function of the left-hand line of the Sixth Prelude as a bass voice and a melody, referring to an unpublished analysis by Schenker himself.[60] Two themes are explored – the relationship between a compound or 'polyphonic' melodic line and the larger polyphonic organism out of which the melody flows, and the significance of different levels of 'register transfer', clearly of special relevance to this prelude. Other Schenkerians have addressed those areas which, rightly or wrongly, have been regarded as deficient in Schenker himself. Carl Schachter, for instance, grasps the rhythmic nettle in his analysis of the Third Prelude,[61] accepting, by and large, Schenker's interpretation of the tonal events (Ex.40) and attempting to co-ordinate this with a method of rhythmic or durational reduction[62] which incorporates the notion of foreground prolongation as durational expansions of a background regularity. Ex.41 gives just the back-

Op.28 No.3

Ex.41

ground and foreground graphs of the Schachter analysis, omitting his two middle-grounds. In relation to Ex.41 Schachter discusses the relationship between the work's asymmetrical proportions and its underlying symmetry and goes on to examine the implications of the metrical position of the final tonic in the *second* half of a 'hypermeasure'. In discussing the middle ground, Schachter demonstrates, among other things, how an element of durational rhythm – the extension of and emphasis on IV – clarifies a tonal function, helping to give the goal tonic a sense of finality, while on the foreground he draws attention to several interesting details, notably the way the 'extra' bar 11 highlights an enlargement of motivic neighbour notes e-d and c-b. Schachter's analysis of the Third Prelude is part of his presentation of a general theory of rhythm in several recent articles. It is symptomatic of the richness of Schenker's methods that they continue to inspire such fresh and widely ranging analytical researches.

10

Scherzos

Preceding pages have shown how a multiplicity of theories, many of them contradictory and competing, have been brought to bear upon the preludes. It would probably be inappropriate for a general study of Chopin's music to approach its subject from any one theoretical perspective, and in any case the present author has little inclination to do so. Musical language is an integrated whole and it seems unlikely that *any* single analytical method can convey this and explain it completely, though the promise of a comprehensive model remains subtly seductive.[1] No less seductive is the idea that different approaches might in some way be combined to form a single global view of a work. As Dunsby implies, a pluralist approach to theoretical positions which are often mutually exclusive is clearly untenable.[2] A great deal hinges on the extent of our ambition. Partial insights into different aspects of a work can often be sharpened and focused with the aid of models, if only through an examination of the 'force-field' generated between musical realities and theoretical absolutes. A relativist, rather than a pluralist, position would admit the possibility of closing in on the work, as it were, from different angles, diagramming some of the many interacting forces which bear upon it while recognising that a comprehensive diagram is likely to remain out of reach. In making such an examination it seems appropriate to turn to those works of Chopin where stylistic backgrounds are at their least obtrusive. In the scherzos, ballades and fantasies he makes such a personal synthesis of received ideas that comparative analysis yields little information.

Scherzo No.1 in B minor, Op.20

The main scherzo material highlights a central issue in Chopin analysis, the competing claims of texture, melody and harmony for structural priority. We will examine the opening paragraph. There are two sentences after the introductory chords (antecedent 9–24, consequent 25–44). Harmonic information is slight, with a simple diatonic progression composed out through arpeggiations, as in Ex.42(i). Melodic information is also minimal, with phrasing and motivic parallelism generating triadic patterns on two

Op.20

Ex.42(i)

Ex.42(ii)

Ex.42(iii)

levels, one 'embedded' in the other (Ex.42(i)). Given the drive and energy of the music, it is notable that these basic pitch structures are relatively inert. This suggests that rhythmically activated texture or sonority (determined by values independent of precise pitch content – register, density, articulation, dynamics) is a more potent energy source than either melodic or harmonic structures. The thesis is supported, moreover, by the tendency for melodic and harmonic information to be blended or fused into a more generalised content through the *proximity*, both vertical and horizontal, of events.

We will consider the opening paragraph from another viewpoint. The eight-bar introduction functions harmonically as an anacrusis. It also 'measures' the period structure, creating a norm against which the rhythmic irregularities of the subsequent figuration are counterpointed. In both respects it establishes a continuity with the main theme. In other ways, however, it is powerfully oppositional to it – in its homorhythmic character, its minimal density-compression, descending direction and (trivially) reduction of dynamic level. So strong are these oppositional features that the chords can be exploited dramatically at the end of the middle section. While the oppositional relationship of introduction to theme provides much of the energy of the opening bars of the scherzo, that energy is maintained in the theme itself by quite different means. The general character of the rhythm is motoric, but there are more detailed features which create momentum within this broad characterisation, and in particular the elision of initial and terminal impulses at 9 and 11 and the contraction of groupings at 13–16. Both factors generate a surplus of energy in relation to the metric norm established by 1–8, requiring a restorative silence at 16. A rhythmic chart of 1–16 might be as Ex.42(ii).

At a higher rhythmic level 9–16 combines with its repetition (17–24) to form a single anticipative impulse which leads to the downbeat at 25. Here tension is released, again primarily through textural features, a reversal of direction and dynamic slope and a significant change in rhythmic character-isation, from the discontinuity and contracting units of the antecedent to the unbroken flow of the consequent. The transition from this consequent to the second group (46) is expertly achieved. An antecedent of two parallel eight-bar sentences implies a consequent of two parallel eight-bar sentences and Chopin begins as though to realise that implication. The interruption of the process after twelve bars ensures that the head of tension generated by the antecedent is not completely released and the subsequent change of direction and dynamics confirms a further ascent in the intensity curve as the second theme approaches. And in preparation for that theme pitch structures begin to assume greater significance with this interruption, the A sharp–B–C sharp pattern emerging to effect a most subtle link between the texture-dominated first paragraph and the theme-dominated second, as in Ex.42(i). The second theme is recessive in function, less an antithesis to the opening material (opposing or balancing it on equal terms) than a means of dissipating its energy. This is emphasised by the link between the two ideas in that the harmonic closure at 45 is not matched by melodic closure. The A sharp–B–C sharp pattern is strongly implicative and it reaches over the B minor closure to the first note (D) of the new theme (Ex.42(i)). The recessive character of the theme is further established by the gradual descent of the two-note motive to achieve full closure at the double bar (Ex.42(iii)). This is in keeping with the sectional scheme suggested by a 'scherzo', one of the features which Chopin preserves from an otherwise emaciated Beethoven model.

Although the context and mood are often very different, this kind of 'shading' of function between sonority, motive and harmony is very common in Chopin and it is a source of endless fascination. The first section of the B minor Scherzo generates power and energy through figuration and releases it through motive with, as we noted, a subtle transition between the two. The second section, of roughly equivalent length, works very differently. Its phraseology establishes a necessary continuity with the first section, but by 'stretching' the content of four bars (9–12) into eight bars (69–76) and separating the initial and terminal rhythmic impulses, it immedi-ately changes the character of the material, depriving it of its urgency and insistence. As rhetoric declines, texture makes more room for voice-leading as a means of building a sustained, goal-directed progression carrying the music towards its climactic peaks in a much broader sweep than in the first section. Voice-leading had played only a minor role at the opening of the first section. In the second it emerges through the figuration at various

Op.20

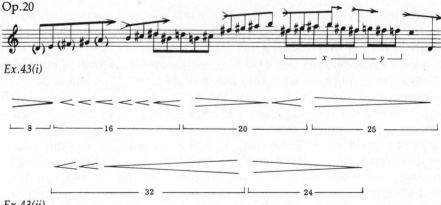

Ex.43(i)

Ex.43(ii)

registral levels, but principally in the top voice and the bass. Ex.43(i) shows
only the top-voice motion, suggesting a balance between strongly directional tendencies and embedded circular movements which relax the
momentum and assume 'melodic' qualities. It is worth noting in this connection that our perception of x is likely to combine elements of both, due to
the effect of repetition, and that the interruption of the pattern at y acts
together with the harmonic symmetries of 102–116 (parallelism and the
diminished seventh) to suspend voice-leading and effect a more conventional, almost cadenza-like rhetoric where texture once more assumes
primary status. This culminates in an inner voice motion at 117–124 leading
to a return of the opening material. The difference in shape between these
first two sections might be represented as in Ex.43(ii).

Apart from the coda these two sections comprise the entire musical
material of the outer flanks of the scherzo. As in late Beethoven the
traditional ternary design of the opening flank is expanded into an ABABA
scheme, while the closing flank leads into a bravura coda, as in ABAB[1]. As
we might expect of a 'scherzo', the larger components of the form are closed
and the divisions clear, and this is emphasised by the symmetrical structure
of the central slow section in the tonic major, again ABABA. This section,
at the heart of the work, is a delicate realisation of a traditional Polish carol,
one of the few instances in Chopin's music where traditional material is
quoted directly. The second limb of the melody is Chopin's own. The carol
forms a still centre to the work, its even rhythm and virtually unchanging
texture-space establishing the strongest possible contrast to the outer flanks.

Our detailed observations on the opening material of the scherzo have
implications for its overall form. Of the four scherzos, this has the most
straightforward design, really just an expansion of a simple ternary form.
Two features call for comment – the amount of repetition necessitated by
that expansion, with the opening paragraph presented unchanged six times,
and the avoidance of any significant tonal contrast beyond the translation
of minor into major for the middle section. In a structure whose principal
building-blocks were harmony and themes these features might well consti-

tute a formal weakness. If, on the other hand, our ear accepts the structure of the scherzo as well-balanced and satisfying, we may adduce this as further evidence that harmony and theme have been obliged to make room for texture and sonority (or 'colour', to use a popular metaphor) as compositional elements in their own right. The prophetic nature of this development is obvious.

Scherzo No.2 in D flat major, Op.31

In any musical succession there will be agents of similarity and continuity and agents of contrast and opposition. In the First Scherzo contrast takes priority over similarity only at the level of successive formal divisions. Within each of the three main sections it is subordinate to similarity and continuity. Partly for this reason, and especially because there is little *tonal* contrast, tempting analogies with sonata-form are unhelpful.[3] The second scherzo, on the other hand, is concerned to integrate contrasts of several qualities – gestural, tonal, rhythmic, thematic and even stylistic – and on several structural levels. In keeping with such concerns it leans rather more towards the sonata principle than does the earlier work, though its formal starting-point is still a 'scherzo' and 'trio'.

Much of the strength of the opening section of the work rests in the colossal tension generated between explosive surface contrasts and the solid framework of symmetrical periods and tonally controlled harmonies which holds them in check. This kind of tension, where components are oppositional yet interdependent, is important in the work and it is expressed both laterally and temporally, i.e. between foreground and background and between part and whole. The first note of the piece has an exclusively metrical function. Although redundant to the theme, its presence is essential to mark an unambiguous starting-point for the first eight-bar sentence and it is omitted in subsequent statements. The regular measurement of this opening sentence is critical so that it can 'contain' the surface contrast of its two phrases, oppositional in texture, rhythm and dynamics and separated by silence. The tension between foreground and background is sustained in the second sentence through a change in harmonic direction. It is greatly increased in the third, where the latent metrical regularity is all but obliterated by disruptive surface features, the absence of a downbeat on 21, the displaced accent in 22 and the daringly protracted silence in 23–25. Strictly measured silence is an important tension-building device throughout the opening section, and it is essential for the performer to take no liberties in this area.

These opening three sentences make up an *aab* structure which is immediately repeated. The one variable factor is harmony and it is time to consider that now. The foreground harmonic direction might be represented as Ex.44(i). The initial progression to the relative major (1–17) is a mirror of

Op.31

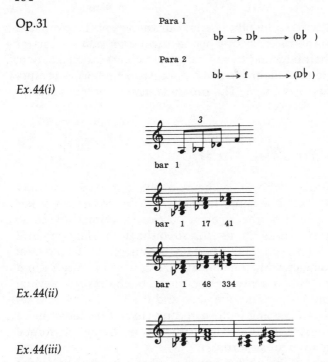

Para 1

bb ⟶ Db ⟶ (bb)

Para 2

bb ⟶ f ⟶ (Db)

Ex.44(i)

bar 1

bar 1   17   41

bar 1   48   334

Ex.44(ii)

Ex.44(iii)

the larger movement of 1–49 and ultimately of the overall tonal progression of the work. Schenker describes it as a Scherzo in D flat major,[4] identifying the F of 49 as the beginning of the Fundamental Line. At the same time the middleground 'tandem' of B flat minor and D flat major is important both here and later in the work. We have noted in the mazurkas and elsewhere Chopin's tendency to associate tonal relatives in this way and it is given its fullest expression here and in the Op.49 Fantasy. The progression to F minor at 41 also has resonances on other levels, expanding the opening motive to an harmonic progression (Ex.44(ii)) and fore-shadowing the third-related regions centred around D flat/C sharp which characterise the larger tonal movement of the work. As Ex.44(ii) suggests, the relationship of detail to structure seems particularly integrative in this work, perhaps because of the overriding concern with surface contrast and opposition.

The power and strength of the structural downbeat at 49 is partly a matter of timing, in that it breaks the pattern of rhythmic repetition initiated at 25, partly of tonality, in that the harmonic outcome of 41–48 could not reason-ably be predicted (later presentations add a connecting and rationalising E flat), and partly of texture. So striking is the spacing of 49 that it constitutes a texture-motive, functioning referentially and ultimately bringing the entire work to a close. The D flat major material which follows (49–132) is strongly oppositional to the opening section. There is the contrast of key, of course, but even more telling is the contrast of musical flow, where for the first time in the work a rhythmic continuity is established in the accompaniment (really a waltz pattern), offering stability and affirmation after the tensions and questionings of the opening. There is further contrast *within* the new section between the enclosed material of 49–64 and the goal-directed sequentially building material of 65–132, initiated, as so often in Chopin, by translating I into V⁷ of IV. There is much subtlety in the cumulative sweep of this music. Variations in voice-leading (especially in the bass) mitigate the sequential repetitions of the melody during 65–88, a deft compression of events from 97 helps build tension thus

$$\left(\begin{array}{cccccc} x & x' & x'' & y & x' & y' \\ 65 & 73 & 81 & 89 & 97 & 105 \end{array} \right),$$

and a brief opening of the structure at 109 strengthens the final cadential affirmation of D flat major. The real significance of this 'opening' becomes clear later in the work, but even in its immediate context it is striking, not least because it represents the first break in an otherwise rigid periodisation of eight-bar sentences. The interruption at 109 and the subsequent phrasing oblige us to interpret y' as $4 + 8 + 8 + 8$.

Irregularities are taken further in the trio, where they form part of a remarkable 'negative' response to the events of the scherzo. There are close parallels in the sequence of ideas between scherzo and trio, despite the obvious character contrasts. Again there is a 'resolution' of halting, unstable material on to stable, flowing material, sequential in presentation, and the tonal sequence is again a third step to D flat/C sharp, as in Ex.44(iii). The structure of the opening material is *ccd ccd*, echoing the scherzo's *aab aab*, but the instability is achieved by diametrically opposed means. Where the scherzo confined contrasting materials within a regular period structure, the trio presents similar materials in an irregular period structure, as

$$\text{Para 1} \quad \frac{c}{4} \quad + \quad \frac{c}{8} \quad + \quad \frac{d}{8}$$

$$\text{Para 2} \quad \frac{c}{4} \quad + \quad \frac{c}{9} \quad + \quad \frac{d}{12}.$$

Even the succeeding material in C sharp minor, opposed in the nature of its musical flow, preserves this similarity in its thematic substance, building the principal shape of 265–309 into both melody and accompaniment motive, as in Ex.45(i). The real contrast in this section is neither of theme nor harmony, but rather of style, as the urgent development of Ex.45(i) gives way to a waltz in E major, unmistakable in its *moto perpetuo* arabesque. It is the last new material in the work and its tonal setting confirms the third-related basis of the overall tonal scheme. A diagram of principal regions would expand earlier presentations to Ex.45(ii). As with the scherzo material, the trio is repeated to 467, and there is once more an affirmative cadential figuration signalling, one might assume, the return of the scherzo.

Op.31

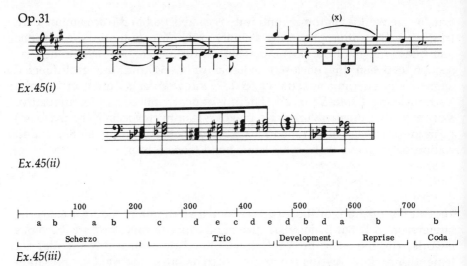

Ex.45(i)

Ex.45(ii)

Ex.45(iii)

One of the gains of Chopin's maturity is a capacity to conceive material not just in relation to its intrinsic beauty or its immediate contextual function, but also in an awareness of its later potential. His early extended works are deficient in this respect, so that certain stages in the structure appear prescribed or unmotivated. It is not that Chopin achieves, or seeks to achieve, the organic motivic growth of Beethoven, though the B minor and G minor Sonatas glance in that direction. Rather he is alive to the possibilities his materials may offer for unexpected openings in the structure, where previously self-contained ideas can suddenly take exciting new directions. Something of the sort has been noted in Op.50 No.3 and it is powerfully evidenced in the Second Scherzo. The expected reprise of the scherzo material is replaced by just such an opening of the form at 476, using the cadential figuration to initiate a powerful development section. That figuration is totally transformed from a cadential gesture into an agent of driving momentum. This leads in turn to an extensive development of Ex.45(i)(x), reaching through sequential working towards a major structural downbeat at 517, important in that it brings back the B section of the scherzo in the newly clarified tonality of E major. It is another new direction, striking through the power of tonal association and thematic juxtaposition, and its intensity is sustained through the return of Ex.45(i)(x) as part of a dominant preparation for the reprise. It is especially beautiful to hear the same motive employed both to build and to release tension. The approach to the reprise is masterly not just because of the thematic transformation to the opening motive, but because the pacing of the 'recession' from 544, is expertly gauged to enable the reprise to creep in while still on the ebb of a single extended rhythmic impulse. The moment has all the structural weight of a sonata-form recapitulation.

Within the relatively short span of the reprise Chopin opens the form on two further occasions. The first (692) is an expansion of that earlier opening at 109, generating an even more powerful drive to the D flat major cadential figure at 708. The second is the unexpected and highly dramatic interruption of that figure by the B section of the scherzo, now in a wholly unexpected A major region. In a sense this completes a process, in that both cadential figures (to the trio and the scherzo) have now initiated a new direction, in sonata terms a 'development' and 'coda' respectively. Although the A major of 716 functions essentially as a neighbour note inflection to the dominant (an interrupted cadence), its very unexpectedness and even more its association with B may well encourage some of us to hear a connection to the earlier E major statement of B and even to the A major of the trio, a final brief reference to a 'sharp' argument which counteracts the overall B flat – D flat progression. The tonic is soon reinstated, however, as elements of B are transformed into a triumphant coda, rushing headlong to the final reference to the striking texture-motive of 49. It is a fitting conclusion to a work whose goal-directed quality – contrasts synthesised through development – is more akin to the world of the sonata than anything we might expect of a scherzo. That quality is emphasised, moreover, by an acceleration of the rate of formal change – immediately evident in the formal synopsis (Ex.45(iii)) – investing the later stages of the piece with the character of an apotheosis.

Scherzo No.3 in C sharp minor, Op.39.

We return to the simpler design of the First Scherzo. The introduction is an unusual structure, though not perhaps meriting cries of 'weird', 'extraordinary', 'seventy-five years ahead of its time' and so forth.[5] Chopin was fond of the elliptical opening, the gradual clarification rather than immediate establishment of a tonality. Nor was there anything new in that. Harmonic ambiguities which only gradually home in on a tonic were already a feature of several Classical introductions and they were to become much loved of the Romantics. All the same Chopin employs the device more consistently than any of his contemporaries, and at times the pitch structures of his introductions resist easy explication. The broad characterisation in Op.39 is an interplay between 'non-tonal' symmetries and tonal hierarchies, with a gradual shift in emphasis from the former towards the latter. There is a background of descending $^6_3$s as in Ex.46(i), but several features are obfuscatory in relation to it. One is the choice of notes 3 and 4 of the motive, in that they contradict rather than support the implied harmony. Another concerns the rhythmic shape of the passage. On its first presentation the motive will be heard as iambic (v —), and its immediate repetition establishes a pattern and an expectation. The third presentation preserves essential features of this pattern – the semitonal sequence and an intervallic invariance for pitches 2–4 – but the superimposed appoggiatura C-B (the parent cell of the piece) is disruptive, suggesting a trochee (— v) rather than an

Op.39

Ex.46(i)

Ex.46(ii)

Ex.46(iii)

iamb and 'resolving' the C prematurely in relation to the implied harmonic background. By disturbing the rhythm of the descent in this way, the third presentation rationalises the recalcitrant notes 3 and 4 of the motive, as they are now conformant to the harmony. These factors give momentary privilege to the B major stage of the background descent. And from this point harmonic considerations (hierarchies) increasingly take precedence over the integrity of the pattern (symmetries). Phrase 2 removes some of the ambiguities of phrase 1. The ear will now carry an awareness of latent trochaic grouping from the start of the phrase, while the notes of the motive are modified to support an emerging harmonic direction, as Ex.46(ii) suggests. The precise tonal destination may not yet be clear, but by 21 the range of possibilities has been substantially narrowed.

The theme itself emerges with striking clarity from the tonal and rhythmic vagaries of this introduction, defining both the triple metre and the C sharp minor tonic. It may be noted in passing that its double octave presentation, demanding a heavy arm technique, is one of several features in the scherzo which remind us of Liszt. The rhetorical chords of the introduction are also Lisztian (cf. the opening of his E flat major Concerto) as is the final gesture of the piece, where a C sharp pedal acts as a springboard to ever wider octave leaps. Both antecedent and consequent of the main theme are eight-bar sentences, but as so often in Chopin there are internal subtleties dictated by the grouping of the structural notes of the theme, as shown in Ex.46(iii). The motivic parallelism at 35 will disrupt our count as from 33, encouraging us to hear 35 at least partly as an initiating impulse and conveying a sense of formal compression or foreshortening when the antecedent returns. This is retained at the equivalent point in the varied repetition (49–57) and it partly explains the two bars (58–59) which remain outside the otherwise consistent eight-bar sentence structure. It is almost as though these bars replace the time which has been 'lost' at 33–34 and 49–50.

As in the First Scherzo the trio is a hymn in the tonic major, not a quotation this time, but chorale-like in character. For all its simplicity this music perfectly evokes the genius of the piano, the rich sonorous chords and tenor melody answered by a light spray of delicate figuration in the upper register. The larger rhythm is measured and regular, barely disturbed by the extended wash of colour in the middle (243–286). The return of the trio at 448 is in the relative major, a distant echo of those earlier tonal structures in Chopin where the tonal schemes of exposition and reprise are reversed in relation to Classical precedent. Here the effect is expressive, the more so when the material is translated into the minor with exquisite transformations.

As both scherzo and trio are relatively self-contained components, special interest attaches to mediating or transitional material in the work. The rhythmic shape of the 'chorale' (Ex.47(i)(*a*)) is already present in the consequent of the scherzo theme (36–39), but the shape here is less clearly defined, due to its position within the eight-bar sentence (Ex.47(i)(b)), an ambiguity which has been discussed. The disturbance at 130–131 is most apparent in melodic and harmonic terms, a substitution of B major for G sharp minor with the necessary adjustments to line, but the change in rhythm is hardly less significant. For the first time the rhythmic shape of the motive is conformant to its position in the trio (Ex.47(i)(c)), facilitating a smooth link to the chorale theme. Unfortunately the subtlety of this is all too often killed in performance. We may note in passing one other important continuity. The striking contrast in texture and dynamics in the last two bars of the consequent at 39 and 121 loses much of its disruptive quality at 143 due to the regularisation of rhythm as already examined. Much of its former aggressively anticipative quality is also lost for the same reason and it becomes partly 'reactive' in quality. This, combined with the melodic transformation, relates it specifically to the delicate 'afterthoughts' of the trio, as in Ex.47(ii).

To effect a return to the scherzo Chopin opens one of the closed phrases of the chorale, treating it sequentially, supplying it with a new consequent and finally stretching it into an anacrusis to the octave theme. The point of departure for the process is 312 where the expectation is a closure in D flat major and, as a foreground graph suggests, the entire transition is really a prolongation of the tonic harmony (Ex.47(iii)). Within this prolongation, however, the illusion of harmonic movement is very strong, and necessarily so given the tonal stability of the areas to be connected. The new quaver figure which separates the chorale phrases (336–339 and 344–347) functions quite differently to the earlier 'afterthoughts' of the trio, no longer gently

Ex.47(i)

Ex.47(ii)

bar 287   367
Ex.47(iii)

amplifying and supporting the cadence but pushing the phrases apart, sustaining the tension and heightening the sense of expectation. The final stages of the transition superimpose the scherzo and trio themes and dove-tail them into an urgent reiteration of the 'parent cell' A-G sharp.

After the second trio in E major and minor the music takes a surprising turn. Far from building tension in preparation for a final statement of the main scherzo theme, Chopin actually slows down the sense of forward momentum. The steady tread of the chorale is reduced to virtual stasis as the harmonic rhythm drops at 517 to a single change at each eight bar sentence until 541. At this point a quite new texture is introduced, as a flowing quaver accompaniment supports a sustained line growing out of the chorale theme but transforming it from a detached litany into an expansive melody of warmth and breadth. Following the terse, short-breathed octave theme of the scherzo (really not much more than the A-G sharp cell) and the broken phrases of the trio, this is a moment of great beauty, initially consolatory in tone but gaining in passion and intensity until the explosive octaves of 567 signal a bravura coda. Once more Chopin has opened the form unexpectedly in a powerful sequence whose expansiveness is all the more telling after the enclosed material of the scherzo and trio. The coda emerges as the culmination of this gradual transformation of the chorale theme, a final apotheosis with little thematic basis which balances the earlier material much more successfully than any conventional thematic recall. It is a gesture with origins in the *stile brillante*, but it has here been transformed into an essential formal component, a natural, seemingly inevitable outcome of the preceding argument. The closing pages of the F minor Ballade were to give consummate expression to this kind of non-thematic bravura coda.

Scherzo No.4 in E major, Op.54

For Chopin the genre title made few demands of his material. Each of the scherzos is uniquely characterised, sharply differentiated from its fellows in mood and technique and united to them only in metre and in a rough-and-ready allegiance to the scherzo and trio design. Formally the most ambitious is the second which embodies all the conflicts and drives of a sonata movement. The first conforms in pattern to the historical archetype, but in the nature of its material it has other aspirations, generating a thrust and power which counteracts the static design. The third also appears conformant, but here the subversive elements extend from the material into the structure. In relation to these first three scherzos the fourth is unusual in its untroubled acceptance of the closed components and clear divisions of the ternary design, however expanded, and in its avoidance of affective extremes, its predominantly sunny, cheerful temper.

   It is interesting to trace the technical sources of this equanimity. We might begin with the obvious, but pertinent, observation that it avoids extremes of dynamics. As Zofia Chechlińska has pointed out,[6] 721 of the work's 967 bars are kept in a *piano* level. The phrase structure also supports the equable disposition of the work. The eight-bar sentence rules, and with little of the tension generated by those internal ambiguities which ruffle the surface of so much of his music. Rather we have an harmonious balance of components which are texturally and rhythmically diversified. The first four eight bar sentences present four components (*a, b, c, d*), each distinct and contrasted, yet at the same time related. It is a judicious balance of opposition and similarity. There is a relationship between *a* and *b* through the dominant-quality chords of 5–8 and 13–16, and between *c* and *d* through the arpeggiated arcs of melody which characterise both. There are further correspondences between *b* and *d* through theme (9–11), 29–33) and between *a* and *d* through (monophonic) texture. The relationship between the four components then is one of poise and balance rather than one of drama or opposition (Ex.48(i)).

Ex.48(i)

Ex.48(ii)

bar 153   bar 249

Ex.48(iii)

Ex.48(iv)

Harmonically too this opening paragraph suppresses disruptive tendencies. It avoids expressive chromaticism on the one hand and tension-building sequence on the other, and it subordinates directional voice-leading to clear diatonic chord connection. Unusually for Chopin, a traditional classification of harmonies in the opening paragraph and its varied repetition would offer a fairly realistic diagram of the basic pitch structures. The lucid diatonicism of the harmony is projected, moreover, on to a higher structural level for the first section as a whole, as in Ex.48(ii). The new arabesque – *e* – which appears at 66, alternating with variants of *d*, further supports the enclosed, rather than implicative, character of the musical material. Like *b* and *c* it describes an arc, a self-contained impulse of departure and return.

The fourth is the most spacious of the scherzos, with the outer flanks each incorporating an extended central passage, somewhat analogous to a 'development section' in its lengthy chromatic prolongations and its admission of the goal-directed quality of the Second Scherzo. The enharmonic shift to A flat major (161) and the subsequent inflections to F major and F sharp major have some weight due to their association with statements of *a*, *b* and *c*, but they are encompassed within a larger voice-leading to V (Ex.48(iii)), and this in turn resolves on to the I of the reprise at 273. The middle-ground, in short, remains firmly diatonic. Within the progression to V, moreover, thematic presentation is relatively self-contained. There is little of the instability, the dependence on a memory of 'complete' statements, which marks thematic treatments in the archetypal Classical development section. Two statements of *a* – *d* are presented virtually complete, to be succeeded by expansions of *e* which preserve its enclosed arc-like contour. The downbeat on V coincides with a new theme *f* in cross-rhythm and this in turn assumes something of the contour of *a* in preparation for the reprise, virtually literal until the approach of the trio.

At this point Chopin briefly extends the material of *e*, isolating the first bar of the arabesque and the left-hand motive and using them to build tension, the first moment in the work which seems to be reaching beyond the pattern of a balanced set of enclosed statements. The process culminates in a striking transformation of *a* (377), questioning rather than assured. It all proves fleeting, a brief glimpse of other possibilities, before the tension is released and the trio is under way. The melody here is in the relative minor, though characteristically associated with the tonic, and again it describes an arc in eight-bar sentences. Even the tension-building transition to the trio had maintained this sentence structure and its invariance emerges increasingly as fundamental to the benign character of the work. In the outer flanks it is usually presented as 4 + 4 (*a* – *e*), though there are later variations such as the 6 + 2 of *f*. In the trio, however, the sentence structure provides a background symmetry for more flexible, pliable phrases. The varied repetition of the opening (409) is characteristic, 'borrowing' an anticipated bar from the preceding phrase and varying the phrasing of the continuation through cadential echoes (423–426) and overlaps as the melody becomes two-voiced (432–433). Ex.48(iv) indicates something of this interplay of symmetries and asymmetries. Even the apparently meandering monophonic line which leads back to the reprise of the trio melody (499) does not disturb the background of eight-bar units and that background is further sustained through the powerful and interesting progression to the return of the scherzo. The relationship of the trio melody to its arpeggiated accompaniment figure subtly changes as the scherzo approaches. Melody declines in interest and accompaniment gains in status, articulating an accrual of intensity determined primarily by harmonic movement. As we reach the dominant, Chopin prolongs the harmony through an extended reference to *e*, initiating a quaver movement which is ingeniously carried over into the fuller scoring of the scherzo reprise.

11

Ballades

Broadly characterised, the scherzos, like the polonaises, build extended structures from simple designs, where the larger divisions are clear, sections are contrasting and closure is optimised. The ballades, on the other hand, favour through-composed, directional structures, where transformation and variation are seminal functions, integration and synthesis essential goals. Within the terms of this generalisation we might add that the Second Scherzo leans towards the condition of the ballades and the Second Ballade towards the condition of the scherzos. There is a further important distinction. In the scherzos and polonaises there is some correlation between Chopin's practice and formal archetypes which, though of fairly recent inception, were nonetheless already clearly defined. By contrast the genre title 'ballade' carries no formal *expectations* whatever, though the composer may naturally take recourse to one or other or several of the archetypes. In this sense there is a useful analogy with the later symphonic poem, whether or not Chopin drew upon literary sources.[1] In both ballade and symphonic poem the innocent ear will have no *a priori* reference point, no clear expectation of a formal scheme. Beyond this rather negative property, there are other features which suggest that Chopin viewed the four ballades as members of a single family. Several writers have pinpointed a 'narrative' quality which is partly adduced by the flowing $\frac{6}{4}$ or $\frac{6}{8}$ time in which all four works are cast.[2] We might add that the ballades draw heavily upon the sonata principle, and particularly upon the *thematic* dualism of the sonata. Each of them finds some way of synthesising an initial thematic contrast.

Ballade No.1 in G minor, Op.23

The introduction composes out a 'Neapolitan 6th' harmony in the manner of a recitative. Chopin had a weakness for Neapolitan harmony, and here it shapes yet another tonally elliptical opening of a kind which is the rule rather than the exception in his major works. The harmonic destination is not clear in the opening bars, but it is strongly implied by the closing fragment of the first phrase (Ex.49(i)). This fragment also serves to define a motivic element *x* and the first note of a foreground 8–1 descent within

Op.23

Ex.49(i)

Ex.49(ii)

Ex.49(iii)

Ex.49(iv)

G minor. The dovetailing of 'recitative' and 'aria' is remarkably subtle here, in that closure is postponed until 9 when the theme is already under way, having been carefully prepared motivically (Ex.49(i)). The placing of such a full closure in the course of the main theme is strikingly original, unusual even for Chopin, and the quasi-cadential harmony continues to lend a very special character to the theme in later statements.

The continuation of the theme, moreover, preserves the $\frac{2}{V} - \frac{1}{I}$ gesture and with it a sense of deliberate discontinuity, mitigated somewhat when the tonic is inflected by III and IV. Here the V – I harmonic pattern is retained, but the melodic line is less final (4 – 3 and 5 – 5 respectively) and in any case pushes beyond the immediate harmonic closure to reach its own goal rather later. The inflection to III can be summarised as in Ex.49(ii). The inflection to IV signals a more substantial prolongation, as the melodic line broadens and the return to I is delayed and ultimately thwarted. The further prolongation to 36 is achieved by a combination of bass voice-leading and applied or 'inter' – dominants which is very characteristic of Chopin. Ex.49(iii) shows the voice-leading.

The paragraph from 36 establishes a continuity with the first theme through motive, as Ex. 49(iv) suggests, but its function is really to take us beyond that world, to generate an increasing momentum and a mounting tension whose release can pave the way for the second theme. The intensity curve is created through a barely perceptible change from motive into pattern (45) and from conformant to disruptive rhythmic grouping (48), supported by changes in tempo and dynamics. The recession to the second theme is marked by a return to conformant rhythm and a change in the function of the figuration, from a primary to a secondary element, now accompanying an emerging left-hand motive as from 56. This motive effects a gradual transition into the second theme, its features preserved through the dominant major ninth and thirteenth of 68. The entire progression from first to second theme is marked then by that subtle shading of functions which is so characteristic of Chopin. We might represent it as an arch: theme – motive – pattern – motive – theme.

The second theme, whose links with the first have been admirably demonstrated by Alan Rawsthorne,[3] emerges almost imperceptibly. This is due not just to the motivic link, but to an harmonic elision which is again typical of Chopin (and incidentally strikingly similar to Skryabin in the present formulation). The 'resolution' of a dominant preparation of the relative major is evaded by assigning to the expected tonic a further dominant quality, so that the true home of the second theme is the sub-mediant. Already in the first theme the members of a diatonic foreground – III, IV and V – were enriched through their respective dominant sevenths and the process is continued in the second theme, where it is supplemented by the appearance of other diatonic sevenths, functioning as much in harmonic as in linear terms. In itself this is merely an extension of Classical procedure, but often Chopin takes the process very far, liberally 'applying' dominants to chromatic as well as diatonic foregrounds to the extent that the diatonic middlegrounds are obscured. Often in such passages traditional harmonic functions, even on the most immediate surface level, are subordinated to other controlling principles, notably voice-leading or symmetrical pitch structures. In this second theme, however, the harmonic impulse remains strong, and the tonal foundations are secured by a stable subsidiary motive affirming E flat major (82). As Ex.50(i) indicates, the underlying harmony accepts a dissonant norm of diatonic sevenths arranged in a fifths cycle, with dominant quality assigning privilege to V and VI as well as I. A passage such as *y*, where an unrelieved seventh quality is composed out through left-hand arpeggiation (note that the melody – its shape *and* its slurring – to some extent disguises the sequence) foreshadows closely a characteristic sound of much late nineteenth-century piano music, notably by French and Russian composers.

Schenker's interpretation of subsequent tonal events (to 138) as a lengthy prolongation of a neighbour note at 69 carries much conviction, especially in view of the long-range bass motion (Ex.50(ii)). Within the prolongation,

Op.23

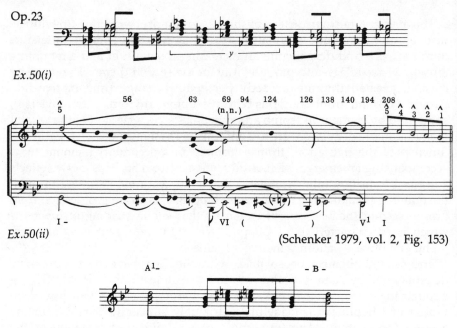

Ex.50(i)

Ex.50(ii)

(Schenker 1979, vol. 2, Fig. 153)

Ex.50(iii)

however, the emphasis on II is strong. There is indeed a fine balance between factors which stabilise II and factors which emphasise its 'passing' quality. The major stabilising element is the repetition – more or less literal – of the early stages of both themes in the new tonal setting, minor for the first theme, major for the second. Yet against this there is the dominant pedal throughout the first theme, the transformations of the later stages of both themes (the affirmative subsidiary motive of the second theme is omitted) and of course the larger voice-leading as in Ex.50(ii). These latter features contribute to a single sweep of tension-building material which reaches its goal only at 124–126, when the return to VI is already intimated. The continuity is striking, and it will not by now be necessary to dwell upon the subtle connections which help to achieve it – the transformations at 90–93 in preparation for the first theme and at 99–105 for the second, which emerges powerfully and unexpectedly, yet entirely naturally, out of the first. Where the two themes described curves of intensity – departure and return – on their first appearances, they are now both tension-building, reaching cumulatively towards the structural dominant at 124–126 which signals a regained E flat major. An interpretation which favoured the stability of II in this section would hear an overall tonal arch, as in Ex.50(iii), rather than or in addition to Schenker's reading. There are no rights and wrongs about it.

The regained VI is celebrated by a 'waltz', rather in the manner of the Second Scherzo. Waltz elements were already implicit in the accompaniment to the main theme, discreet but unmistakable, and now they are extended into a fully characterised dance episode whose phraseology is the *moto perpetuo* arabesque so typical of the independent waltzes. The style counterpoint is rendered rather less abrasive by links to the first theme through phraseology and motive (*x*) in Ex.49(i)) and to the second theme through harmony. As in the Second Scherzo the waltz episode appears after all the thematic material has been presented, acting as a kind of buffer between statement and reprise. It is perfectly possible to hear it as the pinnacle of an overall arch created through thematic pattern (AB AB C BA Coda), while at the same time recognising a goal-directed momentum, achieved through waves of tension and release, which pulls strongly against this purely formal reading. In relation to this 'wave' interpretation the waltz episode initially defuses the intensity of the A major statement of the second theme and then builds it again in preparation for the reprise of that same theme in E flat major.

The pacing and grading of tension here and throughout the ballade is unerring, and no mere description can convey its sense of rightness. A graph would describe a gentle curve in the 'exposition', build steadily through the transformations of both themes to a major peak at 124, drop to the waltz and rise again to a subisidary peak for the reprise of the second theme. It would sustain the line through that theme and allow it to drop again only at the approach of the tonic and the final statement of the first theme. Far from representing a completion, as suggested by the thematic arch, the reprise of this theme is itself tension-building. It is presented over a dominant pedal (in the form of its second statement) and it reaches forward to the highest peak of the intensity curve in the coda. As in the Third Scherzo, the absence of thematic, and in this case also metric, relationship to the main body of the work serves only to strengthen this coda and to enhance its value as an ultimate resolution of earlier tensions, a goal towards which everything in the piece had been striving. The powerful sweep of virtuosity is halted dramatically in the closing bars briefly to remind us of the opening recitative, before the final, aggressively cadential gesture.

Ballade No.2 in F major/A minor, Op.38

In the Second Scherzo and Op.49 Fantasy Chopin's 'progressive' key schemes reflect his intimate association of the tonal relatives within a single key signature.[4] The scheme of the Second Ballade admits of no such explanation and it raises treacherous issues concerning tonal coherence. In the Classical and early Romantic periods exceptions to monotonality in extended works are usually either of the 'Fantasy' type, often following a recitative principle, or multi-partite structures such as opera and oratorio where there is a succession of tonally enclosed numbers. The single-movement or three-four movement extended instrumental work whose tonal scheme is progressive rather than enclosed is a rarity. Interpretations of tonal structure which assume an organic whole (Schenker, Schoenberg) will often explain it reasonably in terms of a 'foreign' opening. Late-Romantic works have also been described (though not by Schenker!) in terms of a foreign ending, or even – in extreme cases – foreign opening *and* ending, without doing violence to the concept of monotonality. This is inadequate to the experience of the Second Ballade, where the weighting of the principal regions will not permit any obvious priority.

An alternative view of 'progressive' tonal schemes might reject monotonality in favour of the interlocking regions described by Graham George in a study which ranges from Bach to Mahler and Nielsen.[5] Here the fundamental, as distinct from the temporary or secondary, tonic will itself change from one musical group to the next, so that tonal coherence will depend upon the association of regions with each other rather than with a central region. This view has particular relevance to works involving key symbolism, a practice common enough in earlier opera, but extended in the later nineteenth century into instrumental works and music dramas where it inevitably threatens tonal integrity. It results in a more flexible view of the relationship between tonality and structure which was eventually to culminate in the purely local hierarchies or 'pantonality'[6] of some twentieth-century harmonic practice.

In relation to this development the intercutting of F major and A minor in the second ballade is the merest chink in the weakening armour of monotonality. Schumann, to whom the work is dedicated, remembered an earlier version which ended in F major, possibly, as Abraham suggests, with a full reprise of the opening material.[7] In a sense this only serves to underline that neither region takes obvious precedence. It is interesting, too, that a Schenkerian reading by H. Krebs interprets the ballade as an interlocking of large scale F major and A minor triads, where each I – V – I progression supports its own Fundamental Line.[8]

It seems reasonable to conclude that the tonal contrast provides just one dimension of a more comprehensive contrast in characterisation between the two themes, perhaps even with a programmatic basis. The deliberate discontinuities, tonal and other, at the first division in the form (46) reinforce this view. We step from one tonal platform to the next as to another world. Yet the new world maintains links with the old. The two regions are related through an emphasis on *both* tonic pitch classes in *each* region, together with a tendency for material in F major to veer towards A minor. The first phrase of the melody (A), emerging imperceptibly from a metrically ambivalent introduction, cadences on $^3_1$, and 3 acts as a pivot to the second phrase (B) where it occupies a full six of the nine accented beats (one less in the first draft K.602[9]). The overall shape of 1–9, repeated 10–17, is as Ex.51(i).

Within this stable structure the harmony is delicately coloured by archaisms, the fifth pedal, parallel fifth progression and unorthodox caden-

Op.38

Ex.51(i)

Ex.51(ii)

Ex.51(iii)

tial part-movement. These, together with the repetitive rhythm, contribute to the music's untroubled simplicity, its gentle, hypnotic charm. The easy flow of the rhythm is deceptive, however, for it disguises subtleties of phrase structure and harmony which enrich the material and even seem to question its innocence. The first paragraph (1–17) is succeeded by brief inflections to III and V, of which the former is heard as unstable, a stage in the progression to the latter. V is given a deceptive stability through a restatement of B (as Alan Rawsthorne indicates the presentation here at 21 obliges us to rethink its earlier phrasing at 5[10]), but a cadential expansion takes us back to I and the return of A. Again there is a deceptive cadence (33), an abrupt shift to III, this time more stable, and a repetition of B in that region. The two inflections to III, together with the emphasis on A as a pitch class, are clearly of significance in relation to the overall tonal scheme, and they are summarised in the final cadence of the opening section by an oscillation of A and F (Ex.51(ii)).

The opening of the stormy A minor theme preserves the relationship by associating the two pitches at the beginning of each right-hand group

(Ex.51(iii)). The rhythmic counterpoint here and in subsequent material (the two-bar unit is grouped as

```
4   +   4   +   4   6           +           6
6   +   6           3   +   3   +   3   +   3)
```

results in an explosive energy which is in strongest possible contrast to the placidity of the first theme. The contrast is sharpened by the strongly directional use of register and the instability of harmony. Sequential treatments predominate in a three-stage structure. The first stage (46–61) is relatively stable, an eight-bar model and sequence. The second (62–67) is disruptive, a more active sequential pattern at the two-bar span creating a characteristic symmetry of minor thirds as in Ex.52(i). There are rhythmic

Op.38

Ex.52(i)

Ex.52(ii)

links with the first theme. The third stage (68–82) briefly stabilises E flat major, thereby undermining any claims of A minor to tonic status at this stage, before sliding through chromatic parallelism to the return of the first theme in F major.

This begins almost like a repeated exposition but breaks off abruptly at the eighth bar[11] to present the second limb (B) in A minor, as at 34. The increasing discontinuity of the progression from I to III within the presentations of the first theme is shown in Ex.52(ii). The break at 87 may again have some hidden programmatic significance, but whatever its origins it serves as a hinge in the overall tonal progression from F major to A minor. As before, the A minor statement of B reverts to F major, but this time a deceptive cadence takes us into an impassioned 'development section' based on the first theme. As Krebs points out,[12] the second major hinge in the tonal structure comes with the alternative dominants presented in 114–131, and from this point we lose sight of our tonal starting point for good. Continuity throughout this critical stage in the structure is skilfully achieved, with the bass line in particular carrying us across the cadences to initiate and contribute to the new canonic motive at 122. This dominates the 'development', sweeping the music towards a brief clarification of B flat major/G.minor, where elements of A and B are combined. Once more there is a deceptive cadence, followed by tenor and bass references to A before the entire process begins again a semitone lower.

It is difficult to be certain about some of the compositional choices in this development section. Its function is clear enough. Having presented as a stark juxtaposition two utterly contrasting materials, Chopin proceeds to mediate between them. The first stage of this mediation is to allow the second theme to subside gradually and imperceptibly on to the first. The second stage (the 'development') is to build the first theme to such a peak of intensity that it can lead naturally into the second. Several features seem to blunt the effect of this second stage, however. One is the repetition of an entire seventeen-bar section, weakening its cumulative character. Another is the recessive effect of a descending interval of sequence for the large-scale repetition (a semitone lower) and also for the material immediately preceding the return of the second theme (first a major, and then a minor, third lower). It is a relatively easy business to pinpoint weaknesses in the music of Chopin's formative years, but it is rare for him to put a foot wrong in the later music. So often do the adverse criticisms of a generation ago raise a wry smile today that we are reluctant to embark too readily on the arrogant path of censuring a great master. Refuge may be sought in autobiography. For this listener at least the progression to 140, however felicitous as to details, always disappoints on the level of structure.

One feature which helps us to accept the appearance of the second theme at 140 is its tonal setting which is not a stable A minor triad as before but a $^6_4$ on A which resolves only after eight bars to a $^5_3$ (the A-F remains invariant to both settings). From this point A minor is secure, confirmed by the reappearance of material from the first theme, drawn briefly into the orbit of the second, and by a new bravura coda theme whose parallelism – both diatonic and chromatic – invariably returns to the tonic. The broader phrasing of this coda strengthens its sense of energy and momentum, with a prolongation through deceptive cadence at 184 strengthening the structural downbeat at 188. Here the second theme returns to drive the music inexorably towards an expected close in A minor, dramatically thwarted by the break in continuity on a French sixth. The whispered reference to the first theme in A minor serves as the resolution, though the effect is less a synthesis than a reminder of the initial contrast, a brief reaffirmation of identity.

Ballade No.3 in A flat major, Op.47

The ballades unfold against a background of the tonal and thematic dualism of the sonata principle, though Chopin's dialogue with sonata-form is free and widely ranging. In particular each work is concerned to bring two initially separate ideas into association. In the G minor the point of contact is 106, where the first theme leads without break or transition into the related second theme as part of a single tension-building paragraph. In the F major/A minor there is a similar mediation of much more sharply contrasting materials, as demonstrated, and a further gesture of accommodation at 156 where the first theme is briefly absorbed into the world of the second.

The Third Ballade goes much further in this direction, welding the two initially separate ideas (A, B) into a fused whole (C) in the 'development section' through an alternation of components from each theme. As Ex.53(i) indicates, the modifications are directed towards opening the closed shape of A to create a single arc encompassing both themes, in effect a new melody. The continuation is ingenious, as the two themes are woven ever more tightly together, building tension in preparation for the tonal and thematic reprise of 213. The $^A_4 + ^B_4$ structure of Ex.53(i) gives way to a $^A_4 + ^B_2$ and then a $^A_3 + ^B_1$. The tonal sequence heightens tension as A appears in an ascending stepwise progression which prefigures the reprise (207).

As so often in Chopin the thematic reprise is a transformation in the character of an apotheosis. More powerful examples were still to come in the Fourth Ballade and the *Polonaise-fantasy*. Here in the Third Ballade the transformation goes beyond the fuller texturing and extends to the voicing of the theme. As a top-voice melody it carries new authority, but sacrifices some of the charm of its discreetly contrapuntal presentation at the opening of the work. The contrapuntal character at the opening becomes clear with the repetition of the antecedent at 5, where the strands are placed in invertible counterpoint, with the melody in the bass. The consequent at 3 also serves as a bass, so that the melody for the entire eight-bar sentence travels from top-voice to bass (1–4) and from bass to top-voice (5–8). Only the second consequent (7–8) has not yet been assigned to the bass. Continuity throughout the remainder of the first theme (to the return of the opening material at 36) is a chain of causal motivic connections, where a

Op.47

Ex.53(i)

Ex.53(ii)

detail in one phrase becomes essential to the next in an accelerating pattern of phrase lengths. The first phrase (9–16) is a varied repetition in the pattern 4 + 4. The rhythm and falling second interval of its second bar ((*a*) in Ex.53(ii)) give rise to the second phrase (*b*), again a 4 + 4 repeated pattern. The rhythm of *its* second bar ((*c*) in Ex.53(ii)) gives rise to the third component (*d*), again a repeated 4 + 4 pattern. And so on, as shown in Ex.53(ii). From this point the repeated patterns are compressed into 2 + 2 and 1 + 1 + 1 + 1 and the process culminates in one of those 4-bar arcs of figuration which are so common in Chopin, sometimes acting as buffers, here as a cadential gesture. The first group ends with an expanded reprise of its opening phrase. The expansion takes the form of a four-bar sequential opening of the first motive 'inserted' between the original two four-bar phrases. It is worth noting that the second consequent now comes in the bass voice, thus completing a process (cf. 7–8 and 48–49).

The second theme takes the iambic rhythm which has dominated the first group and exaggerates its distinctive lilt by harmonising the weak beat rather than the strong. The slightly 'lumpy' effect which this creates is increased by the wide left-hand leaps. To characterise this rhythmic motive as a unifying thread in the work would be to state the obvious at the expense of the central point. In reality the rhythm is so prominent as to create a deliberate monotony, an obsessively repetitive quality which makes implicit demands of the later stages of the structure. The balancing factors are twofold, a change in rhythmic characterisation and a dramatic rise in the intensity curve during the development of the second theme. The former is achieved through a waltz episode whose now familiar *moto perpetuo* semiquaver arcs are supported by a trochaic rhythm, a blessed release from the earlier iambic pattern. The episode is approached obliquely by way of a theme (116) which introduces semiquaver movement but preserves the iambic accompaniment, and which unexpectedly appears as a coda to the work as a whole. It also serves to re-establish A flat major, and this is confirmed by a restatement of the second theme in that region at 146. The tonality to this point has been stable. Throughout the first and second themes, the new semiquaver theme, the waltz episode and the return of the second theme, it encompasses only the tonal relatives within a single key signature. This tonal inertia confirms the effect of that persistent rhythm, reinforcing the need for, and expectancy of, change.

And this brings us to the second factor which redresses the balance of the structure. In general Chopin's mature extended works are end-weighted, very often structural crescendos towards bravura codas. The A flat major Ballade is no exception, but here there is a striking acceleration of change within the formal activity of the work and of growth within its intensity curve. It has already been noted that the reprise of the first theme is in the nature of an apotheosis, the more striking in that the theme has played little part in the argument since its initial presentation. This reprise occupies only the last 29 bars of a work totalling 241 bars, emphasising its cadential role. Moreover the 'exposition' of thematic material, tonally stable and enclosed, takes up a full 156 bars, some way beyond the halfway mark. The development which follows more than compensates for the relative inertia, tonal and rhythmic, of this lengthy exposition, and for its expressive restraint. In its initial presentation the second theme had hinted at a potential for more robust treatment (81 ff), but there is little to prepare us for the powerful expansion of the theme in C sharp minor. It unfolds through three distinct stages, each more impassioned than its predecessor. The first (157–164) is a right-hand statement over a new semiquaver accompaniment, the second (165–173) a left-hand statement with a top-voice dominant pedal and the third (174–183) a 'fully scored' statement which sweeps the music to a magnificent climax. The entire passage (157–183) proves to be the first phase of a two-part development section. The second phase has been discussed. It comprises that fusion of the two principal themes in a tonally unstable context which eventually culminates in the tonal and thematic reprise of 213.

Ballade No.4 in F minor, Op.52.

The Fourth Ballade is one of Chopin's supreme achievements. It is a synthesis of many aspects of his art, ranging from the most popular to the most severe, from the elegance and grace of the waltz to the rigour and logic of strict counterpoint. Above all it is a triumph of architecture, one of the most powerfully goal-directed of all his structures, accommodating within its cumulative sweep elements of sonata-form, rondo and variations. As in the other three ballades there are two principal themes, and the overall scheme is a two-fold progression from one to the other, thus: AAA¹B A²A³B¹. A bipartite interpretation would be strengthened by the reappearance of the introduction X at roughly the halfway stage of the work, thus: XAAA¹B XA²A³B¹. Our picture of the overall design can be filled out a little by including as Y non-recurring material, usually, though not always, of a non-thematic bravura character, and distinguishing a coda as C, thus:

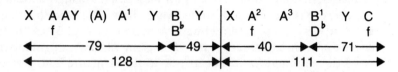

hemes	X	A	A	Y	(A)	A¹	Y	B	Y	X	A²	A³	B¹	Y	C
onal regions		f						B♭			f		D♭		f

The diagram also gives an indication of the proportions of the main sections through bar numbers and of the principal tonal regions. Such a presentation is crude in the extreme, but it may help to provide some initial bearings prior to more detailed analysis.

Of the formal archetypes rondo is the least prominent, but it is suggested as a remote background by the recurrence of A in the tonic key. Sonata-form is also a relevant background, with the second subject modified tonally in the reprise and a middle section creating tonal instability. Variations are suggested by the successive treatments of A. The ballade draws upon all three, but in the end subscribes wholly to none, forging its unique structure in response to the demands of its material.

We may begin with the first theme and its later variations. There are some similarities to the first theme of the G minor Ballade. In both cases an unpromising waltz accompaniment and a succession of short-breathed phrases somehow cohere into an indivisible whole, perfectly shaped and balanced. The secret lies partly in the unobtrusive asymmetries of the phrase structure and partly in an harmonic organisation which describes a single curve of departure and return from 8 to 23, maintaining its flow independently of thematic parallelism. In the three statements of the opening phrase between 8 and 23 the three antecedents are always enclosed harmonically and the three consequents always progressive, though harmonic movement is naturally on the foreground structural level. On its first presentation the consequent progresses to the relative major, enabling Chopin to restate the idea in that region, an association so common in his music as to constitute an element of style. This time the consequent progresses from A flat major to a subdominant harmony of B flat minor. In this region the melody can return at its original pitch (18) but supported by an F *major* (rather than minor) harmony, now functioning as a local dominant rather than a tonic. The consequent on this occasion returns us to the tonic and a very slightly altered restatement of the entire sequence. Ex.54(i) demonstrates this non-congruence of thematic and harmonic structures in the opening paragraph, where a thematic reprise at the original pitch is taken in as part of a broader harmonic progression. The effect of this reprise at 18 is the more striking for its dislocation of phrase structure, compressing the lengths by half a bar in order to compensate for the half-bar extension at 12.

In none of Chopin's ballades is the sense of narrative flow so natural, the progression towards a final apotheosis so seemingly inevitable, as in the fourth. This demands not only a careful pacing of the argument, a strategic 'placing' of the main peaks of the intensity curve, but also a capacity to 'mark time', to wait for effects. Following the double exposition of A there is a passage of some twenty bars – Y (A) in the diagram – before the important tension-building restatement of A at 58 (A^1 in the diagram). This intervening passage is based on elements of A, might indeed be viewed as a development of it, but its role in the structure is to create a necessary diversion, functionally as well as literally to separate the statements of A. It is approached by way of the left-hand figure from 12 which linked the first two phrases of A, its five-quaver shape clearly related to the antecedent of the theme itself. Significantly Chopin omits the figure in the restatement of A (cf. 12 and 26–27), so that the new opening of 36–7 has rather more impact. Again it is worth comparing the relevant passages in the two statements of A to note the tonal and metrical alterations (Ex.54(ii)). Tonally the new section inflates an earlier tendency to exploit the neighbour note to 5 in the sub-dominant region. The overall motion from 36 to the return of A at 58 is a neighbour note prolongation and might be described as in Ex.54(iii). The passage falls into two sections, of which the first (38–46) maintains only a remote contact with the main theme, its left-hand octaves a transformation of 12 and 36–37 and its right-hand repeated notes tenuously linked to the introduction and the consequent of A. The second section (46–57), on the other hand, is an explicit development of A, working its consequent and insinuating for the first time elements of canonic writing which will assume greater importance at a later stage.

Until this point (57) the temperature of the work has remained cool. The variation of A which follows (A^1) achieves the first major growth of intensity, building through its three statements to a climactic point at 72 ff. Much of this growth is activated by the countermelody in constant semiquaver movement which is the principal feature of this variation. Often it is thickened into thirds and sixths and its interplay with the main theme is skilfully achieved. In preserving the continuity of both lines over the waltz accompaniment Chopin calls upon the left hand to make occasional contri-

Op.52

Ex.54(i)

Ex.54(ii)

Ex.54(iii)

butions to the semiquaver movement until by the third statement, it abandons the waltz patterns completely, driving the music relentlessly through
powerful octaves to the 'interrupted cadence' at 72. As in the first two
unvaried statements of A, this first variation arrives at a sub-dominant
region (B flat minor), established through its dominant. The non-thematic

arc of figuration (72–80) characteristically defers a tonic resolution, however, absorbing the head of tension built up by A^1 and gradually dissipating that tension in preparation for the 'second subject' at 80. Earlier progressions to B flat minor are here validated by the B flat major setting for the new theme.

The next complete statement of A (A^2) is at the beginning of the reprise (136). The approach to this statement will be discussed shortly, but it will be sufficient here to point out that it follows a cadenza elaborating a dominant seventh in D minor and that the statement begins in that region. The second half of the theme, as from 146, proceeds in the unvaried manner of its initial presentation and in the same tonal region. The first half is an ingenious transformation, fulfilling the canonic aspirations of earlier material. Ex.55

Ex.55

shows how the initial progression from I to III has been reinterpreted canonically. Chopin simply, but ingeniously, expands the presentation by preceding A^2 as in Ex.55 with a D minor statement, thus preserving the minor third sequence, D – F – A flat. The canonic element is then unobtrusively absorbed into the flow of the original material.

In the second statement of A (23–36) there is a restrained melodic ornamentation of the second bar of the antecedent on each of the three presentations, and this returns at the end of A^2 to form a cue for the exquisite *fioritura* variation which follows (A^3). The synthesising character of the ballade is epitomised in this transformation, as we move from strict counterpoint into the world of the nocturne, with wide bass arpeggiation supporting rhythmically supple arcs of ornamental melody. It is the moment at which the entire work seems to flower, the *fioriture* reaching ever higher in ever more daring transformations of the original. The theme and its variations are shown on Ex.55.

Returning to our diagram of the form we may now note the parallel between these later variations and the 'exposition' section of the work. After the canonic opening A^2 proceeds as A, so that $A^2 - A^3$ follows a similar sequence to $A - A^1$, a 'neutral' statement followed by a tension-building variation. The parallel is strengthened by the approaches to both sections. Characteristically Chopin approaches the main theme obliquely, beginning the work on a dominant rather than a tonic harmony. The opening melody (X), enriched by discreet wisps of counterpoint, is simple but haunting, emerging imperceptibly from the opening repeated octaves and arriving at the main theme by means of a simple triadic descent (Ex.56(i)). Its relationship to A is through the four repeated notes, and it is

Op.52

Ex.56(i)

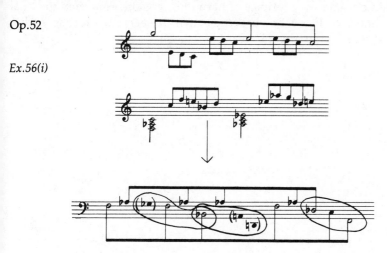

this relationship which Chopin exploits to effect an ingenious approach to the reprise.

The middle section, or 'development' in sonata terms, presents three structures, of which the first two offer a necessary relief from the main thematic materials and from their relatively stable tonal settings, relying largely on sequential treatments of figurative patterns. The second leans increasingly to the A flat major which is established by the third structure. This also re-admits elements of A in a contrapuntal texture which super-imposes modifications of antecedent and consequent, preparing us for the canonic intricacies to come in A^2. The consequent is modified in the direction of the introduction X, so that when the repeated note figure appears it seems to belong to both A and X. With the arrival of a full statement of X in the dominant of D minor Chopin makes the unexpected appear inevitable.

The second theme (B) in B flat major has that easy trochaic flow which distinguished the first theme of the Second Ballade and the second theme of the third. So essential does its first phrase appear that it comes as something of a surprise to note that it never recurs in the work. Rather it is the response (from 84) which is recapitulated after A³, this time in D flat major. The relationship of these tonal regions to the F minor/A flat major of the first theme is set out in Ex.56(ii). The reprise of B is a glorious moment in the work, transforming the original material and building with ever more impassioned fervour towards the structural downbeat of 191. At this point thematic identity dissolves into figuration, generating one of the most powerful passages in all Chopin and reaching a shattering climax with the dominant harmony of 202. A magical sequence of *pianissimo* chords prolongs the dominant. It is a remarkable moment, a brief illusion of repose as we remain poised on a precipice of harmonic tension. And then the final pages, the finest of those bravura codas which seem to exorcise earlier conflicts and tensions in a white heat of virtuosity.

12

Fantasies

Chopin wrote four works incorporating the title 'Fantasy'. There seems little significance attaching to the choice of the term for either the youthful *Fantasy on Polish Themes* Op.13 (really a pot-pourri) or the *Fantasy-impromptu* Op.66, where the description 'Fantasy' was in all probability not Chopin's at all. But in the two later works, the Fantasy in F minor Op.49 and the *Polonaise-fantasy* Op.61, he comes closer to some of the more central associations of an admittedly fairly loosely applied genre title. In the late eighteenth and early nineteenth centuries at least, the term 'Fantasy' was frequently used for works which had something of the character of a composed-out improvisation. This is not, of course, to suggest that there need be anything casual or disorganised in the process of composition. It is rather that the work will often encompass a wider range of contrasting materials than would be usual within the traditional formal archetypes and that, as in an improvisation, several of these materials may never recur. Their characterisation, moreover, frequently owes something to improvisation. 'Preluding' material, either of an arpeggiated or recitative type, is common and the themes themselves often borrow their phraseology from the main treasure troves of the improviser, folksong and popular opera. The two later Chopin fantasies are characteristic in these respects and in some ways they represent the closest meeting-point between Chopin the composer and Chopin the improviser. They are of course separated by several years, years of considerable stylistic change in his music, and their association here should not be taken as having too special a significance as to genre. The linking factor is the influence of improvisation, loosening and stretching the forms respectively of the sonata and the dance piece.

Fantasy in F minor Op.49

The opening material never returns and might be thought of as an introduction or prologue to the main body of the work. Its characterisation as a slow march with dotted rhythm is clearly related to the marches and chorale-like choruses of French opera of the 1830s and 1840s, in particular Meyerbeer, and this in turn is a direct reflection of the popularity of such gestures in

the improvisations of the day. Yet if the character of the material recalls
an improvisation, its presentation is paradoxically a model of Classical
construction. Within the opening four-bar phrase antecedent and consequent stand in time-honoured relation to each other, the modular discontinuity of the former (four units in sequence) answered by the self-contained
whole of the latter, thus:

Other dimensions point up the contrast, again in familiar vein – the unison
texture followed by an harmonised response, the bass register answered
by the treble. The opening of Mozart's 'Jupiter' symphony is a convenient
and easily recalled reference point (see also Ex.2). It need hardly be added
that there is continuity underlying this surface contrast, provided above all
by rhythm and harmony.

Important motivic premises are also established in these opening bars,
both in the falling fourths and in the four descending scalar steps which
they outline (Ex.57(i)). A neat elision introduces a varied restatement, and
this establishes at the outset an important *tonal* premise in its colouring of
the F minor tonality by A flat major. Chopin's association of tonal relatives
within a key signature has already been noted on numerous occasions in
this study, and it is given its clearest expression in Op.49, not only through
the overall tonal progression from F minor to A flat major, but in the detail

Op.49

Ex.57(i)

Ex.57(ii)

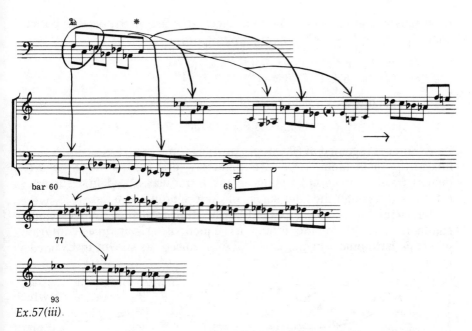

Ex.57(iii).

of the harmony. Here in the second phrase the momentary progression to A flat is the pretext for a felicitous two-bar phrase extension returning us to F minor and incorporating contrapuntal and rhythmic subtleties as in Ex.57(ii).

The entire 4 + 6 sentence is then repeated with an harmonic deviation which arises naturally out of a tendency within the opening two-bar phrase. Rather than accommodate the falling steps tonally, as in 2, 6 and 12, Chopin preserves the sequence to arrive on C flat at 16, affording a brief glimpse of E major harmony before the cadence in F major. It is the first of several moments in the work where the material threatens to veer sharpwards, perhaps foreshadowing the central B major episode of 199. Operatic evocations are even stronger in the second part of the introductory march. Tonally it confirms the tonic major, prolonging V–I progressions by means of descending scalar steps, and its phrase structure is regular, a repeated eight-bar sentence with a six-bar cadential extension.

The new material of 43 suggests further associations with improvisation, taking a 'preluding' arpeggiated figure through changing harmonic contexts. The pause bars reinforce the association, especially in conjunction with a punctuation figure, the distinctive octaves passage of 52–3 which acts as a point of orientation throughout the work. Again the construction of the passage is rigorous, however, emphasising that influences from improvisation do not penetrate beyond the character of the materials and the overall conception into its detailed working. As Lew Mazel has demonstrated, the harmonic structure of this 'prelude' not only confirms the third-related tendencies of the introduction, but presents a microcosm of the tonal scheme yet to come.[1] The two stages, divided by the octaves punctuation figure, outline the following scheme, from 43 to 60:

F   A flat   C   E flat   (G   E flat)
E flat   G flat   B flat   D flat   (F   D flat)   F

Elision facilitates a complete cycle of thirds as

F   A flat   C   E flat   G flat   B flat   D flat   F

As F minor is regained at 60 Chopin devotes some care to effecting a skilful link to the main theme, or as we might say 'first subject' at 68. Ex.57(iii) demonstrates motivic links between the introduction and first subject as established through the later stages of the preluding material.[2]

The theme itself is underpinned by the third-related harmonies already summarised in the prelude, though its sequential basis, in broad conformity with this harmonic scheme, is skilfully disguised, as shown in Ex.58. The

Op.49

Ex.58

broader tonal movement of the theme inflates these progressions in that its second contrasting limb appears at 77 in an A flat major context. Even more than the introduction, then, the first theme associates F minor and A flat major as a sort of composite tonic. Like all the other thematic elements presented so far this second limb of the first subject is immediately repeated. Its motivic links with earlier material are clearly established through the diatonic descent of four scalar steps, balancing the chromatic ascent of its opening phrase.

A sequential linking passage, somewhat in the character of an informal inversion of the preluding material, takes us to the 'second subject'. The tonal setting of C minor continues the overall third-related progression and its immediate repetition in E flat major confirms the tendency. First and second themes can now be characterised tonally as f – A flat and c – E flat respectively. Chopin strengthens E flat major by deviating from it through an eight-bar sequential working of the two-bar 'reactive' phrase (95–97), so that it can return with renewed stability at 109. The completion of the 'exposition' after this point is in two stages, both tonally stable, though affirming E flat major in different ways. The first stage is rhetorical, sacrificing thematic interest in favour of gestures which articulate simple harmonic assertions of E flat, with another sharpwards deviation strengthening the cadence at 126-7. The second stage is a new codetta theme, a march-like melody again characterised by four descending steps and underpinned by the clearest of diatonic harmonies.

Some of the terminology used here will already have suggested sonata-form models and there is a sense in which both these E flat major sections do conform to archetypes of the later stages of a sonata exposition. Non-thematic, tonality-affirming material and codetta themes were both well-tried methods of clinching the tonal destination of the exposition. Yet the analogy can be as misleading as it can be helpful. Undoubtedly Chopin composed the fantasy against a background of traditional formal archetypes, in particular sonata-form. But the music's dialogue with that background is extremely free, rather as it might be in improvisation. We need only consider the proportions of the 'exposition' from the appearance of the first subject. First and second subjects together occupy no more than 33 bars, while the remainder of the exposition takes a full 42 bars. Mazel sees it as an almost symmetrical 33 + 8 + 34, giving privilege to the regained E flat major at 109 and interpreting the eight-bar sequential passage as a central pivot.[3] Moreover the weight and importance of the opening march and prelude (67 bars) are very much greater than anything we might reasonably expect of an 'introduction' to a sonata-form exposition of 75 bars. This is confirmed by the tonal structure. The lengthy passage of stable E flat major material would clearly be hopelessly unbalanced in relation to the tonal settings of the first and second subjects, but it does make sense if we include in the reckoning the long introductory material in F minor. Sonata processes and patterns are best thought of loosely, then, providing a kind of framework which binds together a range of contrasting characterisations of a kind common in improvisation – slow march, prelude or recitative, sonata, and later chorale.

Returning to the tonal scheme, we may note that the reprise of the first subject (235), 'announced' by the last appearance of the octaves punctuation figure, is in the sub-dominant, enabling Chopin (like many before him) to bring the second subject into the tonic region while preserving the tonal relationships of the exposition. The scheme is as follows:

Exposition	Reprise
f - A♭ c - E♭	b♭ - D♭ f - A♭

In other respects the sequence of events in the reprise continues exactly as in the exposition, and the codetta theme culminates in the same dramatic gesture. A closure on the tonic is unexpectedly thwarted by an harmonic interruption, as in Ex.59. Ignoring for the moment the spelling of the chromatic chords (x) in both exposition and reprise it is clear that they have the potential to function *within* the given tonal context as German sixths. On its second appearance the chord does indeed behave in this way,

Op.49

Ex.59

resolving, albeit elliptically, on to the tonic of A flat major, so that its disruptive tendencies are in a sense accommodated.

At the beginning of the middle section, on the other hand, the chord is modulatory, and it introduces an area of tonal instability in association with the preluding material. Chopin teases the ear, suggesting E major and then D flat major and 'punning' enharmonically with a three-note motive which had played only a minor role on its first appearance in the 'prelude' at 50. D flat seems assured when the octaves punctuation figure appears on A flat, but the entire harmonic focus shifts down to introduce a reference to the first subject in a C minor region. Thematically this is a complete statement, so much so that Mazel refers to elements of sonata-rondo, and it continues to follow the earlier sequence right through the eight-bar 'pivot' to the point at which we expect the second subject. Harmonically, however, there are subtle differences. The third ascent is from C minor to E flat *minor* rather than major (158) and the melodic restatement of the opening phrase is a third higher than in the exposition, taking us to *its* relative major G flat for the second part of the theme (164). In effect this extends the thirds cycle one stage further to G flat, thus: f – A flat – c – E flat – G flat.

To this point the middle section has involved little of the working-out of material which we might associate with a sonata-form development section. Its concerns have been tonal, presenting the prelude and first subject more or less in their original form but in a tonal context which overlaps with and then extends beyond the original third-related regions. The sequence of events as in the exposition is altered at 180 when the second subject is replaced by a further working of the prelude, separating the quaver figure from its related motive. Again the tonal settings overlap, thus:

f – A flat – c – E flat
c – e flat – G flat
e flat – G flat – B

and the passage culminates in a hushed reference to the octaves punctuation figure on G flat, an exquisite moment which clearly augurs something new. The G flat major now functions as a dominant as the octaves figure announces a quite new and magical chorale-like episode in B major.

There are several ways of interpreting this new tonal colour. Despite several premonitions it represents the first moment in the work where a sharp region is stabilised, lending special beauty and distance to this central episode, especially as it remains outside the third-related sequence which has governed the tonal direction of the fantasy to this point. At the same time it is possible to see the B major clarification as the completion of a more arcane process within the third-related sequence. The exposition outlines the related pairs f – A flat and c – E flat. The middle section then extends each pair by a further minor third, thus:

Viewed in a longer span the B major episode can be further understood as an enharmonic parenthesis. The tonal goal here is the B flat minor of the reprise, approached by way of a German sixth harmony on G flat. This relates back across the B major episode to the G flat major of 188–198, so that the episode is taken in as part of an inner voice motion, as in Ex.60.

Op.49

Ex.60

The entire process is neatly 'framed' by the octaves punctuation figure on G flat. However we hear the B major episode, we may now note the special significance of the sub-dominant reprise. Apart from allowing Chopin to preserve the tonal relationships of the exposition, it enables him to complete the cycle of thirds, thus:

$$f - A^b - c - E^b - G^b - (B) - b^b - D^b - f - A^b$$

The harmonic scheme outlined in the prelude has now been inflated to a level of tonal significance.

The B major episode clearly plays a pivotal role in the structure of the fantasy. Motivic links have been demonstrated,[4] but its principal function is contrast. It forms a still centre to the work, embedded in the preluding

material which flanks it on both sides. There is contrast of theme, tonality
and texture (chorale-like chordal movement), but most striking of all is the
contrast of metre. In all these respects the episode is set apart so that it
functions almost like a brief 'slow movement', not unlike the 'slow movement' in Liszt's later B minor sonata. Moreover its role as a central point
of stasis and stability is strengthened by a regular phrase structure of three
eight-bar sentences forming a ternary design, the chromatic instability of
the central sentence perfectly offset by the diatonic stability of the outer
flanks. The apparent centricity of the episode calls for some comment, as
it is not in fact literally at the centre of the work. The proportions are as
follows:

Intro	Prelude	Exposition	Middle section 'Slow movt'			Reprise	Coda
42	25	75	56	+ 24	+ 12	75	23

Intro + Prelude + Exposition = 198 ◄──► Middle section + Reprise = 134

Total = 332

The Golden Section comes then at the beginning of the second phrase of
the B major 'slow movement'. I have no desire to make much of this point.
Had such things been a part of Chopin's conscious planning it is more
likely that it would have coincided with the beginning of the entire episode
at 199. Yet it does draw our attention to the ambivalence surrounding
notions of symmetry and arch structures in music. As music unfolds
through time our perception of the proportions of a work is constantly
changing, the more so as the diverse characters of the material influence
that perception. It is dangerous to generalise too much about these matters,
but it does seem that an impression of symmetry and balance in music is
less likely to result from a division at the precise halfway mark of a structure
than at some way beyond the halfway mark as with this B major episode.
The strength of the Golden Section rests in its formalisation of this tendency.

There is one final reference to the melody of the 'slow movement'. The
preluding material of the coda resolves on to a cadential A flat major by
way of a brief reference to the central episode. It is less a reprise than a
reminiscence in the nature of an interruption, composing out a straightfor-
ward $\frac{6}{4} - \frac{5}{3}$ progression through a recitative-like extension of the first phrase
of the melody. The memory is very soon blown away by the bravura
affirmation of A flat major in the closing bars of the work.

Polonaise-fantasy in A flat major, Op.61

Even more than the F minor Fantasy this resembles a stylised improvisation.
In the Op.49 Fantasy, as in the ballades, we are permitted an analytical
inroad to the music through Chopin's dialogue between an unfolding

'narrative' and formal archetypes which, however far in the background, dictate many of the basic structural premises. The *Polonaise-fantasy* is much further removed from such archetypes than any other extended work by Chopin. Like an inspired improvisation, it embraces a wide range of characters – slow introduction, dance elements, sonata-like development, nocturne-like ornamental melody, 'slow movement' – and all within a design of apparent profligacy. Some of the material which assumes a clear thematic identity never recurs, and the sequence of events is largely unpredictable, scarcely even paying lip service to inherited conventions. Yet for all its broad rhapsodic sweep the structure of the work is entirely satisfying and cohesive, even if frustratingly resistant to explication.

Thematic recall is clearly a potent resource of form-building in music, and Chopin avails himself of it in the *Polonaise-fantasy*, as in all his extended works. Its role can be overstated, however, and often *is* in traditional formal analysis, so that a work whose thematic patterning is unconventional and involves non-recurring material may be susceptible to adverse criticism. Several issues need to be considered. We might note for one thing that in the Classical forms a good deal of non-recurring material is deemed acceptable when it functions in other than thematic terms, as tonality-defining passage work, for instance. In the *Polonaise-fantasy* too there are non-recurring episodes, such as Y (66–91), where thematic identity is subsidiary to other functions. Another consideration is the unity of substance which can underlie diverse thematic surfaces. Leaving aside questions of unconscious process, there is plenty of musical evidence that Chopin was increasingly preoccupied with thematic unity in his late extended works, and the *Polonaise-fantasy* is no exception. Paul Hamburger has demonstrated motivic links between all the principal thematic elements of the work.[5] Exact motivic and intervallic correspondence need not be the only basis for an association of thematic shapes, of course. Similarities between lyrical passages based on contour, texture and rhythm are no less telling. The non-recurring melody at 116 can be related in these respects to the later theme at 182 and 216; indeed the relationship is so close that they may be labelled B^1 and B^2. Perhaps most important of all is the relative weighting of tonality and thematicism in the definition of structure. The fecundity of melodic invention in Op.61 is balanced by a tonal structure which, for all the complexity of its harmonic detail, provides a solid foundation to the musical architecture. The outer sections of the work are securely in A flat major and fifth-related regions.

This is not to deny that there are difficulties in grasping the 'shape' of the *Polonaise-fantasy*, but merely to argue that the difficulties will be exacerbated if we rely on thematic patterning as the main criterion of structure. It would seem that Chopin was setting out to recreate something of the spontaneity and rhapsodic flow of an improvisation in this work, and even more than usual he cultivates the unexpected, at least where the sequence of ideas is concerned. An obvious starting-point, though an approach largely ignored in the literature, is to consider the changing role played by dance characteristics. Unlike the polonaises, even the most ambitious of them, Op.61 uses its dance ingredients sparingly. Three rhythmic elements associated with the polonaise gradually infiltrate the slow introduction X:

a ♩. 𝅘𝅥𝅯𝅘𝅥𝅯𝅘𝅥𝅯 𝅘𝅥. 𝅘𝅥𝅯 (4); *b* 𝅘𝅥. 𝅘𝅥𝅯 𝅘𝅥. 𝅘𝅥𝅯 𝅘𝅥. 𝅘𝅥𝅯 (13); *c* 𝄾 𝅘𝅥𝅯𝅘𝅥𝅯 𝅘𝅥𝅯𝅘𝅥𝅯𝅘𝅥𝅯 (22).

Of these *c* is clearly the most characteristic and it remains a background presence as the main theme (A) unfolds at 24. The episode at 66 (Y) is concerned less with new thematic presentation than with the crystallisation of such dance elements. Motive *c* is joined by two other polonaise figures:

d — 𝅘𝅥𝅯𝅘𝅥𝅯𝅘𝅥𝅯 | 𝅘𝅥𝅮

and the closing gesture

e 𝅘𝅥𝅯𝅘𝅥𝅯𝅘𝅥𝅯 𝅘𝅥 𝅘𝅥𝅮 ,

All three (*c* – *e*) can be found in abundance in Chopin's earlier polonaises.

There is, then, a gradually ascending curve of prominence culminating in Y (66–91), which represents the most clearly defined exposition of the dance basis of the work. From this point polonaise elements recede to the background. Even the ensuing reference to the main theme (92ff) loses its accompaniment motive *c*, paving the way for a middle section whose only (and tenuous) connection with the polonaise lies in the retention of *d* as a component of B^1 (116) and B^2 (182). The re-emergence of dance elements at 226 signals a tonal and thematic reprise, with the extended anacrusis (226–241) bringing with it motives *b* and *c*. The reprise of the 'slow movement' at 254 is then accompanied by motive *b*. Dance elements therefore form one basis for a tripartite division, and this is supported by the work's tonal structure. Within the episodic middle section several ideas are presented in a complex sequence, but the clearest landmark, tonally and thematically, is the 'slow movement' (C) in B major, whose role as a still centre to the work inevitably invites comparison with the episode in the same key in the F minor Fantasy.

Nor is this the only link between the two works. A comparison of the interval structure of the two introductions makes the point clearly (Ex.61). The introduction to the *Polonaise-fantasy* is one of Chopin's most beautiful and arresting openings, its discontinuous gestures clearly of an improvisatory, preluding character. Only gradually does it assume a continuity to the main theme. Harmonically the introduction sets the adventurous tone for the work as a whole, beginning, as so often in Chopin, outside the A

Ex.61

flat major tonic and preserving a delicate balance between tonal tendencies and equidistance. The melodic sequence is not paralleled by an exact harmonic sequence, and modifications tend to suggest a *very* remote tonic-dominant progression in A flat minor for 1–5 (Ex.61). While this may be the end-product, it was not an important consideration in the compositional process. Chopin felt his way to these harmonies in a more intuitive way. In the sketches for the work (K. 815 and 816) the opening has three flats in the key signature and is designated F minor (Ex.62).[6] Chopin begins a major third higher with a C minor chord and continues in sequence until 6, where there is an alignment with the final version. The 'echo' at 7 originally began a tone lower, moreover, leading directly from 6 as in the final form. In both cases the changes were made to gain a smoother link and greater continuity, rather than for reasons of tonal integrity. We have the first of several indications here of a local (and at times not so local) flexibility as to tonal and harmonic setting. As finally constituted, the opening motive creates certain harmonic expectations based on symmetry, expectations which are mildly thwarted. The phrase as a whole then creates a further expectation of its 'echo' in the dominant minor, and this in turn is thwarted by the cadential extension of 10–22. The means of doing so are highly characteristic, with the flattened sub-mediant (C flat) refusing to function as expected within E flat minor and generating instead an enharmonic parenthesis of E major. The part-movement at this point (10–22) is of a sophistication only found in Chopin's later music and it gradually takes on the character of a canonic pre-echo of the main theme. We can watch this part-movement take shape in the sketch, which is less 'neutral', and allows dance elements more prominence.

The theme itself represents the first clarification of A flat major, though it is characteristic of a polonaise theme in its prolonged melodic/harmonic 'upbeat' – three bars of $\frac{2}{4}$ followed by a single bar of $\frac{1}{4}$. Even then the closure is fleeting, for the harmony immediately opens to permit a sequential repetition of the four bar phrase. The subsequent course of this theme reveals Chopin at his finest as a melodist, achieving a quality and maturity

Op.61

Ex.62

which gives telling measure of the distance travelled from those early salon and concert pieces of the Warsaw years. The entire theme occupies 42 bars and it will be worth examining its construction in detail. The first eight-bar sentence (A^2), which suggests a stanzaic continuation through its sequential structure (4 + 4), proves rather the necessary anchor for breath-taking flights of asymmetry (A^2 and A^3), thus:

$$
\begin{array}{cccc}
A^1 & A^2 & A^1 & A^3 \\
4 + 4 & 12 & 4 + 4\ (+4) & 10
\end{array}
$$

Within A^2 and A^3 the sense of a spontaneously unfolding, strongly impassioned line is marked, but it is held in check through a discreet motivic parallelism. The motives grow naturally from preceding material, but their relation to metre and harmony is such that similar events are heard in different ways, and the entire paragraph assumes a calculated ambiguity, rich and complex, powerfully affecting.[7]

Ex.63 presents the melodic line of A^2 and attempts to pinpoint some of the correspondences and implications which enliven it. The rhythmic flexibility might be noted, and especially the breaks in continuity within a single melodic shape (34–35), imparting a sense of urgency and mounting

Ex.63

intensity, and encouraging us to hear pitch groupings which do not conform to the underlying rhythmic schema. The published version, incidentally, moderates intensity in the interests of continuity, as the earlier sketch includes a further quaver rest at the beginning of 37, suppresses 39 (i.e. runs from 38 to a form of 40), retains the original rhythmic shape of the motive at 40–41 and approaches the cadence at 44 by way of a syncopated melodic descent.[8] The texture is enriched throughout the passage by a cogent interaction of other voices with the melody, generating a contrapuntal interest which includes the permeation of motives from the melody into the 'accompaniment'. The second statement of A[1] is tension-building, exploding into A[3], whose recessive character is emphasised by a descending bass motion through the octave. The sweep of the harmonies here, and throughout the entire opening melody, is as bold as anything in Chopin, both in its elaboration of an underlying stasis by complex chromatics (52–55) and in its enharmonic adventures in the course of connecting structural harmonies (56–65). Through the entire 42 bars closure is avoided, so that the first clear affirmation of the tonic triad is the structural downbeat at 66, introducing the second theme Y.

As already noted, this has a primary function of establishing clearly the dance characteristics of the work, and its harmonic structure is typical of the polonaise in its series of cadence figures which are not actually cadences. Even the melodic pattern at 70 is a cadential *cliché* of the polonaise, though its placing here a bar *before* the cadence is typical of Chopin's desire to undermine the familiar while in the process of establishing it. The section unfolds over static harmonic platforms in an irregular phrase structure as follows:

A flat	C	E	F sharp	G sharp
6	8	4	2	2

The detailed formulation of its bass pattern was originally consistent with the opening two bars,[9] but Chopin probably felt that the constant repetitions of the ascending scale figure were excessive and later introduced the descending figure as at 68–69 ff. In other respects the sketch for this section remains faithful in general outline to the final version, though the punctuation figure at 92 (repeated 97), reintroducing the main theme in E flat major, was an afterthought.

The dance episode acts in a sense as an interruption of the course of the main theme which resumes at 92. Its setting is now quite different, however, sacrificing polonaise features in favour of a more lyrical manner with occasional melodic elaborations and a flowing triplet accompaniment. The first limb of the melody is treated sequentially, but far from generating tension, the descending sequence (three statements with the third emerging from the left-hand figuration) keeps the temperature low until 105. There follow three bars in which the unit of sequence is compressed and there is

Op.61

Ex.64

a contrapuntal intensification of a kind familiar in Chopin's late style. Until
this point the sketch is mainly instructive as to changes in local detail,
though the harmonic changes in the introduction clearly raise larger issues.
It becomes more revealing at 105, whence Chopin clearly had the greatest
difficulty in proceeding. There are several attempts at a link which would
create intensification and prepare a downbeat at 108 (Ex.64). It seems probable from the sketch that he then proposed to introduce the new melody
B¹ (116ff in the final form) at this point, though it is difficult to draw firm
conclusions about the sequence of sketching. We can at least be certain
from the endings of the several versions of the link that it was *not* at this
stage intended for its final destination. In any event a sketch for B¹ (strictly
speaking non-recurring material) follows immediately.

   From the start Chopin conceived B¹ as a nocturne-like melody, gracefully
elaborated with *fioriture*. But his first draft differs in several respects from
the final version. It begins differently and includes an elaborate *fioritura* in
its second bar, for example. Most important of all, the entire passage is
sketched a semitone higher, a decision which will be discussed later. The
progression to the 'slow movement' is not completed in this sketch of B¹.
The music appears to be seeking a closure at 135, and the sketch goes as

far as the deceptive cadence at that point (still a semitone higher). It is interesting that in the final version the effect of interruption here reaches beyond harmony into texture. The figurative pattern of 132–133 is interrupted by two bars of melody and accompaniment texture, before resuming at 136. The role of such interruptions will also be discussed later.

First, however, we must return to the link at 105. Chopin remained dissatisfied with this link, whether or not it was intended for the new theme. If it was so, he may have felt that the three bars of 105–107, as in the first draft, were insufficient to prepare the structural downbeat of 116, that there was a need for a more sustained increase in intensity before the theme. Or there may have been some concern for larger proportions, given that the first presentation of A occupied a full 42 bars. In any event he 'inserts' a further eight-bar passage before the new theme (108–115), again working A sequentially, but now in a quite different layout, and in a tension-building ascending sequence. Before arriving at a final approach to this new material, Chopin drafts another two versions of the link at 105–107 (Ex.65). His sketch then continues as in the final form as far as 113, where the linking passage into B¹ causes difficulties. Chopin's first thought was

Op.61

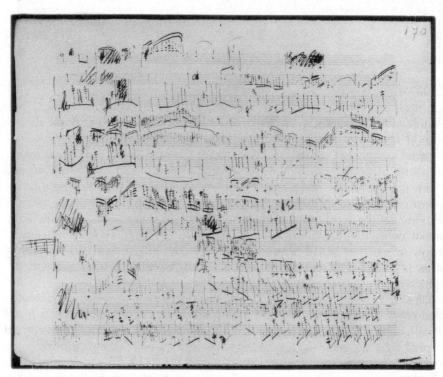

Ex.65

Op.61

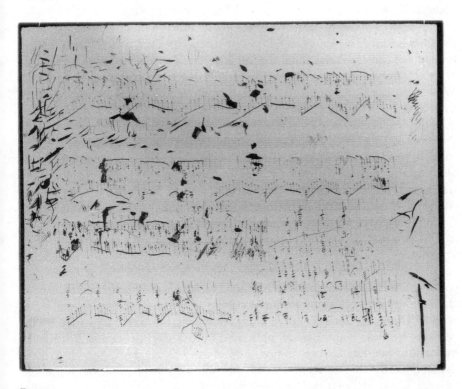

Ex.66

to intensify the triplet movement after 113 and he composed a further five bars (Ex.65) which were rejected in favour of the final version of 114–115, leading into B[1] at 116.

All this suggests that Chopin's greatest difficulty lay not in drafting the main themes of the work, but in arriving at a satisfactory arrangement for them and, above all, in constructing convincing bridges to connect them. Having conceived the lyrical paragraphs without difficulty, he would then make constant play upon the junction points, adjusting them in several ways to suit particular continuations and particular sequences of events. This impression is reinforced by the sketch for the 'slow movement' (C) which comes at 152 in the final form.

The sketch for C (see Ex.66) begins after the introductory chords (148–151) and continues more-or-less as in the final sequence, apart from changes of detail, as far as 181. Chopin was clear from the start that this point should represent a new stage in the structure, even to the extent of using a double bar in the sketch. It seems, however, that he was not yet clear about what would follow, and there are further difficulties with the links, both here and at the beginning and end of the 'slow movement'. There are several drafts of 181 itself, and there is an alternative, later rejected, ending to the section, as at 213.

The most remarkable feature of the slow movement sketch, however, is its tonal setting, which is not B major as in the final form, but C major. Indeed we can trace the tonal discrepancy back to 128 in the sketch. Once more this raises questions as to the long-range tonal planning of Chopin's music. No hard and fast rules can be drawn up. The structure of a work such as the Op.49 Fantasy strongly suggests a rigid pre-compositional determination of tonal outlines, while here in Op.61 Chopin was happy to alter the tonal setting for an important and lengthy section. His reasons for doing so were probably two-fold. In the first place the overall tonal scheme of the work to this point is on the flat side of the tonal spectrum, moving stepwards around the cycle of fifths, thus: A flat – E flat – B flat. The reprise confirms A flat, and the immediately preceding clarification is of F minor. Chopin may have felt that his original intention to place the slow movement in C major just two further steps around the cycle left the tonal structure unbalanced and decided therefore to distance the section further as a 'sharp' counterpole to the rest of the work, rather as in the F minor fantasy. A contributing factor may have been the association of B major with music of stability and quiet beauty, already evidenced in Op.49 and in several other works. There are indeed other ways in which the tonal structure of the work as a whole is greatly strengthened by the shift of section B^1 to B flat major and section C to B major, and they will be discussed in a more detailed study of the work by the present author. It is enough for the present to remark that it is an intriguing reflection on creative process that such a happy outcome can result when a passage of some 98 bars, no less than a third of the piece and comprising several formally differentiated sections, has been lifted bodily down a semitone.

The junction at 181 leads in the end to a new theme B^2, sketched on a separate page and *still* a semitone higher. Again it is the transitional passage (195ff) which causes problems, with several attempts at a continuation before the notorious triple trills at 199–205. Intriguingly the trills represent the point where Chopin drops the pitch to its final form, outlining a dominant harmony in B major. Yet the sketch for the succeeding material – the resumption of the slow movement – is in C major, suggesting that it was sketched before B^2. In effect B^2 represents another 'insertion', interrupting the course of the slow movement by a nocturne whose relationship to B^1 at 116 is explicit, based on rhythm and texture. It will be clear by this stage that in the *Polonaise-fantasy* the ebb and flow of the music incorporates interruptions and insertions in an uncannily original way. They are not employed *dramatically*, as in many another work by Chopin, but as part of a new freedom in the sequence of ideas within a discourse. This deliberate formal discontinuity is no less apparent in the subsequent material. The slow movement is followed by brief references first to the Introduction X and then to B^2, now in F minor. This gives way to an extended anacrusis (226–241) to the apotheotic reprise of A and C.

The sketching practice encourages us, moreover, to view the overall scheme of the work in terms of interlocking elements, where the sense of continuity is disturbed by interruptions of, and insertions into, the unfolding of the main thematic shapes. The process is especially marked in the 'intercutting' of the middle section (B^1 C B^2 C X B^2), though a mere tabulation conveys little of the actual *sense* of discontinuity. Even the reprise separates its climactic statements of A and C by a passage tonally and rhythmically dislocated from its context, its harmonic setting briefly reminding us of the B major of the slow movement. It is, in short, a formal process which achieves on the large scale something of the fluidity and asymmetry which marks the structure of the principal themes themselves.

It is difficult to say whether the *Polonaise-fantasy* might have instigated new directions in Chopin's music. Certainly it strengthens the impression already given by some of the later mazurkas that any subsequent involvement with national dances would have transcended the simpler types of dance piece. On the formal process we must be more cautious, in that the fluidity and discontinuity was undoubtedly prompted in large measure by the associations of the genre title. Even so, the achievement is a remarkable one, not because of the 'freedom' of the structure, but because that freedom has resulted in a work of such compelling cohesion. Chopin seems to have relied here to a degree barely approached in any of his other extended works on an intuitive, subconsciously functioning sense of form and balance, untrammelled by too close an adherence to conventional design, yet unerring in its control of the pacing and proportioning of large dimensions. Only one major work followed the *Polonaise-fantasy*, the Cello Sonata, and that, as we have seen, presented Chopin with new problems and new challenges. It is tempting to speculate about future directions. Both works represent new departures, of form and genre respectively, demonstrating clearly that Chopin was approaching his art more and more in a spirit of exploration and renovation. Either could have formed the gateway to future paths. A Violin Sonata? A Fifth Ballade?

Epilogue

It is a commonplace of music history that Chopin forged new paths for musical language, that he was an innovator of major significance. Yet in a sense this is the least important aspect of his music. All great composers are innovators, even where they appear to accept without difficulty the forms and conventions of today's, or even yesterday's, music. The converse is by no means true, however, and Chopin's innovations would be of little account aside from the *quality* of his music. That quality can never be demonstrated by drawing attention to this or that feature of his harmony, melody, rhythm or texture, however much this may tell us about details of style. His musical language is a fused whole, and it is only through an interparametric approach that we might begin to examine the source of its vitality and the strength of its structures. It has been a primary aim of several preceding analyses to initiate such an investigation, and in so doing to reveal not only the subtleties and felicities which abound on the surface of a Chopin work but the many levels on which it functions. For it is surely a condition of great music that it should so function on different related, though often non-congruent, structural levels, that its events should be susceptible to multiple interpretation, that it should imply more than it realises, that it should as a consequence emerge as somehow larger than oneself.

The best of Chopin's music, including the most apparently simple miniature, conceals beneath its usually beguiling surface just such a wealth of implication and of multi-levelled complexity. It renders in short a density of information which elevates it far beyond the range of the salon pieces for which it served as a model. And there were many such pieces. As with any truly distinctive idiom, the external characteristics of Chopin's musical language proved irresistible to composers of lesser talent, and his influence on this surface level was immense in the later nineteenth and well into the twentieth centuries. The extent and nature of that influence are subjects of much interest, but they belong properly within the field of reception and remain well outside the scope of this study. My concern here is to explore some aspects of his legacy which bear more directly on the history of musical language.

Whatever its limitation as a means of investigating quality in music, a parametric approach can tell us much about the nature of influence. Composers (unlike analysts!) need feel no uneasiness when their attitude to the music they value lacks even a pretence of objectivity. In their search for creative stimulus they will ruthlessly, but quite properly, dissect the organic whole of another's music, picking and choosing from it those elements which serve their purpose with scant respect for the unity of their source. So we find many late nineteenth-century composers benefiting from Chopin's harmonic innovations, for instance, while remaining poles apart from his music in almost every other respect. And it is precisely those harmonic innovations which have most often been cited in the literature as evidence of the prophetic nature of Chopin's achievement. It may be helpful to outline in very general terms some areas of influence. The dominant and other diatonic seventh and ninth harmonies which are sustained through arpeggiation in many a Chopin accompaniment, often sacrificing resolution, form a basic harmonic colour of much late nineteenth and early twentieth-century piano music, especially by French and Russian composers. The connection is at its most explicit in the music – especially the early music – of Fauré and Skryabin, both of whom benefited directly from Chopin's example.[1] Chopin's fondness for harmonic symmetries, often based on the uni-intervallic diminished seventh and often too involving parallelism, exact and inexact, also bore fruit in later music. Initially this class of harmony found its way into the keyboard passage-work of later nineteenth-century music, and Liszt was not the least of Chopin's legatees in this respect. Eventually, however, in the later music of Liszt himself, in Rimsky-Korsakov and of course in Busoni and Debussy, it played a more substantial and less decorative role, helping to shape some of the new conceptions of tonal coherence which arose at the turn of the century. One might also mention here the impact of Chopin's folkloristic modality, particularly on later 'nationalist' composers. Smetana was only one of several who paid direct tribute to him in this regard. But it is Chopin's expressive chromaticism, realised through semitonal part movement, through an almost unprecedented compression of chromatic chord-types within a short span-of-context and through wayward harmonic explorations in parenthesis to the main tonal goals, which has attracted most interest and which has not infrequently earned him recognition as a forerunner of Wagner.

Such claims require careful evaluation. We owe it above all to Schenker, though not of course exclusively to him, that chord-by-chord 'functional' analysis of Chopin's harmony has largely been discredited, and that much of his rich chromatic elaboration can be properly perceived as ornament, however profuse, or prolongation, however extended. The fifth relationship is so common on the foreground of Chopin's harmony that its strength of tonal attraction is weakened, even neutralised, and we must therefore recognize a difference in *quality* between its function on this level and its function on higher levels where it is powerfully structural.[2] To assume an invariance of levels, perceiving tonal order as merely an inflation of harmonic order, is to evade interpretative decisions. Schenker's basic insights easily survive any disagreements we may have over specific readings or even over more fundamental issues of theory and method. His achievement was to reveal the lucid diatonic space outlined in the middle ground of Chopin's harmony and the strength of its contrapuntal framework.[3] It may be dangerous then to assume, despite all the procedural parallels in their voice-leading, that it is merely a step of degree (rather than of kind) from the harmony of Chopin to that of Wagner, where tonal integrity, as an *ursatz*, is indeed threatened.

Aside from harmonic language, Chopin's points of contact with later German music (apart from light salon music) remain intermittent and peripheral, though there are interesting connections with Brahms.[4] The case is very different when we look beyond Austro-Germany and beyond harmony. In its most characteristic form the Chopin melody is of a kind defined by Mersmann in his *Musikästhetik* as 'ornamental'. As such, it displays closer affinities with the Italian operatic aria than with the theme of a German sonata-symphonic tradition. Such affinities extend beyond the character of the melody into its treatment. Motivic play is of course common enough in Chopin, especially in the sonatas and, in a rather different way, the mazurkas. But his true genius lay in drafting long arcs of rhythmically supple, chromatically curving lines and in the subsequent variation of these lines through an ornamentation which may act as an expressive enhancement of the original, as a source of energy and tension, or (and increasingly in later years) as a means of underlining a point of structure. In their priority of decoration and variation over dissection and development, Chopin's thematic treatments suggest parallels not only with Italian opera but also with later developments in Russian and French instrumental music.

Nineteenth-century Russian composers, partly because of the folkloristic basis of many of their themes, often preferred to proceed through repetition and variation, rather than through motivic working. They were thus particularly receptive to Chopin's achievement and several of them, notably Balakirev, responded directly to it. Such parallels in melodic treatment point towards other affinities. Harmonic connections have been noted, but we may add here the similarities of texture or 'facture'. The keyboard textures of Chopin's maturity, and especially those of his nocturne manner, are quite different in character from those of Beethoven, Schumann and Mendelssohn and even of early and middle-period Liszt. To a large extent they instigated a tradition of piano-writing whose true originality and value were grasped not by his immediate successors but by French and Russian composers of the late nineteenth century, extending up to the early works of Debussy, in particular his ballade, nocturne, mazurka and waltz. Debussy studied Chopin's music closely, performing it, preparing a broadly faithful edition for Durand, and later dedicating his own studies to Chopin's memory. His mature piano music was of course to relinquish the obvious debts to Chopin found in his early pieces. Indeed, along with Ravel's, it was to open up a quite new world of keyboard textures which was as fresh, original and influential for our century as was Chopin's for the nineteenth. Yet despite the distance separating them in time, and the very different surfaces of their mature music, the connection remains a potent one, and it is of central importance to any understanding of the ultimate significance of Chopin's achievement.

His musical language sprang from unpromising parentage, the concert and salon music of early nineteenth-century pianism. While he never disowned his origins in such 'popular' music, he greatly enriched and enhanced its materials by drawing upon other musical worlds, in particular the keyboard music of Bach, the florid arias of Italian opera and the thematic working of the Austro-German sonata. From all these musical worlds he maintained the distance which is possible for the outsider. That distance enabled him, moreover, to 'comment' upon his models through the selectivity with which he drew upon them. In doing so he was of course making a positive statement first and foremost. At the same time the nature of that statement rendered an element of creative, if unwitting, criticism of the mainstream of nineteenth-century instrumental music, and such criticism was to grow in importance as the century progressed. There are dangers in viewing any aspect of an historical period as normative. Yet even when we allow for the impositions of historiography, it is clear that the instrumental music of the Austro-German tradition assumed *at the time* the status of a privileged 'high' art to which other musical cultures responded through imitation, rejection or dialogue. The development of that art, notably shy of eclecticism, culminated in an (inbred?) crisis of expression in the early twentieth century, when vital sonata-symphonic composition made its way to centres far from central Europe and vital music in central Europe rejected the traditional instrumental forms, at least until they were subject to renovation in Schoenberg. Mahler emerges as a figure of central significance in this development, not least because, uniquely, he could criticise the tradition both from within and without.

In fact the 'criticism' had begun long before Mahler. In their quite different ways Berlioz and Chopin began to propose alternatives to a Classical inheritance (on which of course they also depended) and it is no coincidence that both of them exerted a major influence on Russian composers of the later nineteenth century. It was in nineteenth-century Russia, isolated geographically, culturally and politically from Western Europe, that such alternatives to · Austro-German procedures gained strength, culminating in radical changes in musical language in the early years of the twentieth century. These changes involved new formulations of the tonal principle, new approaches to musical discourse and form, and a reassessment of the relative structural weighting of the basic dimensions of musical sound. They amounted to nothing less than a challenge to the Classical hegemony of pitch, whose *preservation* was so determinedly sought by Schoenberg in Austro-Germany.

If any single composer emerges as crucial to that challenge it is Debussy. His music, with respect to its new tonal synthesis, its sense of musical flow and its formal organisation, marks the point where earlier alternatives fuse into an independent, self-consistent voice, where a gradual accumulation of changes becomes qualitative and the modern age in music decisively begins. Chopin and Debussy stand then at opposite ends of an important development in the history of musical language, representing the beginning and end of a process of fundamental change. It is more useful to consider points of contact in this light than to explore areas of direct influence, though these certainly exist. The essential point is that Chopin proposes, against a background of Classical harmony, texture and form, certain expansions and modifications which later become part of the substance of Debussy's musical thought, their meaning and context now changed utterly.

Harmonically, for instance, Chopin introduces chromatic substitutions, modalities and symmetries which in no way disturb the diatonic foundation of his music. We can measure the increasing weight of all three features (potentially disruptive of Classical tonality) as they are taken up by Russian composers in the later nineteenth century and eventually by Debussy. In Debussy, however, their meaning has changed. Rather than simply colouring or prolonging diatonic harmony, they have achieved the status of participants (on an equal footing with diatonic harmony) in a new tonal synthesis, a synthesis depending on constant and subtle interactions between different harmonic classes. With melody too it is possible to go a little way beyond the generalised parallels based on variational and ornamental treatments. There are hints in late Chopin of that melodic fragmentation which is so characteristic of Debussy, though the effect of separation achieved by Debussy is lessened in Chopin by the unifying function of harmony.

In piano 'facture', too, we may note in Chopin the early stages of some characteristic features of Debussy's music. This goes beyond subtle differentiations of articulation and of dynamics, to occasional inversely proportional relationships of dynamic level and density, such as are characteristic of Debussy.[5] Such procedures can lead, moreover, to a Debussy-like stratification of texture, though in Chopin other elements, and of course the pedal, tend to be integrative in function, whereas in Debussy they tend to accentuate the stratification. In Chopin's figurative devices there are similar pre-echoes of Debussy, not just in the character of the figuration but in its occasional capacity to reach beyond evolutionary, form-building functions to create more static colouristic values. Again the pedal plays a vital role.

More significant than specific parallels of harmony, melody and texture, however, are parallels in the relative structural weighting of such elements. As previous analyses have tried to show, the borderlines between melodic line and figurative pattern, and between harmonically motivated accompaniment and autonomous sonority are not always clearly demarcated in Chopin. There is often a delicate shading of function between them. Frequently, too, melody and harmony will 'dissolve' into texture, so that the latter gains a new compositional importance, itself a means of shaping the idea, even at times of directing the phrase. Moreover the detailed information within some of Chopin's textures, often a 'counterpoint' of minute particles, is much more dense than anything, say, in Liszt, and this too increases their weight as elements of structure. In all these respects he seems to point ahead towards Debussy. Once more, however, the relationship to Debussy is embryonic rather than directly causal. In Chopin's music texture still concedes to melody and harmony the main responsibility for structure. Yet in his occasional use of texture-motives, his purposeful shaping of texture-space and his often rapid texture-rhythm, he already demonstrates how texture will begin to assume major structural functions more than half a century later in Debussy.

Notes

Prologue

1 Franz Liszt, *Frédéric Chopin*, Paris, 1852.
2 Orga (1976), Jordan (1978), Marek & Gordon Smith (1978), Zamoyski (1979), Attwood (1980). For publication details see bibliography.
3 Gastone Belotti, *F. Chopin l'uomo*, 3 vols, Milan and Rome, 1974; and Józef Chomiński, *Fryderyk Chopin*, Leipzig, 1980 (originally published in Polish, Kraków 1978).
4 Gerald Abraham, *Chopin's Musical Style*, London, 1939.
5 Frederick Niecks, *Chopin as a Man and Musician*, 2 vols, London and New York, 1888, 2nd ed., 1902, Repr. New York, 1973.
6 Alan Walker (ed.), *Frédéric Chopin: Profiles of the Man and the Musician*, London, 1966.
7 The proceedings are published as *The Book of the First International Musicological Congress devoted to the Works of Frederick Chopin*, ed. Zofia Lissa, Warsaw, 1963. Hereafter *The Book*. A second congress is planned for 1986.
8 Notably Wojciech Nowik, 'Proces twórczy Fryderyka Chopina w świetle jego autografów muzycznych', unpub. Ph.D dissertation, University of Warsaw, 1978.
9 Krystyna Kobylańska, *Rękopisy Utworów Chopina. Katalog*, 2 vols, Kraków, 1977. The later German version (*Frédéric Chopin: Thematisch-bibliographisches Werkverzeichnis*, ed. Ernst Herttrich, tr. Helmut Stolze, Munich, 1979) incorporates a thematic catalogue, but excludes much of the manuscript description in the original version. The reader's attention is drawn to Jeffrey Kallberg's instructive reviews of both versions of the *Katalog* for a full discussion, notably on the inadequacies of information on publication history in both Kobylańska and Brown, *19th Century Music*, 3, 1979, pp. 163–9 and *JAMS* 34, 1981, pp. 357–65. It may be added that, as we must expect of such a catalogue, an increasing number of inaccuracies come to light through constant use. Throughout the present book, manuscripts will be identified with reference to the *Katalog* (K.)
10 M. J. E. Brown, *Chopin: An Index of his Works in Chronological Order*, London and New York, 1960, rev.ed., 1972.
11 Jeffrey Kallberg, 'The Chopin Sources: Variants, and Versions in Later Manuscripts, unpub. Ph.D. dissertation, University of Chicago, 1982. There are also major articles by Kallberg in *Notes* and *Journal of Musicology*.
12 See J.-J. Eigeldinger's comments on the glosses on Jane Stirling's copies in his introduction to *Frédéric Chopin: Oeuvres pour Piano*, Paris, 1982.
13 For an evaluation and comparison of complete editions see Thomas Higgins, 'Whose Chopin?', *19th Century Music*, 5, 1981, pp. 67–75.

14 An introduction to this work in English is provided in several contributions to The Chopin Society's *Studies in Chopin*, ed. Dariusz Zebrowski, tr. Eugenie Taska, Halina Oszcygiel and Ludwik Wiewiórkowski, Warsaw, 1973. A more detailed case study involving close examination of autographs and early editions in order to arrive at generalisations concerning performance practice and reception is Zofia Chechlińska, 'Ze studiów nad źródłami do scherz F. Chopina', *Annales Chopin*, 5, 1960, pp. 82–194.

15 As in Adam Harasowski, *The Skein of Legends about Chopin*, Glasgow, 1967.

16 James Huneker, *Chopin, the Man and his Music*, New York, 1900, repr., 1966.

17 Schenker's copious analytical comment on Chopin appears scattered throughout his published and unpublished work.

18 Arnold Whittall comments on this in his contribution to 'Musicology in Great Britain since 1945', *Acta Musicologia*, 52, No.1, 1980, pp. 57–62.

19 Raymond Williams, *Culture and Society 1780–1950*, London, 1958.

20 Karol Szymanowski, *Z pism*, ed. Teresa Chylińska, Kraków, 1958, p. 185.

21 Goethe, quoted in F. Blume, *Classic and Romantic Music, a Comprehensive Survey*, London, 1970, pp. 106–7.

Chapter 1 A biographical sketch

1 J.-J. Eigeldinger argues that the concert featured the E minor concerto and not the F minor, as usually reported. See 'Un concert inconnu de Chopin à Paris', *Revue musicale de Suisse romande*, xxxiv/l, 1981, pp. 2–9.

2 William Weber, *Music and the Middle Class*, London, 1975, p. 16.

3 This had also been programmed for the first concert, but there were difficulties over Chopin's copies of the orchestral parts.

4 Quoted in Niecks, 1973, Vol.1, pp. 99–100.

5 Op.cit., p. 101.

6 *Korespondencja Fryderyka Chopina*, ed. B. E. Sydow, Vol.1, p. 161.

7 Ibid., p. 164.

8 Ibid., pp. 185–6

9 Louis Spohr, *Autobiography* (Eng.tr.), London, 1865, vol.2, pp. 88–90.

10 See Chomiński, 1980, pp. 34–5.

11 Liszt, 1852, p, 119.

12 Jean-Jacques Eigeldinger gives a fascinating picture of Chopin as seen by his pupils in *Chopin vu par ses élèves*, Neuchâtel, 1979.

13 Charles Hallé, *Life and Letters*, London, 1896, p. 31.

14 Adam Czartkowski and Zofia Jeżewska, *Fryderyk Chopin*, Warsaw, 1970, p. 392.

15 The most comprehensive account of Chopin's dealings with his publishers is in Kallberg, 1982. See also his 'Chopin in the Market-place', *Notes*, 39, 3 and 4, March and June 1983.

16 Works with opus numbers from 66 to 74 were published posthumously by Julian Fontana mostly in 1855. The editions were prepared from copies rather than autographs, and where the latter exist discrepancies have been shown to be wide.

17 Chopin was introduced to Mendelssohn in December 1831 by Ferdinand Hiller and later spent some time with him (1834) at Mendelssohn's Lower Rhine Music Festival. It was in the following year that he first met Schumann at the home of Clara Wieck's father.

18 Józef Chomiński even questions that some of the amorous references in Chopin's letters from Vienna are directed towards Konstancja, reminding us that she is not mentioned by name. Chomiński, 1980, pp. 180–2.

19 I do not propose to grind out yet again the arguments for and against the

Chopin-Potocka letters. It is worth drawing attention, however, to the
Ordway Hilton report as presented in Marek and Gordon Smith.
20 Curtis Gate, *George Sand: A Biography*, Boston, 1975, p 486.
21 Most recently by William Attwood in *The Lioness and the Little One*, New York,
1980.
22 *Correspondance de Frédéric Chopin*, ed. Bronislaw Sydow, Suzanne and Denise
Chinaye, and Irène Sydow, Paris, 1954, vol.2, p. 291.
23 Ibid., p. 310
24 Kallberg, 1982.
25 Josef Filtsch in *Selected Correspondence of Fryderyk Chopin,* ed. A. Hedley, p. 217.
Eigeldinger (1979, pp. 201–3) raises some doubts about the authenticity of
the Filtsch letters noted by Hedley.
26 George Sand, *Oeuvres Choisies*, Brussels, 1851, vol.3, p. 218.
27 Adam Zamoyski, *Chopin: A Biography*, London, 1979, p. 214. The diary entry
refers to Chopin's gift of a manuscript and this has subsequently been
identified as Op.9 No.2 with glosses by Chopin. See Virginia Fortescue, 'The
Unknown Chopin: An Alternative to the Cadenza of the Nocturne Op.9
No.2', *South African Journal of Musicology*, 1, 1981, pp. 45–51.
28 Arthur Hedley, 'Chopin the Man', in Walker, 1966.

Chapter 2 Apprenticeship

1 Kobylańska has demonstrated the existence of at least fifty pieces composed
before 1825. Poland's troubled political history has taken a cruel toll of
essential documentation in all branches of scholarship and many Chopin
manuscripts have fallen victim to it.
2 Much of the international interest in the polonaise resulted from the adoption
(mainly in the seventeenth century) of rural prototypes by the Polish nobility
when it was transformed into a 'cultured' ceremonial court dance. To the best
of my knowledge, however, the name *polonez* was only widely adopted in the
eighteenth century.
3 The most recent of many studies of Telemann's celebrated links with Polish
music is Zofia Stęszewska, 'Elementy polskie w twórczósci George Philippa
Telemanna', *Muzyka*, Nos. 3–4, 1981, pp. 71–84.
4 Ogiński's teacher Józef Kozlowski (1757–1831) also composed polonaises. Most
of his later life was spent in Russia, so he had little impact on Polish music,
but he laid the foundations for a thriving nineteenth-century interest in the
polonaise in Russia.
5 Many of Kurpiński's polonaises began life in his operas.
6 Like so many of the more talented composers in Poland at this time, Janiewicz
emigrated at an early age, moving first to Vienna and eventually settling in
England.
7 Lipiński made several arrangements of Chopin's music for violin and piano,
including the B minor Prelude, Op.28 No.6.
8 Although he lived until 1838, Lessel gave up composition in 1822. His surviving
music is among the finest produced in Poland in the early years of the
century.
9 Waclaw Poźniak, 'Neueste Forschungen über Leben und Werke Chopins',
Schweizerische Musikzeitung, vol.CIV, pp. 224–31. Chomiński, 1980, p. 38.
10 Jan Ekier gives the date of the G sharp minor as 1824 (see his chronology in
Wstęp do wydania narodowego, Warsaw 1974), thus contradicting earlier
authorities who give 1822. Professor Ekier is currently preparing a paper on

chronology to be published as part of a symposium dealing with documentary studies in Chopin.

11 One might also cite Hummel's *Six Polonaises Favorites* Op.70 and Weber's Polonaise Op.72. In general there are striking affinities between Chopin's early piano writing and that of Weber.

12 There are indeed 'rondos' which conform in no particular to the formal archetype. See Tovey's remarks on the finale of the F minor Concerto, *Essays in Musical Analysis*, vol. III, p. 106.

13 There are several variants between the autograph of this piece and the copy by Chopin's father. The latter was Fontana's source for the posthumous edition.

14 Chopin went with Kolberg to see *La gazza ladra* after his final examination at the Lyceum in July 1826. When he left with his family for Bad Reinerz (a vain attempt to cure his younger sister Emilia's tuberculosis), he gave Kolberg the polonaise as a parting gift.

15 Dance rondos were fairly common at the time – there is, for example, a *polonaise en rondeau* by John Field – but it is less usual to find the mazurka so stylised.

16 Abraham, 1939, pp. 8–9.

17 An earlier D major Mazurka is considered of doubtful authenticity. The publication history of the G major and B flat major is rather complicated and the reader is referred to Kobylańska, 1977, pp. 357–60.

18 As Jeffrey Kallberg has suggested to me in correspondence, the style of the piece, the handwriting and the paper all argue against accepting this date, though there is no doubt that Kolberg did put the date there.

19 The only significant difference is an additional countermelody at bar 73ff.

20 *Korespondencja Fryderyka Chopina*, vol. 1, p. 109.

21 See Marie Kubień-Uszokowa, 'Stosunek Chopina do Beethovena' in *Chopin a muzyka europejska*, ed. K. Musiol, Katowice, 1977, pp. 25–41.

22 Very detailed instructions as to dynamics, fingering, expression marks and pedalling are provided on the autograph (K.1086).

23 Gerald Abraham's view (1939) that Chopin favoured the rondo because of an insecurity about extended structures seems less convincing.

24 It was partly in protest at such sets that Mendelssohn called his own cycle *Variations sérieuses*.

25 This may be apocryphal. It was reported by M. A. Szulc (*Fryderyk Chopin i utwory jego muzyczne*, Poznan, 1873) based on conversations with Oskar Kolberg.

26 R. Davis, 'The Music of Hummel', *Music Review*, vol. 25, 1965, p. 171.

27 A Tyrolean folksong first published in 1822.

28 Other pianist-composers, including Hummel, wrote 'souvenirs' of Paganini.

29 J. M. Chomiński, *Sonaty Chopina*, Kraków, 1960, p. 13.

30 Chopin was aware of the difficulty and later considered rescoring the top part for viola.

31 Rosen, *Sonata Forms*, New York and London, 1980, p. 319.

32 See Paul Hamburger in Walker, 1966, p. 96.

33 *Korespondencja Fryderyka Chopina*, vol. 1, p. 112.

Chapter 3 Stile brillante

1 J. C. Bach's Op.13 concertos were composed 'for harpsichord or piano'. He is reputed to have been the first to give a public recital on piano in 1768.

2 Quoted in A. Loesser, *Men, Women and Pianos*, New York, 1951, p. 376.

3 Moscheles claimed in his memoirs that he gave the first in 1837.

4 For typical programmes see Isabella Amster, *Das Virtuosenkonzert in der ersten Halfte des 19. Jahrhunderts*, Berlin, 1931, p. 22 and Derek Carew, 'The Composer/Performer Relationship in the Piano Works of J. N. Hummel', unpub. Ph.D. dissertation, University of Leicester, 1981, p. 21.

5 In view of the poor orchestral standards in many cities pianist-composers often *preferred* to play their concertos as solos.

6 Spohr, 1865, vol. 1, p. 279, and vol. 2, p. 168.

7 A valuable recent study is Cyril Ehrlich, *The Piano: A History*, London, 1976.

8 The only major development of Chopin's time was Érard's 'double escapement' action, first devised by him in 1822 and subsequently improved.

9 In volume III of his *Pianoforte School* (Vienna, 1839), Czerny identifies six distinguishable performance styles or schools: Clementi, Cramer and Dussek, Mozart, Beethoven and Ries, the modern 'brilliant' school of Hummel, Kalkbrenner and Moscheles and the new synthesis of Thalberg, Liszt and Chopin which draws upon all the earlier schools in different ways.

10 Clementi also influenced the heavier, fuller chordal style of Beethoven and Ries.

11 Moscheles's performance style apparently moved increasingly from the 'brilliant' towards the lyrical in later years, paralleling to some extent Chopin's own development.

12 Contrary to information in Kobylańska, the so-called 'working autograph' of Op.2 (K.6) is in the Pierport Morgan library. She herself corrects this in 'Autograf roboczy partytury Wariacji B-dur op.2 Fryderyka Chopina', *Ruch muzyczny*, vol. xxiii/23 1979.

13 An examination of improvisation as discussed in the methods appears in Irena Poniatowska, 'Improwizacja fortepianowa w okresie romantyzmu', *Szkice o kulturze muzycznej XIXw*, vol. 4, Warsaw, 1980, pp. 7–26.

14 But not a complete absence. See Eigeldinger, 1979, pp. 215–16.

15 Liszt always required his students at Budapest to graduate in improvisation.

16 The phrase is borrowed from Carew, 1981. Carew's thesis is the most comprehensive account of improvisation in early nineteenth-century piano music. It also includes useful documentation and discussion of concert life at the time. He is currently preparing a 'Dartington Music Paper', *Improvisation in Early Nineteenth-Century Piano Music*.

17 For a discussion of the aesthetic status of an improvisation as a work, see Zofia Lissa, 'Uber das Wesen Musikwerkes', *Neue Aufsatze zur Musikästhetik*, Wilhelmshaven, 1975.

18 Often the inordinate length of slow introductions to light ornamental variation sets would be designed to tease an audience impatiently awaiting the appearance of a familiar theme.

19 Abraham, 1939, p. 19.

20 F.-H.-J. Castil-Blaze, *Dictionnaire de musique moderne*, Paris, 1825, vol. 2, pp. 262–3.

21 Robin Langley, 'John Field and the Genesis of a Style', *Musical Times*, January, 1982, pp. 92–9.

22 'Chopin's Orchestral Style', *The Book*, 1963, pp. 85–7.

23 Niecks, 1973, vol. 1, p. 119.

24 Admittedly there are some Mozart concertos where one perceives the solo entry less as a structural downbeat than a stage in a much broader formal paragraphing.

25 Other pianist-composers of the period have suffered similar indignities. There are still performances of the Moscheles G minor Concerto, for instance, which omit most of the extended symphonic prelude.

26 Abraham, 1939, p. 32.

27 See Amster, 1931, for a much fuller account of such common materials.
28 Aleksander Frączkiewicz, 'Koncerty fortepianowe Chopina jako typ koncertu romantycznego', *The Book*, 1963, pp. 293–6.
29 Peter Gould in Walker, 1966, p. 155.
30 It also echoes, and may even have been influenced by, the 'polonaise' finale of Field's Third Piano Concerto.

Chapter 4 Baroque reflections

1 Naturally the effect of a *sforzando* articulation on an 1830 piano is quite different from that of today's instrument.
2 For further discussion see Dalilo Turlo, 'The Evolution of Dynamics as an Element of Construction in Chopin's Works', *Annales Chopin 6*, 1965, pp. 90–103.
3 Brown's dates for individual studies are by no means authoritative. The bases for his decisions are not clear, and in at least one case, Opus 10, No. 9 he is inaccurate.
4 Only twenty-nine of the pieces are presented in Tausig's later familiar edition.
5 As Robert Collet has pointed out (Walker, 1966, p. 120), there are several important aspects of piano technique which are not addressed by any of the Chopin studies.
6 See Bernard Ott, *Liszt et la Pédagogie du Piano*, Issy-les-Moulineaux, 1978, pp. 205–8.
7 Abraham, 1939, p. 38.
8 The parallel between Bach's first prelude and Chopin Op.10. No. 1 is strengthened by reductive analysis. See Allen Forte and Steven E. Gilbert, *Introduction to Schenkerian Analysis*, New York and London, 1982, p. 190.
9 There are also several melodic variants in this manuscript.
10 For another view see Karol Hlawiczka, 'Chopin – Meister der Rhythmischen Gestaltung', *Annales Chopin*, 5, pp. 31–81.
11 The symbology used in Ex.8 is from Wallace Berry, *Structural Functions in Music*, New Jersey, 1976.
12 Chopin's own phrasing and accents (K. 124) hardly serve to clarify the structure of the melody. If anything they underline the purposeful ambiguity of the music.
13 The final form of this passage was not achieved immediately. In Chopin's earliest autograph (K. 123) the climax is approached less powerfully through an expansion of an earlier phrase, so that bar 14 is as bar 6.
14 Adorno's 'law of complementary harmony', where the second chord produces notes which were lacking in the first, was applied by him to twelve-note music, but it has an (admittedly more limited) application to chord connection in tonal music also.
15 Chopin originally spelt bar 50 as E major rather than F flat major (K.140).
16 The useful phrase is borrowed from Abraham, 1939.
17 Kallberg, 1982, pp. 190–210. Kallberg makes the point rather more directly in 'Compatibility in Chopin's Multipartite Publications', *Journal of Musicology*, vol. 4, 1983.
18 Walter Wiora, 'Chopins Preludes und Études und Bachs *Wohltempiertes Klavier*', *The Book*, 1963, pp. 73–81.
19 Quoted in G. C. Ashton Jonson, *A Handbook to Chopin's Works*, London, 1905, p. 39.
20 Hedley 1947, pp. 143–4.
21 Ibid., p. 121.

22 Alberto Basso (sic), 'Chopin et l'ésprit de la musique instrumentale baroque', *The Book*, pp. 271–4.
23 This 'prelude' was not so titled by Chopin, who gave the piece only a tempo indication.
24 J. M. Chomiński, *Preludia*, Kraków, 1950, p. 22.
25 Quoted in Niecks, 1973, vol. 1, p. 108.
26 In the engraver's exemplar for Op. 28 No.1 (K. 373) Chopin further connects the G-C motive of bars 29–32, later scratching out the connecting beam.
27 Charles Burkhart, 'The Polyphonic Melodic Line of Chopin's B minor Prelude', *Frédéric Chopin: Preludes Op.28*, a 'Norton Critical Score', ed. Thomas Higgins, New York, 1973, pp. 80–8.
28. The ornamental melody of this movement draws attention to yet another affinity between the two composers.
29 See D'Arcy Thompson, *On Growth and Form*, Cambridge, 1961: 'The form of an object is a diagram of the forces acting upon it.' Thompson emphasises the 'dynamical' aspect of form, interpreting in terms of 'forces of the operations of energy'.
30 The approach to the climax is rather less gradual in Chopin's first draft, preserved on the engraver's exemplar (K. 426).
31 For a discussion of value in small forms see Leonard B. Meyer, *Music, the Arts and Ideas*, Chicago and London, 1967, p. 37.
32 Hedley, 1947, p. 148.

Chapter 5 Bel canto

1 Chopin was far from flattering about the piano writing in Spohr's quintet. See Niecks, 1973, Vol. 1, p. 138.
2 See Langley, 1982.
3 David Branson, *John Field and Chopin*, London, 1972.
4 Numbering as in the Liszt edition. No.8 was not published as a 'nocturne' until 1835, but could well have been known to Chopin in its original form as a 'Romance', see Cecil Hopkinson, *A Biographical Thematic Catalogue of the Works of John Field, 1782–1837*, London, 1961, no. 30.
5 This judgment is not universally accepted. Nicholas Temperley, for example, seems to hold Field in higher regard. See his 'Piano Music 1800–1870' in the *Athlone History of Music in Britain: The Romantic Age 1800–1914*, ed. Temperley, London, 1981, p. 407.
6 Marcel Proust, *Remembrance of Things Past*, tr. C. K. Scott Moncrief and Terence Kilmartin, Penguin, 1983, vol. 1, p. 361.
7 Kallberg, 1982, pp. 202–10.
8 Ernst-Jurgen Dreyer, 'Melodisches Fomelgut bei Chopin', *The Book*, 1963, pp. 132–44.
9 Quoted in P. Le Huray and J. Day (eds), *Music and Aesthetics in the Eighteenth and Early Nineteenth Centuries*, Cambridge, 1981, pp. 470–2.
10 Quoted in Blume, 1970, p. 13.
11 I am indebted to Hugh MacDonald who drew my attention to this.
12 Carl Dahlhaus uses the term in his interesting essay 'Neo-romanticism', *Between Romanticism and Modernism*, tr. Mary Whittall, Berkeley, Los Angeles and London, 1980.
13 Edward T. Cone is perhaps unduly cautious in his remarks on analysis and value judgments in 'Analysis Today', *Problems of Modern Music*, New York, 1960, p. 49. A worthwhile study is Leonard B. Meyer's 'Some Remarks on Value and Greatness in Music', *Music, the Arts and Ideas*, Chicago and London,

1967. See also Carl Dahlhaus, *Analysis and Value Judgement*, tr. Siegmund Levarie, New York, 1983.

14 Meyer, 1967.

15 William Thomson, 'Functional Ambiguity in Musical Structures', *Music Perception*, vol. 1, no. 1, Fall, 1983.

16 *19th Century Music*, vol. 5, 1982, pp. 244–7.

17 Ludwik Bronarski, 'Chopin, Cherubini et le contrepoint', *Annales Chopin*, vol. 2 1958, pp. 238–42.

18 Kallberg, 1982, pp. 248–75.

19 See the facsimile in Kobylańska, 1977, vol. 2, pp. 89–90.

20 Chomiński, 1980, pp. 141–2.

21 Jan Ekier has recently demonstrated convincingly that the 'Fantasy' part of the title of Op.66 cannot stem from Chopin. See 'Das Impromptu cis-Moll von Frédéric Chopin', *Melos/Neue Zeitschrift fur Musik*, vol. 4, no.3 May-June 1978, pp. 201–4.

22 Alfred Cortot, in the introduction to his edition of the impromptus.

23 Ferdinand Gajewski, 'New Chopiniana from the Papers of Carl Filtsch', *Studi Musicali*, vol. 11, 1982, pp. 171–7. This information supersedes that in Kobylańska (K. 742).

Chapter 6 The spirit of Poland

1 'Nationalism in Music' in Dahlhaus, 1980.

2 Zofia Lissa, 'Problemy polskiego stylu narodowego w twórczośći Chopina', *Studia nad twórczościa Fryderyka Chopina*, Krakow, 1970, pp. 1–103.

3 Dahlaus, 1980.

4 An argument for abandoning the national perspective in studies of history and art is proposed by Theodore Zelden, 'Ourselves, as we see us', *TLS*, Dec. 31 1982, pp. 1435–6.

5 See, for instance, Gerald Abraham, 'The Factor of Language' in *The Tradition of Western Music*, London, Melbourne and Cape Town, 1974, pp. 62–83.

6 Moniuszko remembered his mother singing some of the *Historical Songs* to him as a child.

7 The chronology and publication history of the songs is complex. The reader is referred to Kobylańska, 1977.

8 Mieczysław Tomaszewski, 'Verbindungen zwischen den Chopinschen Liederwerken und dem polnischen popularen Volks- und Kunstlied', *The Book*, 1963, pp. 404–9.

9 The authenticity of this song has been questioned. The melody itself is a folksong.

10 Hamburger in Walker, 1966, p. 96.

11 Curiously the surviving manuscript and the French and German editions all have 'Fine' clearly written at the end of the *Trio*, not the Polonaise and there is no D.C. indication. Gastone Belotti argues that the autograph and first editions tell the truth in this respect ('Le Polacche op.26 nella concezione autografa di Chopin', *Nuova Rivista Musicale Italiana*, vol. 8, 1974, pp. 191–209, and 'Le Polacche dell'op. 26 nel testo autentico di Chopin', *Studi Musicali*, vol. 2, 1973, pp. 267–313). In a letter to me, Jeffrey Kallberg expresses his uneasiness about this, pointing out that the 'Fine' occurs at the end of a repetition in the M.S. indicated through repeated numbers in sequence and that if there was any place Chopin was likely to err in writing out a manuscript it was at such spots.

12 Hamburger in Walker, 1966, pp. 103–5.

13 Abraham, 1939, p. 46.
14 One is reminded of the ostinato in the second movement of Beethoven Op.135.
15 The achievements of Glinka and later nineteenth-century Russian composers, themselves indebted to Chopin, were of a rather different order. Here forms and procedures substantially at variance with Western European norms could be forged from folkloristic sources precisely because the stylistic distance from these norms was so much greater in the first place.
16 Eigeldinger, 1979, pp. 110–11.
17 See William Thomson, 'Functional Ambiguity in Musical Structures', *Music Perception*, vol. 1, no. 1, Fall, 1983.
18 There are many such studies. Of special importance is the pioneering book by H. Windakiewiczowa, *Wzory ludowej muzyki polskiej w mazurkach Fryderyka Chopina*, Kraków, 1926. A later valuable study is Wieczeslaw Paschalow, *Chopin a polska muzyka ludowa*, Kraków, 1951.
19 There is a similar procedure in Op.6 No. 2, where the effect is heightened by a top-voice pedal. An earlier sketch (K. 31) is weaker in that Chopin changes the pattern after four bars.
20 For a discussion of cyclic unity in multi-partite opuses see Kallberg, 1982.
21 Windakiewiczowa demonstrates the close links between the main theme and a familiar folk mazur, 1926, p. 5 and p. 17.
22 There is some confusion in op. 33 editions over the ordering of the Second and Third Mazurkas.
23 Hedley, 1947, p. 168.
24 An earlier rejected version, described by Kobylańska as a 'working autograph' (K. 718), inserts a further four bars of flowing quaver movement at 105 and moves from there directly to 141.
25 Kallberg, 1982, pp. 189–247. See also his 'compatibility in Chopin's Multipartite Publications', *Journal of Musicology*, vol. 2, no. 4, 1983.

Chapter 7 Salons

1 Weber, 1975, p. 20.
2 Walker, 1966, p. 90.
3 See Kallberg, 1982, pp. 275–307.
4 Andrzej Koszewski, 'Pierwiastek walcowy w twórczośći Chopina', *The Book*, 1963, pp. 196–201.
5 Janos Maróthy proposes a deeper unity underlying this schism in middle-class culture. His *Music and the Bourgeois, Music and the Proletarian*, Budapest, 1974, is an intriguing exploration of the relationships between 'high' and 'low' art.

Chapter 8 German dialogues

1 William Newman, *The Sonata since Beethoven*, Chapel Hill, 1969.
2 Hugo Leichtentritt, *Analyse von Chopins Klavierwerkes*, Berlin, 1921, vol. 2, p. 228.
3 Chomiński, 1960, p. 161.
4 'Chopin and Musical Structure' in Walker, 1966, p. 246.
5 Chomiński, 1980, pp. 112–14.
6 Walker, 1966, p. 247.
7 Quoted in Huneker, 1966, p. 168.
8 Niecks, 1973, vol. 2, p. 227.
9 Ibid., p. 228.

10 There is a short sketch for this section (bars 118–133). See K. 783.
11 Niecks, 1973, p. 229.
12 *Korespondencja Fryderyka Chopina*, vol. 2, p. 175.
13 Ferdinand Gajewski, 'The Worksheets to Chopin's Violoncello Sonata', unpub. Ph.D. thesis, Harvard University, 1980.
14 There are some sketches for violin and piano which suggest that Chopin may have considered other departures from the solo piano medium during these later years.
15 Chomiński, 1980, p. 146.
16 Hedley, 1947, p. 159.

Chapter 9 The preludes revisited

1 David Epstein, *Beyond Orpheus: Studies in Musical Structure*, Cambridge, Massachusetts and London, 1979, p. 6.
2 Hippolyte Taine, *Histoire de la littérature anglaise*, vol. I, Paris, 1863, pp. 3–48.
3 See Carew, 1981.
4 R. Ingarden, *Das Literarische Kunstwerk*, Halle, 1931. See also Jerold Levinson, 'What a Musical Work is', *Journal of Philosophy*, vol. 73, no. 1, Jan., 1980, pp. 5–28.
5 See also Jan L. Broeckx, *Contemporary Views on Musical Style and Aesthetics*, Antwerp, 1979.
6 Meyer, *Explaining Music*, Berkeley and Los Angeles, 1973, p. 14.
7 Broeckx, 1979, p. 129.
8 *Music Analysis*, vol. 1, No.1, March 1982, p. 5.
9 Niecks, 1973.
10 Ibid., p. 256.
11 Huneker, 1966, p. 123.
12 Abraham, 1939, p. 47.
13 'Musicology in Great Britain since 1945', *Acta Musicologica*, vol. 52, no. 1, 1980, pp. 57–62.
14 Derek Cooke, *The Language of Music*, London, 1959.
15 Peter Kivy, *The Corded Shell*, Princeton, 1980.
16 Marion A. Guck, 'Musical Images as Musical Thoughts: The Contribution of Metaphor to Analysis', *In Theory Only*, vol. 5, June, 1881, pp. 29–42.
17 Lwów, 1930.
18 Warsaw, 1935.
19 Notably in his *Angewandte Musikästhetik*, Berlin, 1926.
20 *Harmonielehre*, Stuttgart, 1907.
21 See, for example, his *Harmonielehre in der Schule*, Leipzig, 1930.
22 *Romantische Harmonik und die Krise in Wagners Tristan*, Bern, 1920.
23 Leichtentritt, 1921, vol. I, p. 134.
24 *Muzyka*, 1959, no. 4, pp. 3–25.
25 Chomiński, 1950, pp. 101 ff.
26 Leichtentritt (1921, vol. 1, p. 137) also puts it in $\frac{2}{4}$, but in a different grouping.
27 'Harmonika Chopina z perspektywy techniki dźwiękowej XX wieku', *Studia nad twórczością Fryderyka Chopina*, Krakow, 1970, pp. 445–87.
28 Betty-Jean Thomas, 'Harmonic Materials and Treatment of Dissonance in the Pianoforte Music of F. Chopin', unpub. Ph.D. thesis, Eastman School of Music, June 1963.
29 *Beyond Schenkerism: The Need for Alternatives in Music Analysis*, Chicago, 1977, p. 173.
30 This term is borrowed from Narmour, 1977.

31 Hugo Leichtentritt, *Musical Form*, Massachusetts, 1951, p. 27.
32 Leichtentritt, 1921, vol. 1, pp. 131–3.
33 Ibid., p. 136 and p.149.
34 E. J. P. Camp, 'Temporal Proportion: A Study of Sonata-Form in the Piano Sonatas of Mozart*, unpub. Ph.D. thesis, Florida State University, 1968.
35 Ernö Lendvai, *Béla Bartók: An Analysis of his Music*, London, 1971.
36 Roy Howat, *Debussy in Proportion: A Musical Analysis*, Cambridge, 1983.
37 Michael R. Rodgers, 'Rehearings: Chopin Prelude in A minor Op.28 No.2', *19th Century Music*, vol.IV, No. 3, Spring 1981, pp. 244–50.
38 Grosvenor W. Cooper and Leonard B. Meyer, *The Rhythmic Structure of Music*, Chicago, 1960.
39 For a pungent critique of Cooper and Meyer, see Peter Westergaard, 'Some Problems in Rhythmic Theory and Analysis', *Perspectives on Contemporary Music Theory*, ed. Benjamin Boretz and Edward T. Cone, New York, 1972, pp. 226–37.
40 Edward T. Cone, *Musical Form and Musical Performance*, New York and London, 1968, pp. 39–43.
41 As in the first part of Kurth, 1920. See also his *Musik Psychologie*, Berlin, 1931, especially the later sections on form.
42 New Jersey, 1976.
43 Chicago and London, 1956.
44 Meyer, 1956, p. 96. In later studies (*Music, the Arts and Ideas*, Chicago and London, 1967 and *Explaining Music*, Berkeley and Los Angeles, 1973) Meyer refines his theory considerably, drawing upon information theory in the former study and developing an implication-realisation model for melodic structures in the latter. This model is extended in Narmour 1977.
45 Meyer, 1956, p. 54.
46 Cone, 1968, pp. 88–9 (see n. 40 above).
47 Epstein, 1979, pp. 10–11.
48 For an extensive discussion and useful references see Epstein, 1979.
49 Rudolph Réti, *The Thematic Process in Music*, London, 1961.
50 Alan Walker, *A Study in Musical Analysis*, London, 1962 and *An Anatomy of Musical Criticism*, London, 1966.
51 We might take as an example Walker's analysis of the B flat minor Sonata, and in particular his Ex.23. The compositional flow at this point and the subsequent development of the triplet figure refuse to permit any such union of the first two notes of Walker's x' to form a structural unit. Equally the attempt to demonstrate a unity underlying the first and second subjects of the B minor Sonata (his Ex. 40) founders on a largely arbitrary reductive process when compared to the relatively consistent criteria in Schenker or Meyer. The selection of the pitch D from the second phrase of the second subject is particularly difficult to justify. See Walker, 1966, p. 241 and p.252.
52 Chomiński 1950, pp. 300–33.
53 Schenker was a pupil of Mikuli, who was a pupil of Chopin.
54 Narmour, 1977.
55 As in Abraham's discussion of 'tonal parenthesis', Abraham, 1939.
56 Heinrich Schenker, *Free Composition*, tr. and ed. Ernst Oster, New York and London, 1979, Ex.76 No. 2.
57 Ibid., Ex. 110, No. a3.
58 Oswald Jonas, *Introduction to the Theory of Heinrich Schenker*, tr. and ed. John Rothgeb, New York and London, 1982, p. 44.
59 Felix Salzer, *Structural Hearing: Tonal Coherence in Music*, New York, 1952, Ex. 492.
60 Higgins, 1973, see note 27 to Chapter 4.

61 Carl Schachter, 'Rhythm and Linear Analysis: Durational Reduction', *Music Forum*, vol. V, New York, 1980, pp. 197–232.
62 A further 'Schenkerian' approach to rhythmic analysis is Maury Yeston, *The Stratification of Musical Rhythm*, New Haven and London, 1976.

Chapter 10 Scherzos

1 An interesting and ambitious recent study is Fred Lerdahl and Ray Jackendoff, *A Generative Theory of Tonal Music*, Massachusetts and London 1983.
2 *Music Analysis* Vol. 1, No. 1, March 1982, p. 4.
3 See Alan Rawsthorne in Walker 1966, pp. 64–65.
4 Schenker 1979, p. 26.
5 Walker 1966, p. 69 and p. 247.
6 Zofia Chechlińska, 'Chopin a impresjonizm', *Szkice o kulturze muzycznej XIXw*, Warsaw 1973, pp. 21–34.

Chapter 11 Ballades

1 Mickiewicz is frequently invoked here, but without, as far as I am aware, any precise evidence.
2 See, for example, Alan Rawsthorne in Walker, 1966, p. 43
3 In Walker, 1966, p. 47.
4 See also the waltzes Op.69 No. 1 and Op.70 No. 2.
5 Graham George, *Tonality and Musical Structure*, London, 1970.
6 See Rudolph Réti, *Tonality: Atonality: Pantonality*, London, 1958. Also Edmond Costère, *Mort ou transfiguration de l'harmonie*, Paris, 1962.
7 Abraham, 1939, p. 56.
8 H. Krebs, 'Alternatives to Monotonality in early Nineteenth-century Music', *Journal of Music Theory*, vol. 25, No. 1, Spring 1981, pp. 1–16.
9 This manuscript was the subject of Saint-Saens's essay 'A Chopin M.S.: The F Major Ballade in the Making', *Outspoken Essays on Music*, tr. Fred Rothwell, London, 1922.
10 Walker, 1966, p. 51.
11 In K.602 Chopin completed bar 8 and left bar 9 silent. He was uncertain, it seems, about where to place the break.
12 Krebs, 1981 (see n. 8 above).

Chapter 12 Fantasies

1 Lew Mazel, 'Fantazja F-Moll Chopina', *Studia Chopinowskie*, Kraków, 1965, pp. 17–218.
2 Further motivic links are proposed in Leichtentritt, 1921, vol. 2, p. 271. and Walker, 1966, p. 235.
3 Mazel, 1965, p. 133 (see n. 1 above).
4 Walker, 1966. p. 235.
5 Walker, 1966, pp. 107–8
6 I am grateful to Jeffrey Kallberg for the suggestion that the key signature of three flats and the 'F mol' designation occurred at two different stages in the genesis of the work. Initially the work began as it appears on the first system, then Chopin decided to transpose it up a fourth. Mistakingly taking the first

chord as the tonic for the work he wrote 'F-mol', and then, correctly, indicated the correct beginning, on A flat minor, on staff 3.

7 This ambiguity is evidenced in a way by the variety of phrasing found in different editions, most of it bearing little relationship to Chopin's phrasing on the autograph.

8 The sketch is also instructive on minor detailed alterations. Unfortunately study of this is hampered by the inaccessibility of the original. It is often impossible with a photograph to discover what lies beneath Chopin's heavy cancellations.

9 The first four bars of this section are on a separate sketch, K. 817.

Epilogue

1 See Zofia Lissa 'Chopin i Skriabin', Lissa, 1970, pp. 202–31. Also A. Cortot, *La musique francaise de piano*, Paris, 1930 and W. Landowski, *Frédéric Chopin et Gabriel Fauré*, Paris, 1946.

2 Interestingly the fifth relationship plays a less crucial 'formal' role in Chopin, i.e. as a setting for new themes and cadential articulations.

3 Counterpoint is understood here as applying not at the foreground but at the middle and background levels.

4 See Paul Badura-Skoda, 'Chopin's Influence', Walker, 1966, pp. 258–76. Also Charles Rosen, 'Influence: Plagiarism and Inspiration', *19th Century Music* vol. 4 no. 2, 1980, pp. 87–100, and Charles T. Horton, 'Chopin and Brahms: On a Common Meeting (Middle) ground', *In Theory Only*, vol, 6, no. 7, Dec. 1982, pp. 19–22.

5 This is demonstrated in Chechlińska, 1973 (see note 6 to chapter 10), to which I am indebted in several respects.

Bibliography

1 General reference and background

Amster, I., *Das Virtuosen-konzert in der ersten Hälfte des 19. Jahrhunderts*, Berlin, 1931.

Berry, W., *Structural Functions in Music*, New Jersey, 1976.

Bie, O., *A History of the Pianoforte and Pianoforte Players*, tr. E. E. Kellett and E. W. Naylor, New York, 1966.

Blume, F., *Classic and Romantic Music*, New York, 1970.

Broeckx, J. L., *Contemporary Views on Musical Style and Aesthetics*, Antwerp, 1979.

Carew, D., 'The Composer/Performer Relationship in the Piano Works of J. N. Hummel, unpub. Ph.D. dissertation, University of Leicester, 1981.

Castil-Blaze, F.-H.-J., *Dictionnaire de musique moderne*, 2 vols (2nd ed.), Paris, 1825

Chechlińska, Z. (ed.), *Szkice o kulturze muzycznej XIXw*, vols. 1–4, Warsaw 1973–80.

Cooper, G. and Meyer, L. B., *The Rhythmic Structure of Music*, Chicago, 1960.

Czerny, C., *Complete Theoretical and Practical Pianoforte School*, tr. J. A. Hamilton, London, 1938–9.

Dahlhaus, C., *Between Romanticism and Modernism*, tr. Mary Whittall, Berkeley, Los Angeles and London, 1980.

Dahlhaus, C., *Analysis and Value Judgement*, tr. Siegmund Levarie, New York, 1983.

Ehrlich, C., *The Piano: A History*, London, 1976.

Epstein, D., *Beyond Orpheus: Studies in Musical Structure*, Cambridge, Massachusetts and London, 1979.

Fétis, F.-J. and Moscheles, I., *Méthodes des Méthodes de Piano*, Paris, 1840.

Forte, A and Gilbert, S. E., *Introduction to Schenkerian Analysis*, New York and London, 1982.

George, G., *Tonality and Musical Structure*, London, 1970.

Gerig, R. R., *Famous Pianists and their Technique*, Washington and New York, 1974.

Hallé, C. E. and M., *Life and Letters of Charles Hallé*, London, 1896.

Ingarden, R., *Das literarische Kunstwerk*, Halle, 1931.

Jenkins, G., 'The Legato Touch and the 'Ordinary' Manner of Keyboard Playing from 1750–1850,' unpub. Ph.D. dissertation, University of Cambridge, 1976.

Jonas, O., *Introduction to the Theory of Heinrich Schenker*, tr. and ed., John Rothgeb, New York and London, 1982.

Kivy, P., *The Corded Shell: Reflections on Musical Expression*, Princeton, 1980.

Kurth, E., *Romantische Harmonik und die Krise in Wagners Tristan*, Bern, 1920.

Kurth, E., *Musik Psychologie*, Berlin, 1931.

Le Huray, P. and Day, J. (eds), *Music and Aesthetics in the Eighteenth and Early Nineteenth Centuries*, Cambridge, 1981.

Leichtentritt, H., *Musical Form*, Massachusetts, 1951.

Lenz, W. von., *The Great Virtuosos of our Time* (Eng. tr.) New York, 1899; repr. 1983.
Lerdahl, F., and Jackendoff, R., *A Generative Theory of Tonal Music*, Massachusetts and London, 1983.
Lissa, Z., *Neue Aufsatze zur Musikästhetik*, Wilhelmshaven, 1975.
Loesser, A., *Men, Women and Pianos*, London, 1955.
Marmontel, A., *Les Pianistes Célèbres*, Paris, 1878.
Maróthy, J., *Music and the Bourgeois, Music and the Proletarian*, Budapest, 1974.
Mersmann, H., *Angewandte Musikästhetik*, Berlin, 1926.
Meyer, L. B., *Emotion and Meaning in Music*, Chicago and London, 1956.
Meyer, L. B., *Music, the Arts & Ideas*, Chicago and London, 1967.
Meyer, L. B., *Explaining Music*, Berkeley and Los Angeles, 1973.
Moscheles, C., *The Life of Moscheles with Selections from his Diaries and Correspondence*, tr. A. D. Coleridge, London, 1873 (2 vols.)
Narmour, E., *Beyond Schenkerism: The Need for Alternatives in Music Analysis*, Chicago, 1977.
Newman, W. S., *The Sonata Since Beethoven*, Chapel Hill, 1963.
Ott, B., *Liszt et la Pédagogie du Piano*, Issy-les-Moulineaux, 1978.
Raynor, H., *Music and Society Since 1815*, London, 1976.
Réti, R., *The Thematic Process in Music*, London, 1961.
Riemann, H., *System der musikalischen Rhythmik und Metrik*, Leipzig, 1903.
Rosen, C., *Sonata Forms*, New York and London, 1980.
Schenker, H., *Free Composition*, tr. and ed. Ernst Oster, New York and London, 1979.
Spohr, L., *Louis Spohr's Autobiography*, London, 1865.
Temperley, N. (ed.), *Athlone History of Music in Britain: The Romantic Age 1800–1870*, London, 1981.
Thomson, D., *On Growth and Form*, Cambridge, 1961.
Walker, A., *A Study in Musical Analysis*, London, 1962.
Weber, W., *Music and the Middle Class*, London, 1975.
Williams R., *Culture and Society 1780–1950*, London, 1959.

2 Catalogues, bibliographies, specialist periodicals

Brown, M. J. E., *Chopin: an Index of his Works in Chronological Order*, London, 1960, rev. 1972.
Kobylańska, K., *Rękopisy Utworów Chopina: Katalog* (2 vols), Kraków, 1977.
Kobylańska, K., *Frédéric Chopin: Thematisch-bibliographisches Werkverzeichnis*, ed. Ernst Herttrich, tr. Helmut Stolze, Munich, 1979.
Michałowski, K., *Bibliografia Chopinowska (1849–1869)*, Kraków, 1970 (updated *Rocznik chopinowski* ix, 1975, pp. 121–75).
Wróblewska-Straus, H. (ed.), *Rocznik chopinowski/Annales Chopin*, Warsaw 1956–.

3 Letters

Hedley, A. (ed.), *Selected Correspondence of Fryderyk Chopin*, London, 1962.
Kobylańska, K. (ed.), *Korespondencja Fryderyka Chopina z rodzina*, Warsaw, 1972.
Opieński, H. (ed.), *Chopin's Letters*, New York, 1931, rev. 1971.
Sydow, B. E. (ed.), *Korespondencja Fryderyka Chopina* (2 vols), Warsaw, 1955.

4 Life and works

Attwood, W., *The Lioness and the Little One*, New York, 1980.
Belotti, G., *F. Chopin l'uomo* (3 vols), Milan and Rome, 1974.
Binental, L., *Chopin*, Paris, 1934.
Bone, A. E., *Jane Wilhelmina Stirling 1804–1859*, Chipstead, 1960.
Bourniquel, C., *Chopin*, Paris, 1957, Eng.tr.1960.
Chomiński, J., *Fryderyk Chopin*, Leipzig, 1980.
Czartkowski, A. and Jeżewska, Z., *Fryderyk Chopin*, Warsaw, 1958.
Ganche, E., *Frédéric Chopin: sa vie et ses oeuvres*, Paris, 1909.
Gavoty, B., *Frédéric Chopin*, Paris, 1974.
Harasowski, A., *The Skein of Legends about Chopin*, Glasgow, 1967.
Hedley, A., *Chopin*, London, 1947.
Hoesick, F., *Chopin: życie i twórczość* (3 vols), Warsaw, 1910–11.
Huneker, J. G., *Chopin: the Man and his Music*, New York, 1900, repr. 1966.
Iwaszkiewicz, J., *Chopin*, Kraków, 1955.
Jordan, R., *Nocturne: A Life of Chopin*, London, 1978.
Kobylańska, K., *Chopin w kraju: dokumenty i pamiątki*, Kraków, 1955.
Liszt, F., *F Chopin*, Paris, 1852.
Marek, G. & Gordon-Smith, M., *Chopin: A Biography*, New York, 1978.
Murdoch, W. D., *Chopin: His Life*, London, 1934.
Niecks, F., *Chopin as a Man and a Musician* (2 vols) London, 1888, repr. 1973.
Orga, A., *Chopin: His Life and Times*, Tunbridge Wells, 1976, rev. 1978.
de Pourtalès, G., *Chopin ou le poète*, Paris, 1927.
Sand, G., *Histoire de ma vie*, Paris, 1854.
Scharlitt, B., *Chopin*, Leipzig, 1919.
Szulc, M. A., *Fryderyk Chopin i utwory jego muzyczne*, Poznan, 1873.
Szymanowski, K., *Fryderyk Chopin*, Warsaw, 1925.
Weinstock, H., *Chopin: the Man and his Music*, New York, 1949.
Wierzyński, K., *The Life and Death of Chopin*, New York, 1949.
Willeby, C., *Frédéric François Chopin: A Biography*, London, 1892.
Zamoyski, A., *Chopin: A Biography*, London, 1979.

5 More specialised documentary and analytical studies

Abraham, G., *Chopin's Musical Style*, London, 1939.
Belotti, G., *Saggi sull'arte e sull'opera di F. Chopin*, Bologna, 1977.
Branson, D., *John Field and Chopin*, London, 1972.
Bronarski, L., *Harmonika Chopina*, Warsaw, 1935.
Chomiński, J., *Preludia*, Kraków, 1950.
Chomiński, J., *Sonaty Chopina*, Kraków, 1960.
Cortot, A., *Aspects de Chopin*, Paris, 1949.
Davison, J. W., *Essay on the Works of Frederick Chopin*, London, 1843.
Dunn, J. P., *Ornamentation in the Works of Frederick Chopin*, London, 1921.
Eigeldinger, J.-J., *Chopin vu par ses élèves*, Neuchâtel, 1979.
Ekier, J., *Wstęp do wydania narodowego*, Warsaw, 1974.
Gajewski, J., 'The Worksheets to Chopin's Violoncello Sonata', unpub. Ph.D. dissertation, Harvard University, 1980.
Higgins, T., 'Chopin Interpretation: a Study of Performance Directions in Selected Autographs and Other Sources', unpub. Ph.D. dissertation, University of Iowa, 1966.

Hipkins, E. J., *How Chopin Played*, London, 1937.
Jonson, G. C. A., *A Handbook to Chopin's Works*, London, 1905.
Kallberg, J., 'The Chopin Sources: Variants and Versions in Later Manuscripts', unpub. Ph.D. dissertation, University of Chicago, 1982.
Kubień-Uszokowa, M. (ed.), *Chopin a muzyka europejska*, Katowice, 1977.
Landowski, W. L., *Frédéric Chopin et Gabriel Fauré*, Paris, 1946.
Leichtentritt, H., *Analyse der Chopinschen Klavierwerke* (2 vols), Berlin, 1921.
Lissa, Z., *Studia nad twórczościa Fryderyka Chopina*, Kraków, 1970.
Lissa, Z. (ed.), *The Book of the First International Musicological Congress devoted to the Works of Frederick Chopin*, Warsaw, 1963.
Mazel, L., *Studia Chopinowskie*, Kraków, 1965.
Methuen-Campbell, J., *Chopin Playing*, London, 1981.
Miketta, J., *Mazurki*, Kraków, 1949.
Nowik, W., 'Process twórczy Fryderyka Chopina w świetle jego autografów muzycznych', unpub. Ph.D. dissertation, University of Warsaw, 1978.
Ottich, M., *Die Bedeutung des Ornaments im Schaffen Friedrich Chopins*, Berlin, 1937.
Paschalow, W., *Chopin a polska muzyka ludowa*, Kraków, 1951.
Poźniak, B., *Chopin: praktische Anweisungen für das Studium der Chopin-Werke*, Halle, 1949.
Thomas, B-J., 'Harmonic Materials and Treatment of Dissonance in the Pianoforte Music of Chopin', unpub. Ph.D. dissertation, Eastman School of Music, 1963.
Walker, A. (ed.), *Frédéric Chopin: Profiles of the Man and the Musician*, London, 1966.
Windakiewiczowa, H., *Wzory ludowej muzyki polskiej w mazurkach Fryderyka Chopina*, Krakow, 1926.
Wójcik-Keuprulian, B., *Melodyka Chopina*, Lwów, 1930.
Żebrowski, D. (ed.), *Studies in Chopin*, Warsaw, 1973.

List of Works

The chronology of Chopin's music is anything but well-established. The present list is based largely on Chomiński and Turło, *Katalog Dzieł Fryderyka Chopina* (Kraków, 1990), which differs in numerous ways from Jan Ekier's *Wstęp do wydania narodowego*. Several changes from the Chomiński/Turło chronology have been made, based either on my own research or on Jeffrey Kallberg's dating of autograph manuscripts as reported in John Rink, 'The Evolution of Chopin's "Structural Style" and its Relation to Improvisation' (PhD dissertation, Cambridge, 1989).

1 Original Opus numbers

Opus title	Date of composition	Date of publication
1 Rondo, c; pf	1825	1825
2 Variations on 'Là ci darem la mano', Bb; pf, orch.	1827	1830
3 *Introduction and Polonaise Brillante*, C; vc, pf	1829–30	1831
4 Sonata, c; pf	1827–8	1851
5 *Rondo à la mazur*, F; pf	1826	1828
6 Four Mazurkas, f#, c#, E, Eb; pf	1830–32	1832
7 Five Mazurkas, Bb, A, F, Ab, C; pf (1st version of No. 4, 1825)	1830–32	1832
8 Piano Trio, g	1828–9	1832
9 Three Nocturnes, bb, Eb, B; pf	1830–32	1832
10 Twelve Etudes, pf	1830–32	1833
11 Concerto No. 1, e; pf, orch.	1830	1833
12 *Variations brillantes*, Bb; pf	1833	1833
13 *Fantasy on Polish Airs*, A; pf, orch.	1828	1834
14 *Rondo à la krakowiak*, F; pf, orch.	1828	1834
15 Three Nocturnes, F, F#, g; pf	1830–32	1833
16 *Introduction and Rondo*, c, Eb; pf	1832–3	1834
17 Four Mazurkas, Bb, e, Ab, a; pf	1833	1834
18 Waltz, Eb; pf	1831–2	1834
19 Bolero, C/A; pf	*c.*1833	1834
20 Scherzo, b; pf	*c.*1835	1835
21 Concerto No. 2; f; pf, orch.	1829	1836
22 *Andante spianato and Grande Polonaise brillante*, G; pf, and Eb; pf, orch.	1830–35	1836
23 Ballade, g; pf	*c.*1835	1836
24 Four Mazurkas, g, C, Ab, bb; pf	1833	1836
25 Twelve Etudes, pf	1835–7	1837

Opus title	Date of composition	Date of publication
26 Two Polonaises, c♯, e♭; pf	1835	1836
27 Two Nocturnes, c♯, D♭; pf	1835	1836
28 Twenty-four Preludes, pf	1838–9	1839
29 Impromptu, A♭; pf	c.1837	1837
30 Four Mazurkas, c, b, D♭, c♯; pf	1837	1838
31 Scherzo, D♭; pf	1837	1837
32 Two Nocturnes, B, A♭; pf	1837	1837
33 Four Mazurkas, g♯, D, C, b; pf	1838	1838
34 Three Waltzes		1838
A♭	1835	
a	c.1834	
F	1838	
35 Sonata, b♭; pf (slow movement 1837)	1839	1840
36 Impromptu, F♯; pf	1839	1840
37 Two Nocturnes, g, G; pf	1838–9	1840
38 Ballade, F/a; pf	1839	1840
39 Scherzo, c♯; pf	1839	1840
40 Two Polonaises, A, C; pf	1838–9	1840
41 Four Mazurkas, e, B, A♭, c♯; pf	1838–9	1840
42 Waltz, A♭; pf	1840	1840
43 Tarantelle, A♭; pf	1841	1841
44 Polonaise, f♯; pf	1841	1841
45 Prelude, c♯; pf	1841	1841
46 *Allegro de concert*, pf	c.1834–41	1841
47 Ballade, A♭; pf	1841	1841
48 Two Nocturnes, c, f♯; pf	1841	1841
49 Fantaisie, f/A♭; pf	1841	1841
50 Three Mazurkas, G, A♭, c♯; pf	1842	1842
51 Impromptu, G♭; pf	1842	1842
52 Ballade, f; pf	1842–3	1843
53 Polonaise, A♭; pf	1842–3	1843
54 Scherzo, E; pf	1842–3	1843
55 Two Nocturnes, f, E♭; pf	1842–4	1844
56 Three Mazurkas, B, C, c; pf	1843–4	1844
57 Berceuse, D♭; pf	1844	1845
58 Sonata, b; pf	1844	1845
59 Three Mazurkas, a, A♭, f♯; pf	1845	1845
60 Barcarolle, F♯; pf	1845–6	1846
61 *Polonaise-fantaisie*, A♭; pf	1846	1846
62 Two Nocturnes B, E; pf	1846	1846
63 Three Mazurkas, B, f, c♯; pf	1846	1847
64 Three Waltzes, D♭, c♯, A♭; pf	1847	1847
65 Sonata, g; vc, pf	1845–6	1847

Opus title	Date of composition	Date of publication
2 Published posthumously with Opus numbers by Fontana		
66 *Fantaisie-impromptu*, c♯; pf	*c.*1834	1855
67 Four Mazurkas, pf		1855
G	*c.*1835	
g	1848–9	
C	1835	
a	1846	
68 Four Mazurkas, pf		1855
C	*c.*1830	
a	*c.*1827	
F	*c.*1830	
f	*c.*1846	
69 Two Waltzes, pf		1855
A♭	1835	
b	1829	
70 Three Waltzes, pf		1855
G♭	1832	
f	1842	
D♭	1829	
71 Three Polonaises, pf		1855
d	1827–8	
B♭	1828	
f	1828	
72 Three Ecossaises, D, g, D♭; pf	*c.*1829	1855
73 Rondo, C; 2 pfs (originally solo pf)	1828	1855
74 17 Songs		1857
1 'Życzenie' (Witwicki)	*c.*1829	
2 'Wiosna' (Witwicki)	1838	
3 'Smutna rzeka' (Witwicki)	1831	
4 'Hulanka' (Witwicki)	1830	
5 'Gdzie lubi' (Witwicki)	*c.*1829	
6 'Precz z moich oczu' (Mickiewicz)	1827	
7 'Posel' (Witwicki)	1831	
8 'Śliczny chlopiec' (Zaleski)	1841	
9 'Melodia' (Krasiński)	1847	
10 'Wojak' (Witwicki)	1831	
11 'Dwojaki koniec' (Zaleski)	1845	
12 'Moja pieszczotka' (Mickiewicz)	1837	
13 'Nie ma czego trzeba' (Zaleski)	1845	
14 'Pierścień' (Witwicki)	1836	
15 'Narzeczony' (Witwicki)	1831	
16 'Piosnka litewska' (Witwicki)	1831	
17 'Leci liście z drzewa' (Pol)	1836	

Date of Opus title	Date of composition	publication

3 Works without Opus number (K. = Kobylanska, *Katalog*)

Polonaise, B; pf (K. 1182–3)	1817	1834
Polonaise, g; pf (K. 889)	1817	1817
Polonaise, A♭; pf (K. 1184)	1821	1908
Introduction and Variations on a German air		
('Der Schweizerbub'), E; pf (K. 925–7)	1824	1851
Polonaise, g♯; pf (K. 1185–7)	1824	1850–60?
Mazurka, B♭; pf (K. 891–5)	1825–6	1826
Mazurka, G; pf (K. 896–900)	1825–6	1826
Variations, D; pf 4 hands (K. 1190–2)	1826	1865
Funeral March, c; pf (K. 1059–68)	*c*.1826	1855
Polonaise, b♭; pf (K. 1188–9)	1826	1881
Nocturne, e; pf (K. 1055–8)	1827	1855
Souvenir de Paganini, A; pf (K. 1203)	1829	1881
Mazurka, G; pf (K. 1201–2)	1829	1879
Waltz, E; pf (K. 1207–8)	*c*.1829	1867
Waltz, E♭; pf (K. 1212)	1830	1902
Mazurka, G; voice (K. 1201–2)	1829	1879
Waltz, A♭; pf (K. 1209–11)	1830	1902
Waltz, e; pf (K. 1213–4)	1830	1850–60
Czary, voice, pf (K. 1204–6)	1830	1910
Polonaise, G♭; pf (K. 1197–1200)	1829	1850–60
Lento con gran expressione, c♯; pf (K. 1215–22)	1830	1875
Grand Duo concertant on themes from		
Meyerbeer's 'Robert le Diable', E; vc, pf		
(K. 901–2)	1831	1833
Mazurka, B♭; pf. (K. 1223)	1832	1909
Mazurka, D; pf (K. 1224, 1st version K.		
1193–6)	1832	1880
Mazurka, C; pf (K. 1225–6)	1833	1870
Cantabile, B♭; pf (K. 1230)	1834	1931
Mazurka, A♭; pf (K. 1227–8)	1834	1930
Prelude, A♭; pf (K. 1231–2)	1834	1918
Variation No. 6 in *Hexameron*, E; pf (K. 903–4)	1837	1839
Trois Nouvelles Etudes, pf (K. 905–17)	1839–40	1839
Canon, f; pf (K. 1241)	*c*.1839	
Mazurka 'Notre Temps', a; pf (K. 919–24)	*c*.1839	1842
Sostenuto (Waltz), E♭; pf (K. 1237)	1840	1955
Dumka, voice, pf (K. 1236)	1840	1910
Fugue, a; pf (K. 1242)	*c*.1841	1898
Moderato, E; pf (K. 1240)	1843	1910
Two Bourrées, g, A; pf (K. 1403–4)	1846	1968
Largo, E♭; pf (K. 1229)	1847	1938
Nocturne, c; pf (K. 1233–5)	1847	1938
Waltz, a; pf (K. 1238–9)	1847	1955

Index